# THE FALL OF
# THE ROYAL GOVERNMENT
# IN PERU

# THE FALL
# OF THE
# ROYAL GOVERNMENT
# IN PERU

Timothy E. Anna

University of Nebraska Press • Lincoln and London

*This book has been published with the help of a grant from the Social Science Federation
of Canada, using funds provided by the Social Sciences and Humanities Research Council
of Canada.*

**Library of Congress Cataloging in Publication Data**

Anna, Timothy E.   1944–
   The fall of the royal government in Peru.

   Bibliography: p.273
   Includes index.
   1.   Peru—History—War of Independence, 1820–1829.
I.   Title.
F3446.A53        985′.04        79–9142
ISBN 0–8032–1004–3

*For my son*
*Aaron Bolívar*

# Contents

# Preface

THIS BOOK, like its companion piece on the Mexican War of Independence,[1] is an attempt to remind readers that no really satisfying explanation of the process or meaning of Spanish American independence can be arrived at until we have a fuller understanding of how the Spanish imperial regime lost. For Peru, as for Mexico, the bibliography on the rebels who ended Spain's three centuries of rule is vast. Peruvian historiography is characterized by an eternal fascination with the patriots. And if a person lives long enough he will be privileged to experience the extraordinary outpouring of publications occasioned by some significant anniversary, as we are still enjoying the products of 1971, the sesquicentennial of the Declaration of Independence, and the massive *Colección documental de la independencia del Perú*.[2]

The all-absorbing question in the historiography of Peruvian independence has been why Peru was so slow in achieving its separation from Spain. Peru and Upper Peru (Bolivia) were the last kingdoms of the Spanish empire in continental South America to gain their independence. The military phase of Peru's War of Independence did not even begin until 1820, ten years after the outbreak of armed insurrection throughout most of America, and Peru did not achieve full independence until 1824, three years after the rest of America. Granting that Lima's vice-regal regime was more powerful and more entrenched than those of Bogotá and Buenos Aires, the question remains, Was it truly that much stronger than Mexico's? Or were Peru's rebels simply that much weaker?

In attempting to solve this fundamental problem, historians, while concentrating on the patriots, have tended to lean toward either the nationalist or the interventionist view of whether Peruvians wanted to be independent. It is an age-old dispute that may never be satisfactorily resolved. Some historians, especially non-Peruvians in an earlier era, insisted that it was only the intervention first of José de San Martín and the republic of Chile, with Argentinian support, then of Simón Bolívar and the republic of Gran Colombia that made Peruvian independence possible.[3] Others, particularly Peruvians in modern times, have argued that Peruvians themselves participated spontaneously and fervently in their own independence.[4] Some would go so far as to insist that hardly a single Peruvian supported the imperial system.[5] Still others have pursued a thesis that Peru was in some way unlike the rest of the empire and have ended up writing what is essentially folklore.[6] Allegations of "anti-Peruvianism" and "excessive nationalism" have peppered historical criticism.

It is not my intention to resolve an essentially irresolvable dilemma. I can only plead that a historian best serves the nation that is his subject by helping in some small way to clarify its historical record. And one way to do that is to study the long and by no means inevitable decline and fall of its royalist regime. An inseparable part of the history of the royal regime's almost-successful resistance is, of course, the failure of the regimes of San Martín, Riva Agüero, and Torre Tagle from 1821 to 1824 to complete the process of independence. Thus, in studying the royal regime one must also concentrate upon those members of the Peruvian elite who had to decide for or against independence. Since the Peruvian elite lived and functioned predominantly in the capital city of Lima, which thus exercised hegemony over the rest of the country, it is to Lima that we must direct most of our attention. The great figures of the independence movement, whether Peruvians like Riva Agüero, Torre Tagle, and Sánchez Carrión or outsiders like San Martín, Lord Cochrane, and Bolívar, will be dealt with only as they either failed or succeeded in bringing down the viceregal regime. It is important to shed new light on the process of independence, not to pay homage to individual opponents of Spain, either great or small, Peruvian or outsider. Their story, at any rate, has been told before and will be told again.[7] Thus I argue neither the nationalist nor the interventionist thesis about Peruvian independence, though I do wish to try to explain why both the battle of Ayacucho and the final siege of Callao were necessary and what they meant.

It is worthwhile, however, to refer the reader to a recent article (published as this book was in press) by John Fisher, a historian who has done a great deal in the last few years to clarify historical knowledge about late colonial Peru. Fisher may have provided the first satisfying discussion of the relative function of nationalists and interventionists in Peruvian independence by pointing out that between 1808 and 1815 Peruvian participation in anti-Spanish revolts was regional—occurring outside of Lima, centered in Cuzco, Arequipa, Huanuco and Tacna—and that these unsuccessful revolts largely constituted regional challenges to the role of Lima as capital of the viceroyalty. They failed because Lima, home of the pro-Spanish elite, was "sufficiently powerful to determine the future of Peru."[8] With the defeat of the Pumacahua rebellion in 1815, regional Peruvian rebellion was suppressed, although the attempt of royalist Cuzco in 1824 to have itself proclaimed capital of the tottering viceroyalty confirms the continuity of the interior's regional ambitions. The initiative, or focus, remained in Lima, and it is from that vantage that we will pursue the tale.

Since this book looks at Peruvian independence from the angle of the fall of the established regime, it is based not only on published works but also on many archival documents. This will, I hope, explain why I could not avoid commenting on some of the existing historiography, while I simultaneously acknowledge my debt to the contributions of that historiography.

Let me say a word about how this book relates to my book on Mexican independence. It seemed to me that the processes of independence in Spain's two greatest American colonies were so different that they warranted treatment in quite separate accounts. Whereas I argued in the book on Mexico that the decline and fall of the royal government in New Spain was essentially the product of its gradual loss of authority to rule, in Peru it seems that the question of authority, though still very important, was subordinate to more practical factors. Thus I have chosen in most cases not to make direct comparisons between the two countries because I believe it is important for Peru's historical record to be clarified and to stand on its own.

# THE FALL OF
# THE ROYAL GOVERNMENT
# IN PERU

Chapter 1

# The Reality of Peru

THE FUNDAMENTAL CHARACTERISTIC of the royal regime in Peru—
the feature that runs throughout the story of royal resistance to
rebellion and the gradual fall of the regime—is poverty. It is both
a cause and an explanation of independence. Paradoxically, it is
also both a cause and an explanation of Peru's long resistance to
independence. Just as Peru's poverty defeated the royalists, so it
defeated their successor, San Martín. A number of recent studies
have substantiated the fact that the Peruvian economy was in
deep trouble in the last decades of the imperial era.[1] Consequently, it is no longer possible to accept the stories of Peru's
incredible wealth that were a constant theme in older historiography. Take, for example, Jean Descola's description of Lima: "In
the days of La Perricholi, [Lima] had reached its apogee and
incarnated the glory and opulence of the Spanish Empire in
America." Benjamin Vicuña Mackenna described Lima as "a
nymph of idleness, asleep on the banks of the flowering
Rímac, . . . surrounded by green fields, crowned by rustic
diadems, lifting its voluptuous forehead to the caresses of a
cloudless sky."[2] Descriptions like these leave a false impression
that must be dispelled if Lima's agony in the era of independence
is to be understood.

    The real Lima was far less glorious, though it was no doubt the
most important city of the Spanish Pacific coast. In 1790 it had a
population of 52,547, while Mexico City had 103,189. By 1813

Lima's population had increased by only 6 percent, to 56,284, while Mexico City's in that same year had grown by 16 percent to 123,907. Lima was capital of the viceroyalty of Peru, which counted a total population in 1795 of 1,115,207, while the viceroyalty of New Spain in 1803, according to Humboldt, had a population of 5,837,100. By 1813, both Peru and New Spain had increased by from 4 to 5 percent. Peru's population was 1,180,669, while New Spain's was 6,122,000.[3] Both Lima and Peru as a whole fell far short of being the incarnation of the "glory and opulence" of the Spanish empire in America; that distinction belonged to Mexico City and the kingdom of New Spain.

A far more realistic description of the real Lima comes from a most unexpected source. In February 1818 the Russian naval ship *Kamchatka*, in the midst of a trip around the world, put in at Lima. Her commander, Vasilii M. Golovnin, left an unparalleled account of late colonial Lima, one that was not clouded by ethnocentrism—at least not by Spanish ethnocentrism. His assessment of the city is straightforward and somewhat unsettling: "I expected to find in Lima a beautiful city, but great was my disillusion to see that in all the world there is not another large city that has such a poor appearance." In witty and cutting prose Golovnin punctured the pretensions of his hosts. "The inhabitants of Peru praise their country, and so do the Spaniards who live there. They say that the only inconveniences are the frequent earthquakes and the colonial politics of the Spanish government; and they agree that the second inconvenience is much greater than the first." About Lima's much-vaunted coaches and carriages he remarked: "In all my life I have never seen coaches that were more comical, dirtier or poorer than those here." About the municipal cemetery and pantheon—one of the glories of Viceroy José de Abascal's administration—he said: "The building and site are not worth anything from any point of view, but the Spaniards find it a marvel and show it to foreigners as something rare and uncommon." About the military arsenal and mint: "The two merit very little attention when compared with those of Europe." Concerning the stone bridge that crossed the Rímac behind the viceroy's palace: "The people here who have never been in Europe show it off as a marvel of architecture, but in reality it does not merit mention." Although he admired the rich furnishings and extravagant decor of private homes he visited, he found the houses architecturally undistinguished and in bad repair. The streets, he said, were "long and straight, but very narrow and dirty." Lima's famous enclosed balconies he called "comical." The churches and convents he found large, splendid, but decorated "with a multitude of columns and friezes distributed with little taste." Coming upon a large and dirty market plaza he reacted with dismay: "Who would have imagined that such an unclean place was the principal plaza of the city?" Dining with Viceroy Joaquín de la Pezuela, he remarked upon the table service, which "was not viceregal," and the simplicity of the food. The viceregal palace had numerous magnificent rooms, but many of them were virtually unfurnished. Among all the palace furnishings, the item he found most appropriate was a life-size portrait of the goddess of justice that hung by the viceroy's office door. He remarked wryly that the goddess "does not always help him with her counsel." In short, Golovnin was not impressed by Lima and found that its buildings were all "very poor" and that "none of them would merit attention in a large European city."[4]

Golovnin's assessment of Lima's general appearance is borne out by the most detailed contemporary description that exists, that of William Bennet Stevenson, an Englishman who lived in Peru, Chile, Colombia, and Quito from 1804 to 1827, and who eventually served as Lord Cochrane's secretary. In his *Historical and Descriptive Narrative of Twenty Years in South America* he described Lima, and Peru in general, in great detail. Although much better disposed toward Peru than Golovnin, he still described Lima as a city of low houses made largely of adobe with roofs of cane, many churches made of adobe, stucco, and wood, and few distinguished works of architecture. He testified that the viceregal palace, for example, was poorly furnished and inadequate to the viceregal rank. He judged the archbishop's palace to be the most noteworthy building in the city, though small. He verified that "the churches of Lima have nothing to attract the attention, particularly of a stranger," although the convents of the prominent orders were very rich.[5] For Stevenson, as for most other visitors, Peru's most positive characteristic was the extraordinary vivacity and charm of its people, described in warm and even loving detail by this transplanted Englishman.

Peru was rich in only one commodity—silver. While a recent work by J. R. Fisher has shown that Peru's mining sector remained strong, and indeed even increased production, in the last years before the struggle for independence, the colony's other economic sectors—manufacturing, agriculture, and commerce—presented a picture of gradual decline throughout the eighteenth century. In trade and commerce, Peru's decline started at the beginning of the eighteenth century when the old fleet system was abolished and replaced with single licensed ships, called registros, carrying European goods to Lima by way of Cape Horn and exporting bullion to Spain. Lima's lifeblood thus began to flow from the south rather than from Panama in the north as it had previously done. Single ships, no longer controlled by the fleet system, had to pass Buenos Aires—South America's newest, most vibrant, and most competitive port—before reaching Lima. Buenos Aires, with the undeniable advantage of being an Atlantic port, began its rise to eminence as Lima declined. Lima continued, in theory, to hold the monopoly for most of the eighteenth century, but in fact Buenos Aires and the Chilean ports began to take some of its trade. Simultaneously, Peruvian agriculture declined in productivity and efficiency, owing chiefly to problems in the supply of manpower, capital, and transportation. By 1776 Peru itself no longer supplied all its own agricultural essentials and was increasingly dependent on imported commodities.[6]

In 1776 the most disastrous blow to Peruvian prosperity fell when, as part of its continuing program of rationalization through sweeping economic and administrative reform, the Bourbon monarchy created a new viceroyalty of Río de la Plata, with its capital at Buenos Aires. This removed from Lima's titular control the vast territories of the southern hinterland. More disastrous still, the region of Upper Peru (Bolivia), center of the richest silver mines, was separated from the viceroyalty of Peru and given to the new viceroyalty of Río de la Plata. From that time to this, the blame for Peru's economic troubles in the last half-century of Spanish control has been placed on its loss of control over Upper Peru. Every viceroy and important spokesman for the Peruvian viceregal government fell back upon it. As late as 1811 the archbishop of Lima, Bartolomé de las Heras, gave as an explanation for his inability to make larger contributions to the Spanish war effort the fact that "this kingdom is today a pallid shadow of what it was before being dismembered of the opulent provinces contiguous with Potosí."[7]

The archbishop's explanation, though technically correct, requires amplification. It was not the loss of territorial control over Upper Peru that caused economic decline in Lower Peru. Indeed, the loss of mere territorial control over the vast region was meant to save Lima money. Besides, in 1810, after the uprising of Buenos Aires, Viceroy Abascal reannexed Upper Peru, and throughout the War of Independence the two territories functioned virtually as one.[8] What was important about the loss of Upper Peru was that it dispossessed Peru of its own virtual colony, which was granted to Buenos Aires instead, giving that port a major boost in its objective of replacing Lima as South America's major trading center. Simple geography then determined the winner. Buenos Aires, easily accessible from all parts of the Atlantic, now became the funnel through which passed the vast bullion production of Upper Peru, as well as the European goods needed to supply Upper Peru. In 1776 and 1778 Lima's formal monopoly over the continent's overseas trade was revoked. Separated by a continent from easy access to Europe and now bereft of guaranteed internal markets in Upper Peru, Lima could not compete. Peru continued to dominate the Pacific coast trade, although ports in Chile stole some of its business. The "lesser ports" of Peru itself also began to challenge Lima, and with the granting of "free trade" in 1778—by which other Pacific ports were given the right of direct trade with Spain—Lima began to feel even more competition. Natural market forces were allowed to determine the flow of goods to a greater extent than before, to Lima's detriment. The chief competitor on the Pacific was Guayaquil, although it never equaled Lima. Guayaquil was transferred to the control of the viceroyalty of Peru in 1803, but switched back to the jurisdiction of the viceroyalty of New Granada in 1809.

The loss of Upper Peru set in motion two unfortunate developments. Having lost its traditional hinterland market for manufactured goods, Peru was no longer commercially competitive. Although it remained the chief supplier of agricultural products to Upper Peru—mainly wine, aguardiente, oil, sugar, pimientos, and grain—it ceased to supply it with the cheap

Peruvian-made cloth that had once been the staple of the trade. The market for this product was now taken over by Buenos Aires, which imported European cloth of higher quality and lower price. Furthermore, as Buenos Aires and Chile began to carry European goods into Peru itself, Peruvian textile manufactories lost even most of their domestic market. At the same time, Peru lost control over the export of bulk bullion from the mines of Upper Peru. Traditionally, goods imported from Lower Peru had been paid for with bullion that was then taken to Lima for coinage. After 1777 Lima received from Upper Peru only minted coins that had been produced at the Potosí mint. This paralyzed the trade between Upper and Lower Peru.[9]

Lima was faced with unbeatable competition from European goods. Technically these products were supposed to come only from Spain; but in fact, because of the widespread contrabanding at Guayaquil, smaller Peruvian coast towns, and chiefly Buenos Aires, considerable quantities of English and even Asian goods were available to the consumer. Since imported manufactures were infinitely preferable to local products, Peruvian markets were soon completely saturated with them. Since agriculture was also declining, Peru got in the habit of importing even Chilean wheat, which came to be preferred in Lima to domestic wheat. Although Peru exported some raw materials—mainly cascarilla, cacao, copper from Chile, and some vicuña wool—the only really large-quantity product it could export to pay for its large imports was bullion, still produced in huge quantities at Cerro de Pasco and in other domestic mining regions. The net effect was that bullion came to pay for almost everything. From 1785 to 1789, for example, bullion accounted for 88 percent of Peru's total exports (27,861,700 pesos in bullion against only 3,624,657 pesos in all other products combined), and from 1790 to 1794 bullion made up 85 percent of total exports (23,780,977 pesos in bullion against 4,127,250 pesos in other goods).[10]

Peru thus came to import too many manufactured goods and even food—which naturally retarded the development of domestic industry and agriculture—while it exported too much of its gold and silver. Excessive dependence on bullion was dangerous because the annual output of bullion could fluctuate so wildly as to turn Peru's very existence into a giant game of chance. For example, in 1792 bullion exports reached more than 8 million pesos, but in 1793 they totaled barely 1.5 million, whereas in 1794 they were nearly 4 million.[11]

Fisher shows that Peru's exports in the early 1790s were worth an average of about 5 million pesos a year. Yet in the three-year period 1785 to 1787, Peru imported 24 million pesos worth of goods, an unfavorable balance of trade of 3 million pesos a year. In addition, by 1790 Peru's trade with the Pacific coast of South America itself—with Chile, Chiloé, Santa Fé, and Guatemala—produced an annual deficit of about 445,000 pesos. This added up to a total unfavorable balance of coastal and overseas trade of about 3.5 million pesos a year. The only portion of Peru's national trade that produced a favorable balance was its sale of agricultural products to Upper Peru, for which it was paid both in silver and in other commodities, producing in 1790 a balance of 1,170,190 pesos in Peru's favor.[12] But even this favorable balance did nothing to stimulate internal development. What does a country that produces bullion need with more silver? It simply passed through Peru.

The reply of the Lima Consulado (the merchants' guild) to the accelerating decline of Peruvian manufacturing and the loss of the domestic market to foreign imports was predictable and was repeated with such consistency as to make it one of the prevailing refrains of Peruvian documents from the 1790s to 1821. The Consulado demanded a two-part program to restore the health of the Peruvian economy: a moratorium on direct European and Asian imports into Lima and a total ban on the import into Peru of goods that had passed through Buenos Aires. The first would eliminate or restrict competition from Spanish goods carried directly to Peru. The second would apply chiefly to English goods, which is what the words "via Buenos Aires" meant to the Consulado. Both objectives, it argued, would stop the flow of coinage out of Peru, for that had become a real problem by the 1790s. Indeed, perhaps the ultimate paradox in Peruvian economic affairs was that by the time San Martín took Lima in 1821, the country that was world-famous as a silver producer was chronically short of coinage for domestic market purposes.[13] At any rate, the Consulado never got what it wanted, even though after 1806 it had the outspoken support of Viceroy Abascal himself. Partly it was because the Consulado merchants were too clearly trying to recover lost monopolistic privileges that had the air of a previous century. More to the point, however, there came to be a considerable group of men of affairs in Lima, including many merchant entrepreneurs, who were influenced by the liberal economics of the Enlightenment and who believed free trade was desirable. The writers of the *Mercurio Peruano*, for example, expounded the doctrine that free trade spread prosperity to a greater portion of the population. Whatever the reason, the Consulado, though it was until 1821 the most important voice in commercial and economic affairs, had clearly ceased to be the exclusive arbiter of trade. And it remains that Peru, whatever its pretenses to opulence, simply lacked the domestic manpower and capital to fall back on its own resources and function in isolation in a time of rising consumer expectations. Lima, the entrepôt that had once dominated all trade on the continent, increasingly found it impossible to sell even to other Peruvian centers such as Cuzco or Arequipa, much less to extraterritorial centers. The struggle between supporters of free trade and supporters of monopoly became truly acute during the administration of Viceroy Joaquín de la Pezuela when, as we shall see, the viceroy himself advocated complete free trade with even non-Spanish nations as the only method of rescuing the royal regime.

Mining therefore continued to be Peru's economic mainstay. Despite a widespread assumption that mining was badly harmed by the loss of Upper Peru in 1776, Fisher has shown that, in marked distinction to commerce and agriculture, mining in Peru grew impressively in the last quarter of the eighteenth century. Production increased notably owing to the creation in 1786 of a mining tribunal at Lima, modeled on Mexico City's tribunal, and to the discovery and exploitation of new deposits in the intendancies of Arequipa and, more important, Tarma. Fluctuations in the total output of silver were the result of labor deficiencies, disruption in the supply of mercury caused by the wars in Europe and the nearly total cessation of mercury production by about 1808 at Huancavelica (Peru's only domestic source), fundamental weaknesses in financing the mines, and technological backwardness.[14] From 1790 to 1810 the famous mining mission of the German Baron Thaddeus von Nordenflicht was at work in Peru attempting—unsuccessfully as it happened—to modernize mining and extractive techniques.[15] Despite Nordenflicht's failure, silver production reached its peak in 1799, and, although it declined slightly in subsequent years, it remained high until 1812. After 1812 Peru's silver production finally collapsed, the result of flooding of the mines of Cerro de Pasco (which had produced up to 40 percent of the country's silver) and of disruptions caused by the War of Independence. Mining, at any rate, had remained the one bright spot in Peru's economic picture throughout the long era of commercial and agricultural decline. Fisher concludes that the relatively healthy condition of mining "should not be regarded as an accurate reflection of the situation in the late colonial period as a whole."[16]

Three other elements played a critical role in Peru's economic decline: the shortage (or maldistribution) of labor, the absence of good roads and communications, and the limited investment capital. With a population in 1795 of 1,115,207, Peru lacked sufficient cheap labor to run its agricultural activities. The abolition of the repartimiento system in 1780, the immense disruption caused by the Túpac Amaru uprising, and the fact that the Indians lived in the highlands while the haciendas were in the valleys and the manufactories in the cities, made it difficult for Peru to exploit its Indian population to the extent desired by most property owners. Furthermore, Peru's geographical isolation made the acquisition of African slaves to work its coastal haciendas difficult and expensive. In 1795 there were 40,385 slaves in all of Peru, and of that number 29,781 were in the province of Lima alone.

The extraordinarily difficult terrain of Peru, combined with the lack of adequate roads into the interior, was a crippling weakness for agriculture and commerce. It cost so much money to carry Peruvian sugar or tobacco a few leagues to a coastal port that almost all the rest of the empire could produce agricultural goods more cheaply. Peru was, in truth, bullion-rich and food-poor. By the era of independence most of Peruvian agriculture supplied only a domestic market, and even then, not completely. Taxation added to the paralysis. It was cheaper for Arequipa, for example, to buy imports, whether foodstuffs or manufactured goods, from Chile or Buenos Aires than from Lima. A shipment of linen landed at Buenos Aires and shipped overland to Arequipa, a distance of 800 leagues, was cheaper than the same load brought from Europe around the Cape to Lima and then transshipped to Arequipa, a distance of 200 leagues. By 1810, Lima itself depended so completely on Chilean wheat that it nearly starved when the supply was cut in 1818; yet the valleys in the immediate environs of the capital—Chancay, Huaura, Pativilca, Cañete, and Chincha—produced wheat as well. Even between Lima and its nearby port of Callao transportation was difficult, expensive, and constantly disrupted by either the bad road or bandits. In 1798 a new Lima-Callao road was opened, built at a cost of 343,000 pesos. Yet in 1816 Viceroy Pezuela sent to the Lima city council a long letter scolding it for allowing the Callao road to fall into disrepair. Just because Callao was very near to Lima did not mean it was cheap to send goods there. Indeed, in 1823, after several years of military confiscation of mules had taken its toll, an English merchant testified that it cost more to carry goods from Callao to Lima than to ship them from England.[17]

The net effect of Peru's economic decline, naturally, was to limit still further the capital available for investment. Both individuals and institutions in Peru were far less wealthy, even relatively, than their Mexican counterparts. Whereas Doris M. Ladd found that New Spain in 1810 had seventeen families that were millionaires and nine others with fortunes of 500,000 to 900,000 pesos, in Peru—where the same sort of research has not yet been conducted—only two or three families (among them the Baquíjanos and probably the Lavalles) appear to have been reputed millionaires. The richest man in Peru seems to have been the merchant José Arizmendi, who, when he fled into exile following independence, left behind assets valued at 2,172,000 pesos, much of them in the form of credits owing to him.[18] Nor were there any private houses in Lima like those in Mexico City built at costs of upward of 300,000 pesos. Nor were there elite families in Lima with retinues of more than thirty servants in their town houses as there were in Mexico. There was no Peruvian José de la Borda or Fagoaga family or Sardaneta family like those D. A. Brading has described as investing millions of pesos in Mexican mining.[19] Peru had an aristocracy, of course, and a nobility— indeed, the total of títulos de Castilla was greater in Peru than in New Spain. Peru boasted no less than 105 noble titles, which included 1 duke, 58 marqueses, 45 counts, and 1 viscount, while New Spain had only 63 titles, of which there were 32 counts, 30 marqueses, and 1 mariscal de Castilla.[20] The difference can be explained, perhaps, by the historical precedence Peru had taken over New Spain for the first two centuries of the colonial era, for most of the Peruvian titles dated from before 1772. At any rate, the tables were clearly reversed by the nineteenth century, as can be seen from the frequent requests of the Lima city council, or the ecclesiastical cabildo of the Lima cathedral, or the regiment of the Concordia, or the Consulado to be granted by the crown the same preeminences and titles "as they have in New Spain."

And it is palpably clear that the incomes of Peru's elite fell far short of the incomes of Mexico's plutocrats. To begin with, during the Spanish war against Napoleon, Peruvian contributions and private donations in aid of the war effort, whether on the peninsula or in Peru, did not equal those of Mexicans. There are repeated instances in New Spain of individual donors giving 50,000 to 300,000 pesos to a single drive or fund for the relief of Spain.[21] In Peru the same sort of contributions were solicited at the outset of Spain's war with Napoleon, but the sums produced were pitifully small. Fortunes of such size simply did not exist in Peru. In 1809 Peru sent to Spain, aboard the *San Fulgencio*, a contribution of 1,356,184 pesos for the war effort. Though that seems a great deal of money, very little came from voluntary donations. Indeed, 1,211,187 pesos of the total came from Consolidation collections of the years 1804 through 1808. The Consolidation was the amortization of all mortgages held by pious funds of the church, ordered in 1804 by the peninsular regime of Manuel de Godoy to help pay Spain's massive war costs. It met with such resistance in America and was so destructive—since the pious funds were the largest holders of mortgages in all parts of the empire—that it was abolished in 1808. (Unfortunately, no research has yet been done to assess the effects of consolidation on the Peruvian elite.) Most of the remainder of the 1809 contribution came from the montepío militar (the pension fund for widows and orphans of military officers) and from the media anata (the contribution paid by civil servants for their appointments). The next year, 1810, Peru sent Spain a contribution of 2,771,504 pesos aboard the *San Pedro Alcántara*. This also appears at first to equal the sort of voluntary donations Mexicans were making; but, again, most of the total was not voluntary. Only 633,784 pesos came from voluntary donations, while 231,025 pesos came from voluntary loans to the government. All the remainder consisted of grants from government funds, monopolies, or the Consulado—in a sense, from taxes. For example, 185,951 pesos came from Temporalidades (the fund administering the properties of the suppressed Jesuit order); 240,000 pesos came from the mails; 200,000 came from the tobacco monopoly; 712,487 came from the Casa de Moneda in bars of silver; and 333,000 was a subvention from the Consulado.[22]

Where data are available to indicate individual donations or contributions to the Spanish war effort in 1808–10, they bear out the general impression that Limeños, even peninsulars living in Lima, gave sums that were much more modest than the contributions of wealthy Mexican peninsulars. In this period, for example, Joaquín Mansilla, a lawyer, gave a voluntary donation of 10,000 pesos; Martín de Osambela, an important merchant, gave 5,000; and the marqués de Fuentehermosa gave 4,000.[23] These are about the largest individual private donations that can be found in the documents. They do not compare in munificence to the single contribution of 355,000 pesos given by the Mexican hacendado Gabriel de Yermo in 1810, which was in turn only one of many huge gifts or loans from him and other peninsulars. When Viceroy Abascal contributed 41,581 pesos in 1809, he admitted that it was his entire life's savings from thirteen years of command in America as intendant of New Galicia and viceroy of Peru, and that he had intended it as the inheritance of his only child, Ramona.[24]

In 1808 the city council of Lima gave a flat contribution of 100,000 pesos to the war cause. This occurred, however, in conjunction with its request in November 1808 to the Junta Central for the abolition of the Consolidation, an objective of every member of the city council. The damaging amortization program had, in fact, already been canceled, but Peru was not aware of it until June 1809.[25]

A brief enumeration of the special contributions of the Consulado, which was the one agency in Lima with considerable capital at its disposal, suggests the extent to which Lima was capital-poor at the beginning of the independence era. The Consulado's contributions were mighty—so much so that in 1815 Viceroy Abascal asked that the prior (the conde de Villar de Fuente) and the consuls (Juan Francisco Xavier de Izcue and Faustino del Campo) be rewarded with the cross of the order of Isabel la Católica, as the prior and consuls of Mexico City had been.[26] Yet the makeup of the Consulado's contributions show two characteristics: after 1810 its contributions were entirely directed toward Peruvian rather than peninsular defense, and most of the contributions represented transfers of Consulado funds—which were themselves derived from rights over the customs and other state grants—rather than coming from private capital. Almost every drive to collect cash or pledges from private citizens failed. In 1810, for example, the Consulado raised one million pesos in a campaign, half of which was sent to Spain and half of which was reabsorbed into the viceregal treasury. Yet, Archbishop Las Heras testified that citizens had not contributed as much as had been expected. From 1811 to mid-1813, members of the merchant community supported one thousand men in the army of Upper Peru, at an expense of 480,000 pesos. That was a direct collection. From 1813 to 1815, the Consulado members pledged 35,600 pesos to support the Concordia Regiment. But in any case the Concordia Regiment was a militia composed of merchants and gentlemen, so the Consulado probably merely tabulated contributions made by merchant officers toward their own appointments or to their own troops. In June 1812 the Consulado gave 100,000 pesos for the recovery of Quito. In August 1812 it gave one million pesos to the government. However, all but 50,000 pesos of that sum was borrowed. In April 1814 it gave 104,500 pesos to Cádiz to pay for the transport of the Regiment of Talavera to Lima, but this was in the form of drafts against the Consulado's account in Cádiz. In July 1814 it gave 110,000 pesos cash for the expedition to Chile; in August 1814, 50,000 pesos for the relief of Cuzco; and in September 1814, 50,000 pesos to rearm troops in Arequipa province. A final donation totaling 102,000 pesos came from Consulado members' own pockets for Buenos Aires and the maintenance of troops in Upper Peru.[27]

This seems to be a considerable contribution from the Consulado. The point, however, is that of the total of nearly 3 million pesos in contributions to the state, less than a million pesos was in the form of cash donations out of the pockets of members and other merchants, whereas more than 2 million came as paper drafts, direct borrowing, or future pledges. For example, of the first collection in 1810 of a million pesos, the half that remained in Peru, the Consulado reported, was "entered in the treasury for the use of the viceroyalty, in the form of a refund." In other words, the Consulado merely returned to the government monies collected under privileges granted by the government. It is also impressive that, among the men who pledged in 1811 toward the support of troops in Upper Peru, almost half pledged less than one soldier's pay a month, that is, 16 pesos.[28]

But the strongest evidence of the weakness of Peru's economy before the independence era comes from a "list of the natural and artificial products of Peru," which, though undated, belongs to the period of about 1807 to 1809.[29] It illustrates (see table 1) that Peru's only significant manufactured products were textiles and clothing. The intendancies of Lima and Arequipa were the most productive, followed by Cuzco. This does not correspond to population, since the most populous intendancy was Trujillo, followed by Cuzco, Tarma, Lima, and Arequipa. No value was computed for the intendancy of Puno, which was added to the viceroyalty of Peru only in 1795; nor were the provinces of Mainas and Guayaquil—which were added to Peru in 1802 and 1803— even listed. Nonetheless, the total commercial value of Peru's annual production, less Puno, added up to only 8,745,815 pesos. This does not include, of course, the value of imports; nor, presumably, does it include any attempt to compute the value of food and other goods not involved in trade. In addition, one assumes that the entire inner economic world of Indian barter and trade, by which the majority of Peru's large indigenous population sustained itself, was not amenable to valuation. What this figure does represent is the "wealth" of Peru. Only 8.7 million pesos of productivity is an incredibly small figure. It is certainly too limited a base to sustain a nation that spent approximately 5 million pesos a year on imports and a further 4 to 5 million a year on government. Not only was Peru living beyond its means, sustaining an excessive standard of living, it was living disastrously beyond its means.

Yet the actual economic situation of late colonial Peru was even bleaker than these figures suggest. We must remember that Peru exported most of its gold and silver and some of its agricultural produce. If the nation's annual exports are subtracted from the annual production of 8.7 million pesos it will tell how much of Peru's total production remained in the country for domestic consumption and development. The average annual gold and silver production in the years 1807 to 1809 was 4.3 million pesos.

TABLE 1
NATURAL AND ARTIFICIAL PRODUCTS OF PERU
AND COMPUTATION OF COMMERCIAL VALUE EACH YEAR, CA.
1807–1809

| Product | Value (in Pesos) |
|---|---|
| *Intendancy of Lima* | |
| Fruits, grazing, sugar, | |
| honey, fish, vegetables, saltpeter, brandy, | |
| oil, dates, soap, copper, burros, grain, | |
| sheep, cattle, corn, potatoes | 2,190,349 |
| *Intendancy of Cuzco* | |
| Grain and root crops, mining, | |
| cloth, sugar, cochineal, cotton, potatoes, | |
| corn, livestock, clothing, coca, wood | 1,643,688 |
| *Intendancy of Huamanga* | |
| Sweets, sugar, coca, textiles, | |
| grain, seeds, livestock | 266,505 |
| *Intendancy of Huancavelica* | |
| Sugar, grain, livestock, | |
| vegetables, root crops | 207,826 |
| *Intendancy of Tarma* | |
| Cascarilla, grain, livestock, textiles, | |
| vegetables, sugar, clothing | 1,396,519 |
| *Intendancy of Trujillo* | |
| Grain, saffron, sugar, tobacco, | |
| cotton, indigo, mules, soap, seeds, livestock, | |
| potatoes, gold and silver, cacao | 886,928 |
| *Intendancy of Arequipa* | |
| Grain, vines, brandies, textiles, sugar, | |
| oil, cotton, mining, potatoes, livestock, | |
| fish | 2,154,000 |
| *Intendancy of Puno* | |
| Swine, textiles, carpets, worked silver, | |
| wood, gold, resin, coca, vegetables, vacuñas, | |
| guanacos, livestock, cheese, mercury, silver, quinine, | |
| potatoes, sugar syrup, fish | No sum given |
| Total yearly commercial product | 8,745,815 |

SOURCE: "Estado de los productos naturales y artificiales del Perú en el vireynato de Lima, y computo de su valor comercial cada año," AGI, Indiferente 1525.

Extrapolating from Fisher's figures, it seems valid to conclude that all of that coinage was exported. In the ten-year period 1785–94, for example, Peru exported an average of 5.3 million pesos a year in gold and silver, but the Lima Casa de Moneda produced an average of only 4.8 million pesos a year. This means that not only was the entire silver output exported each year, but an additional half-million pesos in reserve or Upper Peruvian bullion was also sent out of the country. In addition, Peru exported an annual average of 859,000 pesos worth of agricultural goods in these years.[30] In total, therefore, Peru exported an average of 5.2 million pesos of its total 8.7 million peso yearly production, leaving only 40 percent, or 3.5 million pesos, for internal consumption.

In spite of the extraordinary precariousness of the Peruvian economy, the viceregal regime was able to raise an annual revenue that averaged 4.6 million pesos in the 1790s and reached 5.2 million pesos in 1812. In the 1790s the royal treasury had functioned with an annual surplus of more than a million pesos, but by 1812—when its expenditure was 5.3 million pesos—it had got into the habit of deficit spending.[31] Peru entered the War of Independence era with a debt of 8,088,212 pesos. After restoration of the tribute in 1815, conditions improved a little, so that by 1816 the viceregal debt had crept up to only 11 million. But by 1819 the Ministry of Finance in Spain estimated that the Peruvian debt was at least 16 to 20 million pesos, and probably much more. Nobody was counting any longer. The result, according to a memorandum of the ministry, was that "[Peru's] credit has further declined; the bills it sends and the drafts it executes are not paid, and its most sacred loans and deposits cannot be repaid."[32] Since Peru had begun the struggle with a very lopsided economy, it should be no surprise that one year before San Martín's expedition had even landed on the coast, the strain of resistance had already become too much and the country was in default.

There are two explanations for how such an unbalanced economic system could have survived as long as it did. One is that Peru produced and exported gold and silver, commodities the whole world wanted and whose value (if not price) was assured. The other lies in the inequality of colonial Peru's social system. Out of a total population of 1,115,207 persons in 1795, 674,615 (60 percent) were Indian; 244,313 (22 percent) were mestizo; 41,004 were free pardos (in Peru, mixed blacks), 40,385 were slaves, and 140,890 (12 percent) were whites. Yet the 12 percent of the population who were white controlled the nation's economic, political, and social life. Furthermore, most of the political decisions of the era were made in Lima, where the white population was a larger percentage of the total and certainly loomed considerably larger in decision-making. The partido of Lima in 1813 had a total population of 63,809, consisting of 20,175 whites (32 percent), 10,643 Indians (only 16.5 percent), 4,879 mestizos (only 7.5 percent), 10,231 pardos (16 percent), and 17,881 slaves (28 percent).[33] Incidentally, it is not possible to estimate accurately the portion of whites who were peninsulars or creoles, since the 1795 census grouped all whites together as españoles, whereas the 1813 census drawn up to apportion constitutional voting lists called all whites, Indians, and mestizos alike españoles. Given this imprecision in the documents, some authors' estimates of the number of peninsulars versus creoles should be questioned.

The real Peru, at any rate, was a society in which 12 percent of the population in gross terms (and far fewer in actual terms, since many whites would also be poor), enjoyed the benefits of the productivity of the remainder of the population and made the political decisions. The vast majority of Peru's people—the Indians—were not merely depressed; they did not even share in the prevailing economic, political, or social system. Their role in the process of independence was minimal because the predominantly Indian regions of the country had been militarily controlled by regular army garrisons since suppression of the great Túpac Amaru rebellion of 1780.[34] The role played by the mestizo, the pardo, and the slave—in the cities as well as in the countryside—was considerably more important. They formed much of the manpower of the uprisings, of the rebel and royalist armies, and of the guerrilla bands. Some Peruvian mestizos and pardos even shared in the rewards of independence; but these individuals were very few, and only the whites held political power.

The process of independence, then, is the story of an overprivileged minority (even with considerable numbers of poor creoles among them the whites were still relatively overprivileged) trying to select from among alternative governmental systems the one that would allow them the greatest share of wealth, prestige, power, self-fulfillment, or whatever else they sought. The genuine patriotism of some participants cannot be questioned. Yet many others undeniably functioned in terms of the sheerest expediency.

The real decision-making minority of Peru was naturally much smaller than the gross racial figure of 12 percent suggests. In Lima it is possible to delineate in broad terms who made up the colonial elite. Using the 1813 census, we see that while the white population of Lima was given as 20,175, only 5,243 males were granted the right to vote. Another 6,670 white males were excluded from the voting elite, probably on grounds of income, literacy, age, or profession, and 11,460 white females were excluded. But even that is only part of the story, for the 1813 enumeration was badly marred because it was required to adhere to the social categories set forth in the Constitution (to say nothing of the fact that its sums do not add up correctly). The Constitution specifically declared that all Indians and castes were now to be called españoles—a term formerly reserved in America for whites. What we need, therefore, is some tally of inhabitants by profession. The 1795 census—usually accepted as the most accurate colonial enumeration—does not help because it lists only racial categories.

The variable of occupation is provided by only one enumeration—the 1790 census of Lima published by the liberal Sociedad Académica de Amantes del País.[35] This survey (see table 2) not only showed the gross outlines of Lima's population but included a list of male inhabitants by "destino y categoría." This is invaluable, since occupation tells as much about a person's social position and perceptions as any criterion and at the same time suggests his class. The 1790 census is still usable for Lima in the early nineteenth century because the city's population changed very little—from 52,547 in 1790 to 56,284 in 1813.

By the simple expedient of removing from the 1790 list of males by occupation those whose status, occupation, or income would have made them nonelite (admittedly, a subjective undertaking), it is possible to arrive at a working figure representing the elite and those perceived to be or perceiving themselves to be associated with the elite (see table 3). For example, cirújanos can be removed from the elite but not médicos, because of the much lower status of cirújanos. Pulperos can be eliminated, but not abastecedores, because pulperos were corner grocers and retailers while abastecedores were wholesale provisioners and contract suppliers. Artisans, workers, and jornaleros are easily eliminated, but fabricantes are retained among the elite because the term probably refers to owners of manufacturing concerns. Students and religious novices would be minors, or at least would be viewed as not yet mature enough to have entered their professions. Demandantes ("plaintiffs") are probably those members of the elite whose occupation was not clear at the time of the census because they were in the process of applying for royal appointment, were suing for inheritances, or were awaiting action on an application for some proprietary office. Once the nonelite males are eliminated, the occupational elite totals only 2,489 persons. But even this figure is probably inflated. For example, in most instances the 711 professed members of the regular orders (less any prelates) would also have been excluded from active participation in political decision-making, as certainly would many minor royal employees, escribanos, and cofradía employees, leaving the total policy-making population even smaller—only about 1,500 men. Even this sum, though a working figure that expresses membership in the upper middle and upper classes, should not be taken as the same thing as the "ruling elite." Only those men who were active in some corporation, guild, or association, together with the royal officeholders, officers, and prelates, would constitute the ruling class for day-to-day governmental decisions. Since the 1813 census listed 5,243 voting citizens—a number twice as large as even the occupational elite—it is clear why Viceroy Abascal and other absolutists thought the Constitution and Cortes had caused a radical liberalization in the social classification of the day.

The most significant fact that emerges from these figures has to do not with the small number of the elite, but with their occupations. Notice how many of them depended for their position in society not on industry and agriculture, or even on merchandizing and commerce. The vast majority depended on ecclesiastical or royal appointment. The vast majority of the Lima elite were not producers of real wealth but only consumers. Strictly speaking, a mere 26.3 percent of the elite may be classified as producers. But an astounding 41.7 percent were regular or secular religious, a

TABLE 2

1790 CENSUS OF LIMA

| Grand Totals | | | |
|---|---|---|---|
| | Men | Women | Total |
| Secular | 23,182 | 24,614 | 47,796 |
| Religious | 911 | 656 | 1,567 |
| Living in communities | 1,564 | 1,620 | 3,184 |
| Totals | 25,657 | 26,890 | 52,547 |

| Total Secular Population by "Quality" | |
|---|---|
| Spaniards | 17,215 |
| Indians | 3,912 |
| Mestizos | 4,631 |
| Negroes | 8,960 |
| Mulattoes | 5,972 |
| Cuarterones | 2,383 |
| Quinterones | 219 |
| Zambos | 3,384 |
| Chinos | 1,120 |

| Total Secular Population by Civil Status | |
|---|---|
| Single | 29,944 |
| Married | 13,703 |
| Widowed | 4,149 |

| Males by Occupation and Category | |
|---|---|
| Professed members of regular orders | 711 |
| Religious novices | 438[a] |
| Curates | 10 |
| Assistant curates | 19 |
| Secular clerics | 229 |
| Minor ordination | 16 |
| Sacristans | 34 |
| Dependents of Inquisition | 15 |
| Dependents of Cruzada | 6 |
| Hacendados | 90 |
| Merchants | 393 |
| Fabricantes (manufacturers) | 60 |
| Abastecedores (wholesale provisioners) | 48 |
| Employees of private offices | 64 |
| Titled nobles | 49 |

(Table 2 con't.)

| | |
|---|---|
| Royal employees | 426 |
| Fuero militar | 27 |
| Médicos (doctors) | 21 |
| Cirújanos (surgeons) | 56 |
| Students | 366 |
| Demandantes ("plaintiffs") | 52 |
| Pulperos (retailers, grocers) | 287 |
| Lawyers | 91 |
| Escribanos | 58 |
| Notaries | 13 |
| Cofradía employees | 47 |
| Síndicos de religión | 10 |
| Artisans | 1,027 |
| Laborers | 308 |
| Jornaleros | 363 |
| White servants | 474 |
| Servants from free castes | 2,903 |
| Slaves | 9,229[b] |

SOURCE: "Plan demostrativo de la población comprehendida en el recinto de la Ciudad de Lima," Lima, 5 December 1790, AGI, Indiferente 1527.

NOTE: This census is only for the city and cercado (which by 1790 simply meant "environs"), not for the province or intendancy of Lima.

[a]This is the only figure not taken directly from the census. The census shows a total of 1,392 inhabitants of male religious houses—including 711 professed members, 149 slaves, and 94 servants. I conclude that the remaining 438 inhabitants of such houses were novices or youths in various stages of a potential or actual novitiate.

[b]There were only 8,960 Negroes (male and female), but 9,229 male slaves and an unrecorded number of female slaves. Slavery, therefore, was not restricted to Negroes. The 1813 census shows 12,263 male and female slaves.

TABLE 3

THE LIMA MALE ELITE BY OCCUPATION,
BASED ON THE 1790 CENSUS

| Occupation | Total Cases | Percentage of Total Elite | |
|---|---|---|---|
| Professed members of regular orders | 711 | 28.6 | |
| Curates | 10 | .4 | |
| Assistant curates | 19 | .7 | Religion |
| Secular clerics | 229 | 9.2 | 41.7% |
| Minor ordination | 16 | .6 | |
| Sacristans | 34 | 1.4 | |
| Dependents of Inquisition or Cruzada | 21 | .8 | |
| Hacendados | 90 | 3.6 | |
| Merchants | 393 | 15.8 | Business |
| Fabricantes (manufacturers) | 60 | 2.4 | 26.3% |
| Abastecedores (wholesale provisioners) | 48 | 1.9 | |
| Employees of private offices | 64 | 2.6 | |
| Royal employees | 426 | 17.1 | Royal service |
| Fuero militar | 27 | 1.1 | 18.2% |
| Titled nobles | 49 | 2.0 | |
| Lawyers | 91 | 3.7 | |
| Demandantes ("plaintiffs") | 52 | 2.1 | |
| Escribanos | 58 | 2.4 | Others |
| Doctors | 21 | .8 | 13.8% |
| Síndicos de religión | 10 | .4 | |
| Cofradía employees | 47 | 1.9 | |
| Notaries | 13 | .5 | |
| Total Male Elite | 2,489 | 100.00 | |

fact that must surely give fresh meaning to the old cliché of the "priest-ridden" colonial society. Another 18.2 percent were in royal service or permanent residents who held the fuero militar (and this does not include royal army personnel from the peninsula, because they were not vecinos and were not counted). Even the titled nobles, in a sense, may be considered to owe their positions to royal appointment, though each was supposed to be independently wealthy before being given a title. Escribanos, síndicos de religión, and cofradía employees also depended on royal or ecclesiastical appointment, and demandantes were in the process of acquiring their appointments. However, if one is willing to press the point and include titled nobles, lawyers, and doctors as part of the producing sector of the economy, it still turns out that 67.2 percent of the occupational elite were not producers of wealth but depended on royal or ecclesiastical appointment. No wonder Lima was overrun by pretendientes and aspirants to office, and no wonder the royal treasury was pressed to its limit.

Lima's male occupational elite were no doubt considered well off by the criteria of their day. Yet remarkably few of them owed their incomes to anything other than appointment. A list of real estate owners of 1820—drafted in order to assess a special war tax—shows that only 814 males owned real estate in Lima. The remaining proprietors were 571 women and 45 institutions such as colleges, monasteries, hermandades, parishes, cofradías, oratorios, hospitals, and government agencies. Yet the total male elite by occupation was more than three times as large. Two-thirds of the elite, therefore, did not own real estate (at least not in the city), and 84 percent of the voters of 1813 did not. The 1820 list, unfortunately, did not show the value of the properties or tell which owners possessed multiple properties. It is possible to surmise, based on extrapolation from an 1813 census of property owners conducted in Mexico City, that many were actually among the poorer classes—people who owned makeshift adobe houses or huts on the outskirts of the city—while a handful were great proprietors owning many houses and shops. Yet, since the kind of data that exists for Mexico City has not come to light in Lima, any such surmise must remain tenuous.[36] What is clear, at any rate, is that nearly all clergy, royal officials, and private employees lived in accommodations that were provided for them or that they rented. For most Limeños, therefore, "property" meant cash, furnishings, inventory, or investments.

With so large a portion of the elite dependent, either directly or indirectly, on royal or ecclesiastical appointment, the question whether they were creoles or peninsulars may in fact be a distinctly secondary consideration. Their political decisions, especially their attitude toward the all-encompassing question of separation from Spain, would be most influenced by their dependence on the state or church treasury. When the time came to make their decision they would hesitate and draw back in confusion, unable to make the political choice that would necessarily jeopardize their jobs. Until total victory was won, how could they risk everything on an untimely or early declaration of support for one side or the other? On the other hand, how long could the royal regime sustain itself financially in the midst of rebellion when so limited a portion of the elite were productive?

Yet it would be unwarranted to conclude that the Lima elite, because they were necessarily conservative, were also reactionary. On the contrary, the very fact that they depended so heavily on governmental and church positions meant that many would react favorably when independence implied a promise of promotion for the creole—of a final creole takeover of the highest echelons of state and church bureaucracy. The problem was that it was not clear whether independence would be to their best interest. While the young creole José de la Riva Agüero became a supporter of independence because of personal grievances involving promotion and salary, others, like Manuel Lorenzo Vidaurre, found themselves paralyzed by an excess of scruples and a genuine fear of the unknown future. How could they know whether, once the Spanish regime were destroyed, there would be better appointments for creoles? Would a fledgling and no doubt weak independent regime be able to overcome the financial problems the Spanish empire could not solve? Even more frightening, would independence open the floodgates to the lower class's aspirations for status and income? Would the Indians' anger, so recently demonstrated in the Túpac Amaru uprising, rise again to overwhelm stability, order, and good government in a sea of blood? It was precisely because the Lima elite was so sophisticated, so unemotional, and so aware of the risk to status and income that the decision became impossible. Knowing the creoles' grievances against the imperial regime does not explain independence, for their complaints about jobs and appointments, as it turned out, were as great under the San Martín regime.

Royal power, in Peru and everywhere else in the empire, rested on the uniformity between Spanish objectives and the interests of the whites. Political separation from Spain would occur only when politically active Peruvians turned against the crown, and their decision would be taken on the basis of their perceived interest. Yet how were Peruvians to be sure where their future interests would lie? Late colonial Peru, far from enjoying unrestrained wealth, actually had a rather pinched air, which made the conspicuous consumption of the small top elite all the more noticeable and the grievances of middle-class creoles all the more deeply felt. Politically active Limeños knew how inflexible and delicate the economic and social structures were. How could they be certain independence would provide them a greater portion of Peru's palpably insufficient wealth? Since the most ancient bonds of history tied them to the Spanish cause, how could they be certain independence was the solution to their grievances? In the end they never were able to decide, and that, too, is part of the real Peru. The decision was made on the battlefield, outside Peruvian volition.

The poverty of Peru, occasioned by the relative unproductiveness of its population and the massive expenditures of the war, is the key to the eventual collapse of the royal regime; and, paradoxical as it may sound, this same poverty and unproductiveness is the key to the Peruvians' failure to give enthusiastic support to independence.

In this context, therefore, the response of the viceregal regime to the many grievances Peruvians expressed became all the more critical, for Peru would not turn toward independence as long as the imperial system functioned and seemed to possess authority. Only the regime could disprove its own right to exist; only by failing could it be destroyed. In the very period of crisis, as Peruvians were first becoming aware of alternatives to continued Spanish dominance, the royal government of Peru was in the hands of Viceroy José Fernando de Abascal, one of the most remarkable figures of Spanish American colonial history and one of the most successful servants the Spanish crown ever had.

Chapter 2

# The First Stage of the Struggle

ONCE THE FACT OF Peru's relative poverty is established, the grievances of Peruvians toward the ancient imperial regime and the response of royal authority can be seen as part of a continuum that ultimately led to the anomalies of 1821–24. Every grievance reduces to a complaint about commerce, finance, appointment, prestige, or distribution of goods and offices. One can almost trace the Peruvian independence period without regard to the contradictory ideologies expressed by supporters of one or the other side. At any rate, scholars cannot use expressed ideology to determine historical cause in the Peruvian independence movement, for the high-sounding propaganda issued by either royalists or rebels is invariably rendered meaningless by the bitter struggle for economic survival between individuals and between movements. Every ideological faction was an interest group in one way or another. Peruvians who advocated independence acted in their own interests, as did those who opposed it.

Foremost among the opponents of independence was José Fernando de Abascal, viceroy of Peru from 1806 to 1816. In the history of South American independence he is a central figure, for his administration was able to stop the spread of independence throughout most of the continent. Despite his importance, few biographies of him exist.[1] Modern historiography seems to view him as a totally negative force—the man who delayed independence and retarded the natural flow of creole nationalism, the "prior of the colonial American convent," as one author called him.[2] That view of Abascal, however, denies the fact that those who feared independence saw him as their savior. It denies the reality of Peru—that there was a large segment of society to whom the Spanish ethos continued to make sense and to be the only rational basis for government. In the midst of the agonizing confusion of direction that gripped Peruvians after 1808, Abascal stands as a pillar of rectitude, honesty, clear thinking, and leadership.[3] The measure of his accomplishment is that he governed Peru without interruption during the same time that Viceroy José de Iturrigaray of Mexico was overthrown by conservatives and the viceroys of Río de la Plata and New Granada were overthrown by rebels. Abascal's unique record lies in his ability to counteract dissent and to keep royal authority intact. Abascal was an Asturian, born in Oviedo. He came to Peru after four tours of military service in America—in Puerto Rico, Buenos Aires, Santo Domingo, and Cuba—and after service since 1799 as intendant and president of the audiencia of New Galicia in Guadalajara, Mexico. He was originally appointed viceroy of Río de la Plata, but his ship was captured by an English vessel and he was left on the island of San Miguel in the Azores. After returning to Spain, he was appointed to Lima instead. He landed at Buenos Aires and made his way overland to Peru, thereby touring the southern provinces, and arrived in Lima in July 1806. In 1812 he was granted the title marqués de la Concordia Española del Perú, on the petition of the Lima city council.

Even apart from his resistance to independence, Abascal's accomplishments equal those of other famous viceroys. By his initiative or with his guidance, smallpox vaccine was introduced to Peru and the Junta of Conservation and Propagation was created to maintain the supply; the cleaning and ordering of Lima was advanced; the number of night guards was increased; the practice of burying the dead in the churches was prohibited and a large public cemetery was built; steam engines were introduced in the mines; the Lima Casa de Moneda was improved; the Colegio de San Pablo, or del Príncipe, for mestizos and Indians, was rebuilt and reopened; the Colegio de Abogados was created; the Jardín Botánico was built; and the famous medical college of San Fernando was founded. For defense he spent much effort and money in rebuilding and strengthening a number of forts; he reopened the Lima gunpowder factory that had been burned out in 1792; and he raised two new regular divisions, providing them with quarters, arms, uniforms, and training. To defend the region around Lima he created the militia Regiment of Concordia, composed of three battalions and commanded by Lima aristocrats; and he also supervised the creation of a militia battalion of commercial employees. And for the defense of the peninsula itself, Abascal raised so much money that, according to Germán Leguía y Martínez, when he went home he left the Consulado 7 million pesos in debt and the tobacco monopoly 3.5 million pesos in debt.[4]

In simple, even pedestrian, prose, Abascal proudly reviewed these various accomplishments in his *Memoria*, not hesitating to point out his own failures, although he usually blamed any failure on the lack of funds or the inadequacy of his subalterns. His own reflections seem to imply that he felt no task was too great (he admitted that everything was hard in the beginning but got easier with practice) and suggested that America needed magistrates who possessed what he obviously felt were the most important qualities: "a love of humanity, and of work."[5] Incorrectly viewed as a dour despot, Abascal was in fact a thoroughly professional servant of the king who loved work, admired efficiency, had no patience with incompetence, disliked pomp, but enjoyed power. If he was arrogant, it was the product of accomplishment and confidence, not of venality. He knew who he was and why he had been sent to Peru. In 1814 he had a disagreement with the audiencia—with whom his relations were generally bad—over treatment of a rebel sent from Arequipa for trial. When the audiencia referred to their disagreement as a "conflict," the viceroy replied, "I urge you next time to avoid using the word 'conflict' with me, because either you do not understand its significance, or you forget where I come from and what I represent."[6] This certainty of purpose was Abascal's most important characteristic.

Abascal inherited the control of a country that had already been wracked by everything from violent Indian uprising to outraged calls for justice from aristocrats of the highest social level. The Túpac Amaru uprising of 1780–81, the most serious challenge to royal government before the independence movement, was the most terrible Indian rebellion in America history. It was both a race war between Indian and white and an attempted social revolution aimed at securing a more just distribution of political power and affluence for the highland Indians and mestizos. Some Peruvian historians cite the Túpac Amaru uprising as the first round in the War of Independence, insisting that its objective was separation from Spain.[7] It seems more accurate, however, to count 1780 as just another, though the most massive, of the uprisings against social discrimination and economic debasement that occurred frequently in colonial Peru. The program that Túpac Amaru himself proposed included the establishment of a royal audiencia at Cuzco, redress of the economic mistreatment of the Indians and mestizos at the hands of their corrupt corregidores, abolition of the customs duty on trade between provinces, freedom for the slaves, final and total abolition of the repartimiento, abolition of forced Indian labor drafts (the mita), and improvement of working conditions in the mines and obrajes. Túpac Amaru testified repeatedly that he was not rebelling against the crown, nor against religion, but that he wished only to overthrow immoral administrators who were mistreating the Indians in defiance of the laws for their protection. Thus Túpac Amaru struck the fundamental theme of Peruvian complaint from 1780 to 1821—that the best of laws and most just of governments were being perverted thousands of miles away from the center of power in Spain by immoral and greedy royal administrators in Peru. The rebellion was crushed in Lower Peru in 1781 and in Upper Peru in early 1782, with 100,000 lives lost. After the uprising was over, Spain established several basic reforms in the administration of the interior. An audiencia was created in Cuzco, the repartimiento was abolished, and the intendant system, already launched in other parts of the empire, was imported into Peru to replace the corrupt corregidores.[8]

The reforms, however, were oriented more toward imperial centralization than toward meeting Peruvian grievances. Leon G. Campbell has pointed out that the net effect of the Túpac Amaru rebellion was to harden royalist attitudes toward the danger of internal lower-class or creole insurrection. In the immediate wake of the revolt the Spanish began to demobilize the creole and mestizo militias of the Peruvian interior and reverted to the earlier system of dependence on permanent garrisons of veteran soldiers. After 1784 the militias were restricted to the coastal intendancies and the Sierra was returned to small, but well-trained regular garrisons in which creoles were permitted no influence. Not until 1810 would Peru return to dependence on large militia forces. Although Campbell perhaps overstates the issue when he says "Peru remained a bulwark of Royalism by virtue of an army of occupation,"[9] the essential fact remains that the Peruvian royal regime, unique among all the American colonial regimes, had faced and overcome a massive threat to Spanish power in the generation before the movement for independence, thus hardening its defenses and forcing it to alter the primary mission of the army after 1784 from defense against some outside invader to defense against internal lower-class rebellion. This consciousness of the danger of Indian rebellion undoubtedly was an advantage to the Peruvian regime. The Peruvian independence movement would not be initiated by a mass Indian uprising like Mexico's Grito de Dolores of 1810.

Another aspect of the administrative reorganization of the 1780s, in this case not unique to Peru, was the peninsula's policy of gradually replacing American-born royal appointees, especially members of the audiencia, with peninsulars. Mark A. Burkholder and D. S. Chandler have shown that this was an empirewide policy and one of the most critical of the Bourbon reforms advocated by Minister of the Indies José de Gálvez and Peruvian Visitor-General José de Areche. More important than the mere exclusion of creoles was the specific exclusion of Limeños from membership on the Lima audiencia. From the 1740s to the 1770s Limeños and creoles from other parts of America made up a majority of the Lima audiencia; yet by 1803 only one Limeño, José Baquíjano y Carrillo, and one other creole were on the audiencia. This policy, while tightening Madrid's control over American administration, also provoked creoles to feel that they were being denied their fair share of power, a share they had once possessed. The net effect of these reforms was thus contradictory; while they tended to suppress lower-class rebellion, they added new grievances for the middle and upper classes.[10] In Lima, where aspirations to government appointment were particularly acute, the demand that creoles be appointed to at least one-third or one-half of all government positions was a constant refrain from the 1790s to independence.

Nor did complaints of corruption and mistreatment abate after suppression of the Indian uprising. Rather, they spread to the group of gentlemen thinkers in Lima who had been heavily influenced by their reading of the Enlightenment philosophers. This is the group of intellectual precursors about whom so much has been written. The head of this group of enlightened thinkers was José Baquíjano. In 1781 Baquíjano was chosen to deliver the principal address of welcome to the newly arrived Viceroy Agustín de Jáuregui (1780–84). The speech initiated a whole generation of debate and discussion concerning the issue of Spanish policy in Peru. Baquíjano was so outspoken as to criticize the Spanish regime—only four months after the defeat of Túpac Amaru—for its mistreatment of the Indians and to point out the hunger, desolation, and misery from which they suffered.[11]

Although the text of Baquíjano's address was later confiscated by royal order, the new ideas he had dared speak openly became the central doctrine of a generation of liberal thinkers. This liberal philosophy reached its peak in the period from 1791 to 1795 in the publication of a periodical named the *Mercurio Peruano*. Lima's leading intellectuals wrote for the *Mercurio*, using it to discuss openly the status of the Indian and the philosophies of natural law and reason, both of which were viewed by conservatives as potentially subversive. Many figures in this group, most of whom belonged to the Sociedad de Amantes del País, were teachers at or graduates of the Real Convictorio de San Carlos, an institution founded by Viceroy Manuel de Amat y Junient that functioned as the principal colegio of Lima and housed the faculty of humanities of the University of San Marcos. The college of San Carlos not only eclipsed the university as the institution where exciting ideas were being transmitted, it was the main source for the dissemination of Enlightenment philosophy. Under the rectorship of Toribio Rodríguez de Mendoza—the chief teacher and preserver of the new thought—San Carlos turned out many students steeped in the writings of Locke, Descartes, and Voltaire, advocates of the social contract, natural law, and the primacy of reason.[12]

The professors and students of San Carlos provided the most important intellectual criticism of the Spanish system from the 1780s to the late 1810s. Peru produced one of the largest and most significant groups of Enlightenment thinkers in all of South America. Yet it will become abundantly clear in the next chapters that the generation of Baquíjano and the generation that succeeded it by about 1808 and produced such brilliant minds as Manuel Lorenzo Vidaurre, José Faustino Sánchez Carrión, and Francisco Javier Luna Pizarro were mainly critics of the regime rather than rebels. It is important to recognize this distinction. It is often assumed that because Peru produced social critics, libertarians, and advocates of equality, it therefore became independent. Quite the contrary; the advocates of the philosophy of reason were products of or aspirants to membership in the upper class. Though advocating amelioration of the Indians' condition, they also feared the consequences of possible Indian rebellion. Though opposed to the Spanish monopoly system, which placed domination over Peru's internal and external trade in the hands of peninsulars, they sought in its place creole domination. Though opponents of scholasticism, they fought just as scrappily as anyone else for preferment to office and the security of tenure in university, college, protomedicato, civil service, or church. Only a tiny minority of the liberal thinkers, as Pike says, believed that independence would solve what they perceived as Peru's problems.[13] Most sought reform within the imperial structure, equality for creoles, and autonomy for Peru.

It is almost a general rule that the most rational of Peru's thinkers were the slowest to accept the idea of independence. The Peruvian thinkers who depended on empiricism could not automatically reject the imperial ethos of Spain; for as long as the ancient imperialism worked, it was itself rational. The reformers sought "good government," and reform of the existing regime seemed a more expeditious way to achieve it than did rebellion. Consequently, in 1812 Baquíjano is to be found already an oidor, a titled noble, and recipient of the great distinction of being chosen a councilor of state, writing Viceroy Abascal to initiate an investigation of alleged liberal conspiracies in Lima's first constitutional election. Do not expect such a man to be a rebel. Baquíjano accused Friar Segundo Carrión of promoting electoral irregularities, Friar Tomás Mendez of provoking disorder among minors and lower classes, Friar Cecilio Tagle of being a notorious proponent of equality between the classes, lawyer Manuel Pérez de Tudela of "holding the same criminal opinions," Francisco Paula Quiróz of publicly stating these ideas, Joaquín Mansilla of soliciting votes, and the conde de la Vega del Ren of being misled into treasonous opinions.[14]

Despite the subversive role it was playing in Peruvian affairs, the Colegio de San Carlos continued teaching and disseminating Enlightenment philosophy until 1816, when, as the result of a visita ordered by Abascal and conducted by Manuel Pardo, emigrant regent of the audiencia of Cuzco, its doors were temporarily closed and Toribio Rodríguez de Mendoza, rector for more than thirty years, was dismissed and replaced by Carlos Pedemonte. Even so, it is not clear if the college was disciplined because of its politics or merely because its finances and community life were found in need of reform. The final report of Pardo's visita found that the college's income, usually about 18,000 pesos a year in tribute from several haciendas and other government grants and from student tuition, had fallen by 1816 to only 2,500 pesos. By 1816 the college had a rector, two vice-rectors, and eleven professors, but only seventy-three students, not all of whom boarded in as they were supposed to do. All the students were questioned concerning curriculum, community life, and internal management of the college, and it was found that the food was extremely limited and that the strict rules of conduct laid down in the original charter were not being adhered to. Pardo reported that the college library contained some prohibited books, though they were kept under lock and key. A new constitution for the college was proposed, consisting chiefly of much stricter rules for college life, meals, outside contacts, and curriculum, but Pardo admitted that no lasting improvement in the college was possible because of the decadence of the University of San Marcos itself, which he called "no more than an edifice of pure pomp and ostentation." The viceregal regime's slowness in disciplining the college was probably due to the sheer importance of San Carlos to the viceroyalty's educational system. Viceroy Joaquín de la Pezuela, when he sent to Spain the final report of the college's reform, admitted that its decline was all the more deeply felt "because it could be called the only college of its kind in this kingdom."[15]

In many regards, then, the historian who seeks explanations for Peru's independence by concentrating on the College of San Carlos and its graduates will be misled. Many of the foremost lights of the group of liberals the college produced never actually advocated rebellion, and many others joined the movement for independence only after 1820. The college collapsed only in 1816, as a result of its own bankruptcy, and even then Viceroy Pezuela mourned its demise. A more important focus of dissent lay elsewhere.

In addition to the precise and rational critique by Lima's enlightened thinkers, the royal regime was also subjected to a constant barrage of complaints and denunciations that originated in personal and economic grievances. In many ways these personal grievances give a more practical, if more mundane, view of what was troubling anonymous men and women in late colonial Peru. One theme predominates in these grievances, as in all others: accusations of corruption and immorality directed against the peninsular administrators of the viceroyalty and centered upon the status anxiety and economic fears of individuals.

Late colonial Lima's chief characteristic seems to have been a rather unsavory propensity toward name-calling. It can best be illustrated by reviewing the series of outraged letters of denunciation sent to Spain between 1810 and 1817 by two men named Domingo Sánchez Revata and Antonio Pérez. Little is known about either of them except what their many letters reveal. They may be taken to represent, though with considerable exaggeration, the large population of letrados that characterized late colonial Lima, for both were well-educated, unemployed seekers of government appointment. For example, Abascal defined Sánchez Revata's profession simply as "penman."[16] They were more representative of Lima than were the gentlemen thinkers of the aristocracy and the colleges. They impress the reader most of all with their anxiety and frustration. This discontent, deriving from a desire to share more fully in the good things of life that Lima offered, is the core of Lima's confused politics in later years. Personal ambition, anger, and frustration played a significant part in the political decisions Limeños made, or failed to make, in the War of Independence.

The whining, self-congratulatory, half-mad ravings of Domingo Sánchez Revata, despite their excesses, reflect typical fears and concerns of late colonial Lima. Revata seems to have had no other career but writing long letters to a succession of peninsular governments, each aimed at pointing out the multitude of failings of Peruvian officials. In 1791, for example, he sent Spain an exposé of abuses in the collection of the Indian tribute in Cañete, for which service to the state he was rewarded with four charges laid against him by the subdelegate of Cañete, brief imprisonment, confiscation of his mother's goods, and a legal battle to clear his name that lasted fifteen years, finally resulting, he said, in his complete vindication. In 1806 he complained of abuses in the handling of denunciations he had brought to the audiencia, and he was outraged when the viceroy required him to post a bond of 1,000 pesos. Throughout the reign of Charles IV he dispatched reports accusing the audiencia, tribunals, magistrates, subdelegates, and viceroys of unjust acts and countless extortions and abuses of power. He criticized the monopoly system, begging for free agriculture and trade. He proposed reforming the Laws of the Indies; abolishing perpetual city council seats; abolishing the office of viceregal assessor; abolishing the tribute, sales taxes, and state monopolies; abolishing salaries of Consulado officials; increasing the salaries of magistrates and escribanos so that the public could bring cases to court without having to pay a multitude of costs; and abolishing ecclesiastical fees. After establishment of the Constitution he wrote a series of denunciations accusing the viceroy and audiencia of disobedience to the law. Though he accused the elected city council of misuse of funds, he also accused the former perpetual city council of being sycophantic followers of Viceroy Abascal. He accused at least half the members of the audiencia of corruption. He accused Ignacio de la Pezuela, secretary of the Spanish Regency and later minister of state, of being an agent of Viceroy Abascal. In a single sentence he complimented Joaquín de la Pezuela, brother of Ignacio and subinspector of artillery of Peru, for being a genius responsible for improving Peru's defenses and at the same time accused him of being a traitorous follower of Manuel de Godoy. At one point Revata, in his hysterical attempt to be heard, even addressed a letter filled with such charges to George III, king of England.[17]

Revata's preferred targets were Viceroy Abascal, the Lima city council, and the audiencia. Abascal, he charged in various letters, governed despotically, disobeyed royal orders at will, and depended for his power upon a cabal of favorites that included the audiencia members and the city aldermen. In one letter he summarized, "Viceroy Abascal has been the worst of those who have governed, he has been arbitrary . . . . His principal object has been to acquire crosses, to be ennobled, and to amass money to give to his daughter Ramonsita, whom he offers in marriage to everybody." The viceroy's secretary he called "a mulatto, the adulterous son of a theater comic." The cabildo, he insisted, was nothing but "a great mayorazgo for its members." But the audiencia and all its functionaries were beyond words. In one letter Revata summarized the multitude of faults of the magistrates by concluding, "Not only do they not know the law but they do not have one single book in their studies." Exhausted by his own rhetoric, he concluded another letter by saying: "The viceroys in Lima do what they want . . . and all of them have made themselves so ridiculous, that upon hearing their imaginary accomplishments celebrated by themselves, it seems to me that I am hearing Don Quixote celebrate his Dulcinea del Taboso." [18]

Revata is cited here to illustrate the extent of anger felt by some Limeños. Many of his charges were demonstrably untrue. At one point, for example, he said that Abascal had sent out "millions" of pesos to Panama for his daughter Ramona's inheritance, when in fact Abascal never profited personally from his administration. Just as inaccurate was his letter to Spain dated 8 April 1810, in which he charged the Peruvian church with extortion in the collection of fees for baptism and marriage. This was one of the few Revata letters that provoked a reply. The Regency ordered Archbishop Bartolomé de Las Heras of Lima to moderate the fees. In reply, Archbishop Las Heras, a man whose rectitude and honesty have never been questioned, told the Regency that although he would obey the order, it would scandalize his clergy, for he emphatically denied they received excessive fees. [19]

Not surprisingly, Revata incurred the wrath of the upright Abascal, who ordered him arrested on two occasions. In early 1812 he was jailed on charges of being the author of subversive papers and of distributing proclamations from the Buenos Aires insurgents. Replying to Revata's charges that the regent of the audiencia, Manuel de Arredondo, was guilty of collusion and conspiracy in the confiscation of estates in the Valley of Cañete belonging to supporters of the French, Abascal said that Revata was one of "those pamphleteers . . . who conspire with their detestable writings to provoke disorder . . . and to take the superior tribunals by surprise with complaints and grievances that exist only in their disconcerted minds." Again in December 1812, during the first constitutional elections in Lima, Abascal ordered Revata confined at Magdalena on charges of electoral conspiracy and sent guards to search his house for signs of treason. When Viceroy Abascal requested information about Revata from a selected group of trusted gentlemen in Lima in 1813, only one reported knowing him. José Banquíjano replied that Revata "is a wicked man in the fullest meaning of the word."[20]

Obviously, Revata's condemnation of nearly everybody in power in Lima is not credible. Some of his charges accurately reflect the worries of ordinary people, whereas others were clearly false. All were motivated by personal ambition, outraged pride, and, to judge from the often incoherent style of his letters, more than a hint of insanity. Revata was simply the most hysterical of many other complainants who wrote to Spain accusing the viceregal authorities of despotism, corruption, and tyranny. Popular perceptions of reality, as much as the reality itself, are important to the historian.

The denunciations of Antonio Pérez were more specific than Revata's but no more credible. In a series of letters, Pérez attacked the audiencia and the church; his prevailing theme was the widespread immorality of Peru. Referring to the church, he charged that prelates and priests were living openly with concubines and their children; that prelates absorbed one-third of the church's income for their own support while poor priests lived in great want; that regular orders had greatly deteriorated through loss of discipline; that some runaway members of regular orders joined bands of robbers and rapists; and that many fathers were consigning their daughters to religious life at ages as young as twelve.[21]

The audiencia remained Pérez's favorite target. In one letter he specified the commonly held complaints against the oidors. Only the creole Miguel de Eyzaguirre, fiscal de lo crímen, a universal favorite among Peruvians, was above suspicion. All other members of the audiencia, he said, were corrupt and venal. Domingo Arnaiz had abandoned his wife and was living with his concubine in a bread shop he had opened for her; Manuel María del Valle y Postigo was a famous braggart who owned several haciendas and who had defrauded his sister-in-law of 80,000 pesos; Manuel García de la Plata was also a braggart who had robbed the cofradías of large sums of money; José Pareja owned a large hacienda and a mantequería, and he notoriously extorted money from people engaged in lawsuits; Juan del Pino Manrique, though not a braggart and not engaged in commerce, was still venal, as was Tomás Ignacio Palomeque, who had run up gambling debts of 31,000 pesos; Juan Bazo y Berri lived apart from his family; and José Muñoz, the viceregal assessor who was very unpopular with creoles, lived in the greatest immorality. In another letter Pérez complained of the excessive salaries of royal officials and denounced Abascal as a despot. In yet another, he complained of the immense costs of the war effort and of the 400,000 pesos General Pezuela spent in rebuilding the capital's defenses, and he claimed that commanders were employing soldiers as servants in their houses. He said the members of the Lima city council were all poor men who managed to keep only the central streets of the city in proper repair while the rest deteriorated, exactly duplicating a charge Revata made. Since the slaves who sold food and water in the streets were the property of the city councilors, nothing was done to control weights and prices.[22]

The many letters of Revata and Pérez were by no means the only such denunciations of government authorities. Mariano Tramarria wrote in 1816 to repeat the charges against the audiencia members. Extending his complaint to include the entire government, he said that "from the Captain General down to the lowliest public employee . . . they are all tyrants in the shadow of the royal mantle." A highly placed government bureaucrat, Joaquín Jordán, interim treasurer of the national monopolies, wrote on several occasions to accuse the regent, Manuel de Arredondo, of collusion in the buying and managing of haciendas. Meanwhile, an anonymous denunciation dated 10 August 1810 carried the name-calling to its extreme by specifying three members of the audiencia who were adulterers and naming the women they lived with; charging Manuel Valle with having been trained as a blacksmith before coming to Peru; Juan Bazo y Berri with being the son of a Mercedarian friar and being married to a mestiza; Gaspar Osma with being an insurgent; Tomás Palomeque with stealing from a silver shop; and José Baquíjano with corrupting the morals of the young nobles and being a Protestant.[23]

The chief value of these letters of denunciation is what they reveal of the environment of late colonial Lima. It was a society characterized by suspicion, name-calling, deep-seated personal feuds, and rapacious ambition. The air was poisoned with recrimination and selfishness. Yet, the dissension was founded on status anxiety and the scramble for office, not on resounding principles of the social contract or the rights of man. Simón Bolívar would later despair of it, saying "this country is afflicted with a moral pestilence," and "every scoundrel wants to be supreme." Basil Hall was to declare that Lima was "characterized by an engrossing selfishness."[24] This was no figment of the imagination; many visitors noticed it, and the Limeños' own letters testify to it. There were too many aspirants to fill the positions that were necessarily restricted by limited resources and by conscious imperial policy. For all their complaints, of course, the discontented pretendientes of Lima would rally to the crown when threatened with the overwhelming disaster of Indian rebellion or French invasion, but when those dangers were not present they turned again to in-fighting. It was in this milieu that Viceroy Abascal had to function. Of all his accomplishments, the greatest was that in such an environment he was able to maintain the strongest and most effective of all the royal governments in the rebellious Spanish American empire.

The status anxiety that reigned among Peruvians, and their inability to agree among themselves, was Abascal's greatest ally in the political crisis that swept the Spanish empire in 1808. On 9 August 1808 the city council of Lima received word from the viceroy that King Charles IV had abdicated in favor of his son Ferdinand VII.[25] In other parts of the empire this revelation, and the events immediately following it, led to a sustained period of constitutional crisis over the possession of sovereignty. In Lima, though it would be an overstatement to say there was no shock, the abdication of the king and the overthrow of his chief minister Manuel de Godoy did not lead to revolution or to an attempt to create local self-government, as it did in Mexico City, Caracas, Bogotá, and Buenos Aires.

Only four days before the news of the abdication arrived, the city council of Lima recorded in its minutes a discussion of the state of Peru's defenses. Deciding that Viceroy Abascal, who had been in power for two years, was largely responsible for the improvement in security, the council determined to send a letter to the king asking that Abascal be allowed to remain in power "without taking account of the [usual viceregal] term of five years, or anything else, and without naming a successor."[26]

Although the letter was probably not sent on this occasion, the cabildo later wrote similar recommendations. Preferring security to disruption, the creoles rallied to Abascal. The viceroyalty of Peru was governed in 1808 by a man who had the general confidence of even the creole city council of the capital, something that occurred nowhere else in America. Thus girded against the storm that was about to break, Lima began to make plans for the fiesta it would conduct to honor Ferdinand's accession, with the viceroy setting 1 December as the date for the formal oath of allegiance to the new king.

Then on 4 October the news arrived, via Chile, that Ferdinand VII had also abdicated and had been imprisoned by Napoleon at Bayonne. The city council noted that this event "caused an inexplicable sadness and general emotion" among all the population. But still there was no crisis of confidence in the royal regime. The viceroy informed the city council that Ferdinand would still be recognized as the only legitimate king, and that was that. Abascal moved the date for the oath of allegiance forward, from 1 December to 13 October. After hurried plans, the oath-taking occurred on the appointed day amid considerable pomp. Only a month earlier, Viceroy José de Iturrigaray of Mexico had been overthrown in a coup d'etat led by conservative peninsular merchants who feared he was not sufficiently loyal to the new king. In Lima there was no such confusion. Whereas the city councils of Mexico City, Bogotá, Santiago, Caracas, Quito, and Buenos Aires took the opportunity of the king's captivity to proclaim the doctrine of popular sovereignty and to strike out for autonomy under provisional juntas created in the king's name, the Lima city council mustered only enough boldness to ask the viceroy, on 15 October, to suspend collection of the amortization ordered in 1804 by the Cédula of Consolidation.[27] Unknown to the Lima aldermen, suspension of the Consolidation had already been ordered by the Spanish Junta Central.

The Junta Central was the government formed in mid-1808 by the various provincial juntas that had sprung up throughout Spain to resist the French invasion and conquest after Ferdinand fell prisoner. It first met in late September 1808, and for sixteen months it was the only legitimate government in Spain and the empire, with its seat first in Seville, then in Cádiz and the Isle of León. When creation of the Junta Central was announced in Lima on 9 March 1809, the capital again responded quietly and loyally and immediately recognized it as the legitimate government.[28] Lima remained quiet and untroubled in the midst of the greatest political crisis that had ever swept the empire. Despite the massive discontent of Peruvians with the regime, when the storm came the elite found Abascal their beacon of safety.

Between 1808 and 1810 Viceroy Abascal worked out for himself the basic response to the successive waves of political crisis that followed—a policy of moderation and prevention. While he worked feverishly to refurbish the viceroyalty's defenses, creating the Regiment of Concordia in 1811 and spending large sums of money on General Pezuela's defense works, he also took care not to offend prominent Peruvian creoles who seemed on the verge of dissent. His hand was everywhere, moderate when needed, firm and aggressive when that was required. His master policy, as it turned out, was to prevent the spread of insurrection into Peru from its neighbors.

When Abascal needed to be moderate, it was remarkable how mild he could be. Shortly after news of the Napoleonic usurpation of the throne reached Lima, a group of prominent medical doctors began to hold meetings in the Medical College of San Fernando to discuss the political events of the empire. They included José Pezet, who was then editor of the official government periodical, the *Gaceta de Gobierno*; Hipólito Unánue, chief figure in the medical college; Gavino Chacaltana, professor of anatomy; and perhaps ten or fifteen other professors and students. These people were important to Abascal and to the capital; they had raised the practice of medicine to a more professional level and removed its control from the hands of the quacks and cirújanos who had previously dominated it. Besides, they were too articulate to have as enemies. When Abascal received a denunciation, perhaps from a student of the college, he determined, instead of bringing the doctors to trial, simply to warn them to desist from further political discussions. When he had privately warned each man in turn, they kept quiet.[29]

But when conspiracy appeared among the lower classes, Abascal could strike with speed. Following the uprising of Quito in August 1809, for example, a group of relatively lowly inhabitants of Lima hatched a plot to establish a provisional junta and to force the viceroy to sanction the plan. Although the undertaking never advanced beyond the talking stage, it was denounced to the viceroy, and the members of the conspiracy were arrested and jailed on the night of 26–27 September 1809. The chief conspirators were Antonio María Pardo, a business agent who had the protection of Francisco Zárate, son of the powerful marqués de Montemira; and Mateo Silva, a young creole lawyer. They were joined by a peninsular, José Antonio Canosa; a lottery employee, José María García; a native of Cajamarca, Juan Sánchez Silva; a young night guard, Pedro Zorrilla; and several young cadets. Another important connection came in the membership of José Santos Figueroa y Villacorta, who was an employee of the cabildo syndic, Manuel Pérez de Tudela, perhaps Lima's most important liberal lawyer. After a two-month investigation, oidor Juan Bazo y Berri gave out such harsh sentences as to make the plot seem more serious than it really was. All the conspirators were sentenced to prison.[30] Vicuña Mackenna calls this the most important plot before the Pumacahua uprising of 1814, which adequately points out the relative lack of conspiracies for independence in Abascal's Peru.

Thus, though some Peruvians began to drift toward political dissent, the majority rallied around the viceroy in the name of their new and as yet unknown king. Peru experienced an emotional resurgence of loyalty to the mother country and to the prince who, so Peruvians thought, had been caught up and destroyed in a political disaster created by the aggression of the French tyrant and the cupidity of his own father. Since Ferdinand's true colors were as yet unknown, he became "the desired one" (el deseado), the hope of the future security of the empire. Eventually Ferdinand showed that he was not worthy of his people's affection, but for the moment everyone, from viceroy to peon, placed him on the pedestal created by national pride and outrage against the French conquerors and their Spanish collaborators.[31]

José Manuel de Goyeneche, an Arequipa-born officer sent to South America in 1809 by the Junta of Seville to confer with the authorities and to strengthen loyalty to Ferdinand VII, traveled overland from Buenos Aires to Lima, visiting the various centers along the way. In April 1809, after witnessing Lima's oath to the Junta Central, he wrote Spain to testify to the fidelity of both Cuzco and Lima. He defined Lima's loyalty to the king as being "electric." It was largely the work, he said, of Abascal, General Pezuela, and three or four members of the audiencia. He did, however, strike a note of warning about Chile. Although he had not visited it, he testified that Chile had been poorly governed for some years, its loyalty was not strong, and it was defenseless. He prophesied, "[Chile] is the throat of South America; once lost, Peru is lost."[32] Abascal appointed Goyeneche temporary president of the audiencia of Cuzco, from which point the Arequipeño later became one of the most important royalist military commanders in the Upper Peruvian theater.

In this brief period of general enthusiasm, the first signs of the revolutionary changes of government soon to come in Spain were greeted in Peru with a mixture of joy and trepidation. In January 1809 the Junta Central in Spain announced that the vast overseas territories in America and Asia were integral parts of the Spanish nation rather than colonies, and each viceroyalty and captaincy-general of America was invited to send a delegate to take part in the Junta. In Peru each cabildo chose one nominee and submitted his name to Viceroy Abascal, who selected three he thought were qualified to serve. The finalists were José Baquíjano, José Manuel de Goyeneche (who had already departed for Cuzco), and José Silva y Olave, a doctor of law from the university. The three names were placed in an urn, and Abascal's daughter Ramona chose by lot the name of Silva.[33] Silva left for Spain via Mexico, where he was informed of the dissolution of the Junta Central, whereupon he returned to Lima.

The Junta Central in Spain dissolved itself in January 1810 in favor of a newly created Council of Regency. The Regency proceeded, although with some reservations, to fulfill the announced intention of the former Junta to call together in Cádiz a Cortes, or parliament, of all the empire. The American dominions were to be represented in the Cortes on the basis of one deputy to each 100,000 white inhabitants. This was an unequal proportion, despite the Junta's declaration of American equality, since the peninsula was allotted one deputy for each 50,000 inhabitants, plus one for each provincial junta and one for each major city. In addition, the large castizo population of the overseas territories was not counted in the apportionment of seats. Such obvious discrimination guaranteed that the Cortes would consist of a majority of peninsular deputies even though the colonial population outnumbered the European. Even so, the creation of a parliament provided Peru a new focus for expressing its grievances. The duality of response that characterized Peruvians throughout the entire independence period was already clear: loyalty in the face of extreme crisis, combined with unrelenting complaints of Spanish tyranny.

On 27 August 1810 the city council of Lima chose by lot from among three nominees the name of Francisco Salazar, brother of the alcalde Andrés Salazar, as its Cortes deputy. He left for Spain in January 1811, his expenses paid by the city council. The Cortes, which governed the empire from 1810 to 1814, convened in Cádiz on 24 September 1810. Since there had not been time for the delegates from America to arrive in Spain, the Cortes began its sessions with substitute overseas delegates chosen from among the many colonials residing in the peninsula. Peru, having been allotted five substitute seats, was represented by five Peruvians living in Cádiz—Vicente Morales y Duarez, a native of Lima and a doctor of law and theology; Ramón Olaguer Feliú, a native of Ceuta but a graduate of the College of San Carlos; Dionisio Inca Yupanqui, a member of the Inca dynasty of Cuzco, but educated in Spain; Antonio Suazo, a creole military officer who had lived the past twenty-six years in Spain; and Blas Ostolaza, an ultraroyalist from Trujillo and former tutor and chaplain of Ferdinand VII.[34] These five deputies—later joined by the deputies elected in Peru itself—collectively represented the position of creole Peruvians before the Spanish government.

By the week of the Cortes's first meeting, almost all of America, with the exception of Peru, Central America, and the Caribbean islands, was in revolt. Quito had already risen in 1809, and in 1810 insurrections commenced in Venezuela on 19 April, in Buenos Aires and Upper Peru on 25 May, in New Granada on 20 July, in Mexico on 15 September, and in Chile on 18 September.

For the next four years, therefore, Abascal's challenges consisted of rebellion on Peru's borders and political revolution in the mother country. Only the neighboring rebellions were amenable to action from the viceroy, since he could not control the direction taken by the Cortes. Abascal's Peru, militarized and efficiently ordered, held back the flood of rebellion in Quito, Chile, and Upper Peru. With an initial regular army that in 1809 numbered only 1,500 men, Abascal was at first forced to rely on the viceroyalty's various militias, which together numbered more than 40,000.[35] These forces, under command of the four great royalist generals—José Manuel de Goyeneche, Joaquín de la Pezuela, Juan Ramírez, and Mariano Osorio—were thrown time and time again against Quito on the north, Chile on the south, and, most important, against the armies of Buenos Aires in Upper Peru. In July 1810 Abascal reannexed Upper Peru, removing it from the titular control of the now independent Buenos Aires. Furthermore, when it was not possible to send troops, Abascal sent funds to help reinforce royal governments under assault. In 1811, for example, Peru granted 300,000 pesos to Montevideo, and further grants were given to Quito and Upper Peru. In 1812 Lima spent more than 1,275,000 pesos (one-fifth of total viceregal revenues) in defense of other territories, including Upper Peru (820,000), Montevideo (188,000), Chile (67,000), Quito (100,000), and Acapulco (16,000). In January 1814 Abascal declined a request that he also aid Bogotá and Panama, pointing out that the Peruvian treasury was already supporting Upper Peru, Chile, and Quito and paying the salaries of the refugee oidors from those places. As if all of that were not enough, Abascal also had to face four regional rebellions in Peru itself before the outbreak of the major uprising at Cuzco in 1814. These were the short-lived rising of Francisco Antonio de Zela in Tacna in June 1811, the seizure of Tacna by Enrique Paillardelle in May 1813, the revolutionary conspiracy in Huamanga in 1812, and the rebellion of Huanuco in February 1812.[36]

For almost five years Peru was the bulwark of Spanish power, and its military success was impressive. By 1815 only Buenos Aires remained independent, while viceregal arms had destroyed and routed rebel governments in Quito and Santiago, had several times driven rebel occupiers out of La Paz, and had crushed internal Peruvian rebellion in Cuzco and Arequipa. A century later, Germán Leguía proudly claimed that Abascal's extraordinary success proved that the Peruvian people, if well governed, and Peruvian soldiers, if well commanded, were invincible. Furthermore, Peru accomplished all this virtually without reinforcements from Spain. Not until 1812 did the first reinforcements arrive—the 700 men of the dreaded Talavera battalion. Only after restoration of the king were there further peninsular reinforcements. In 1815 a reinforcement of 1,600 men arrived, part of Pablo Morillo's forces, consisting of the artillery regiment of Extremadura commanded by Mariano Ricafort, the Fourth Hussars Regiment of Ferdinand VII, the Fourth Squadron of the Dragoon Regiment of the Union, and a company of infantry. In 1816 there came the regiments of Gerona and Cantabria (Colonel Juan Antonio Monet); in 1817 the first battalion of the Regiment of Burgos; a squadron of the King's Lancers, and some others; and in 1818 further battalions of the Cantabria.[37] Though the backbone of the viceroyalty's military power remained creole, mestizo, and pardo militiamen, by 1816 there was also a large contingent of European expeditionary forces that provided officers for the militia as well as front-line troops, highly mobile and well trained, to resist the rebellion when it finally spread into Peru itself.

Even as the viceroy was launching what would turn out to be his successful military resistance to insurrection, the Cortes of Cádiz, which began meeting in September 1810, debated the demand of the Americans that overseas territories should have equal representation. All five Peruvian substitute delegates spoke firmly in favor of equal representation and of recognizing the equality of the Indian with the Spaniard. Feliú declared that "America is no longer . . . a child who, put to bed with promises, will forget them when he awakens." Suazo declared that Americans were "tired of hearing brilliant and pompous decrees in their favor." Yupanqui passionately defended the Indian culture against whites' assumptions of its inferiority. The most prominent Peruvian delegate, however, was Vicente Morales y Duarez. A creole of firm liberal persuasion, he was a proponent of free press, racial equality, American equality, and protection of the Indian. In defending the Indians from the calumnies of peninsular delegates who claimed they were inferior and fit only for slavery, he declared: "There are men who seem born for slavery, because in reality they were born under it. . . . There are slaves by nature, because they were made slaves against nature." Morales so impressed his fellow deputies that on 24 March 1812 he was elected president of the Cortes, but he died only six days later from natural causes. After the death of Morales, Peru's total representation in the Cortes extraordinarias—which sat until 1813 when the first Cortes ordinarias gathered—was twelve. This figure included the four surviving substitute deputies and eight more who were elected in Peru and who were able to reach Cádiz. The deputies elected in Peru who actually sat in the Cortes extraordinarias were Francisco Salazar for Lima, José Lorenzo Bermúdez for Tarma, Pedro García Coronel for Trujillo, and José Antonio Navarette for Piura (these four arrived in time to sign the Constitution), and José Joaquín Olmedo for Guayaquil, Tadeo Gárate for Puno, Juan Antonio Andueza for Chachapoyas, and Nicolás Aranívar for Arequipa (all of whom arrived later).[38] Despite the intensity of American feeling, equal representation was never granted.

The various demands presented to the Cortes by the Peruvian deputies provide the clearest expression of Peruvian grievances against the imperial regime. In December 1810, for example, the Peruvian deputies joined all the other American and Asian Cortes members in presenting a list of eleven fundamental reforms that the overseas territories required. They were: (1) equal proportionate Cortes representation, with Indians and castes being counted; (2) freedom to plant and manufacture all previously prohibited commodities; (3) free trade with any part of Spain and with allies and neutrals; (4) free American trade with Asia; (5) free trade with Asia from any American or Filipino port (6) suppression of all state and private monopolies; (7) free mining of mercury; (8) equal rights of Americans to government employment; (9) distribution of half the positions in each territory to natives of that territory; (10) creation of advisory committees in America to select the creoles to be given those public offices; and (11) restoration of the Jesuit order in America.[39] These objectives were particularly attractive to Peruvians; the Lima city council sent copies of them to other cabildos throughout the country.

Although all the Peruvian deputies endorsed the general demands, a more detailed and specifically Peruvian list of demands came in the Lima city council's instructions to its deputy Francisco Salazar. In August 1814, after the Cortes and Constitution had been annulled, Salazar wrote the secretary of the Indies recapitulating not only his instructions, but the outcome of each demand. Lima had requested the abolition of Indian tribute and of the mita, and the Cortes had granted both. Salazar specifically said that the cabildo was concerned with the status of the coastal Indians and those who lived in Lima. The cabildo requested free trade in mercury, and the Cortes granted that also, although the quantity of mercury available to Peru did not increase to any significant extent and free mining of mercury was never permitted.

All the other demands of the Lima city council, however, the Cortes failed to grant. Lima requested the restoration of the right to mint local coinage, both copper and silver, as it apparently had done before José de Areche's visita general. The lack of coinage available in Peru, caused by the export of bullion to Spain, had seriously weakened internal trade. "I presented to the Cortes a long memoria demonstrating the necessity of creating a provincial money for Peru," Salazar wrote, "but since it was passed on to a subcommittee, no report was ever forthcoming."[40] The cabildo also requested the abolition of all monopolies and special rights over Peruvian trade and commerce, especially as they concerned production and sale of aguardiente, upon which several provinces depended. Salazar said the various monopolies had caused the export of aguardiente to fall from 15,000 or 20,000 bottles a year to only 2,000 or 3,000. The cabildo also demanded that the insatiable demands of the pretendientes be met by giving half of all government appointments to creoles and by absorbing Lima's militia Regiment of Dragoons into the royal army. Salazar insisted that "it is very important to open an honorable career to the sons of Lima's chief families" and testified that "the absolute lack of careers in Peru . . . causes the sons to study merely to be hacendados, priests, or lawyers," a claim that is borne out in the statistics.

Furthermore, the Lima city council requested the abolition of all internal customs duties between the provinces of Peru, leaving only the port duties and customs at the capital, but neither the Cortes nor the appropriate subcommittee dealt with this demand. Salazar himself presented the Cortes a memorial asking for reduction of the customs duties on interprovincial mule sales from Tucumán, which the Cortes did accept but never implemented.[41] The cabildo also asked for abolition of the sugar monopoly. Sugar was one of the main products of the haciendas in the Valleys of Cañete and Chincha—where the city councilors and other members of the Lima elite owned properties. With the rebellion in Chile, these sugar producers lost a major market. They now requested permission to sell to Buenos Aires and asked that Buenos Aires be prohibited from buying Brazilian sugar.

Finally, the Lima city council asked for four to six months' grace in the collection of taxes on aguardiente and other products of viniculture—in which the Lima creole elite were also heavily involved.

Salazar also presented a set of demands given him by the city council of Yca. Very similar to Lima's, they included a request for the abolition of the tax on aguardiente, free trade in aguardiente to Panama and Guayaquil, relief from the necessity of buying essential ingredients for aguardiente from monopolies, and restoration of a tax on chiles that had previously been assigned to the Yca city council.

This concluded Salazar's instructions from Lima and Yca, but he added another request of his own. He asked that the American ports be made equal to Cádiz; in other words, that they be allowed free trade with all parts of the empire, including Manila. Salazar argued that Peru had single-handedly kept South America subject to the Spanish crown, and at great cost to itself. These services should be rewarded by the grant of free trade.[42]

With the slowness that characterized its handling of controversial matters, the Council of the Indies spent four long years studying Salazar's demands, just as the Cortes had previously occupied four years. In 1818 the fiscal for Peru concluded that though these demands were of general interest to all of America, no specific action should be taken because some of them had already been decided, some were under discussion, and some were questions of municipal jurisdiction in any case. No nation in the world was as expert as Spain at sidestepping fundamental colonial complaints.

There exists yet another indication of the objectives of the Lima creole elite and city council at the outset of the Cortes era, one that also came to nothing. In November 1810 the cabildo issued instructions to Salazar to press for permission for Lima merchants, under the official sponsorship of the cabildo rather than the Consulado, to send a total of six annual expeditions to trade "at the port of Canton, and on the coasts of Coromandel and Malabar." Each expedition would carry 500,000 pesos in Peruvian silver, and other colonial products. The cabildo argued that these expeditions would allow Peruvian merchants and producers to make up for their losses during the wars with Great Britain; it would produce an estimated 4 million pesos for the royal treasury in import and export taxes; it would meet the need for Asian goods in Peru, which the officially licensed Company of the Philippines was unable to do; it would allow Peruvians to buy on the coast of Asia at producers' prices rather than in Manila at middlemen's prices; and it would permit the city of Lima to pay off its large debt.[43] Needless to say, the Cortes did not grant this request either, for free Asian trade was firmly resisted by the Consulado, the Company of the Philippines, and Viceroy Abascal. The Cortes met in the Spanish port city of Cádiz, center of the peninsular trade with America. What was good for Cádiz was good for the Cortes, and that put an end to any colonial argument for expanded trade with either Asia or Europe.

Throughout the first half of 1811, the Lima cabildo continued to press for free trade and the abolition of the monopolies. The city's syndic, Ignacio de Orue, attacked viceregal plans to increase taxation in order to raise money for sending troops to Upper Peru, claiming that the viceroyalty's economy was already so depressed, as a result of the many restrictions on trade, that any new taxation would further weaken it. Instead, he suggested that Abascal should arrange an armistice with the insurgents in Buenos Aires so that the normal trade patterns of the two territories might be reestablished, and the cabildo as a whole endorsed this representation.[44]

There was, of course, an important political implication in the creole demands for economic and commercial autonomy, one that the creoles themselves did not always understand. Many prominent creoles, of whom Baquíjano is perhaps the best example, were totally unaware of the implication of their demands for Peruvian control of the economy, for though they opposed independence, they advocated the very principles that would lead to the disintegration of the empire. Viceroy Abascal and the audiencia, on the other hand, clearly perceived the consequences of these demands for reform. The majority of the peninsular officials, for example, opposed the abolition of the monopolies, recognizing that even though the monopolies were anachronistic and inefficient they nonetheless guaranteed peninsular and Consulado control of the economy. The viceroy and audiencia also considered abolition of the Indian tribute tantamount to fiscal and perhaps even social suicide, for the tribute was the mark of Spain's control of the vast majority of the population. Peninsulars opposed Peruvian local coinage because Peruvian bullion had to be preserved as the exclusive privilege of the motherland and was essential to Spain's survival; furthermore, a Peruvian coinage would in effect constitute a national currency. No imperialist could agree to incorporate the creole-dominated militia into the regular army, for that would constitute the establishment of a Peruvian national army. And of course no Spanish ruler could agree to giving half of all government offices to Peruvians, for that would mean virtual administrative autonomy. In short, the creoles' demands may appear mundane and limited—and so the creoles themselves viewed them—but they were laden with explosive political import. In 1812 Abascal put his finger precisely on the implications of the creole demands when he wrote that free trade "would be tantamount to decreeing the separation of these dominions from the Mother Country, since, once direct trade with foreigners was established on the wide basis which they demand, the fate of European Spain would matter little to them."[45]

What passes, therefore, as merely a selfish attempt to maintain the privileges of a few European monopolists was in reality a struggle to maintain the artificial political, institutional, and economic structures that made Peruvians think Spain was necessary to their existence. Consequently, any act or event that questioned this dependence tended directly to the weakening of Spanish sovereignty. In this process the Cortes played a critical role, for although the peninsulars in the Cortes were unwilling to grant all the economic and institutional reforms demanded by Peruvians, they nonetheless adopted policies inimical to the continuation of the old absolutism by which Abascal governed. Thus Abascal had to resist both the South American rebels and the Spanish Cortes.

The first stage in the struggle had thus begun in Peru. It was a contest between imperial absolutism and colonial autonomy, expressed in terms of Peruvian complaints—some petty, others fundamental—over trade, commerce, finance, and appointment. The struggle had been brewing since 1780, and the collapse of metropolitan government in 1808 brought it to a crisis stage. There was a great difference, however, between Peru and much of the rest of Spanish America. Whereas in Buenos Aires, Bogotá, Santiago, and Quito this crisis of American aspirations versus imperial needs led directly to the desire for independence, in Peru it was merely the first stage. There was as yet no significant Peruvian aspiration for independence, with the exception of the suppressed Huanuco rebellion of 1812. The War of Independence, which began in other countries in 1810, would not begin in Peru until 1820, after the viceregal government had gone bankrupt and after the Chilean Army of Liberation had arrived. Despite the intensity of their grievances, Peruvians on the whole supported the viceregal government for the next ten years. More certain of the dangers inherent in independence—which would unleash the ambitions of the Indians and other oppressed classes—politically active Peruvians were more reluctant to find in independence the answer to their complaints.

Chapter 3

# Tribute and the Press in the Cortes Era

WITH GREAT SKILL and considerable cunning, in the years 1810 to 1814 Viceroy Abascal resisted not only the rebellions around him, but also the decrees and enactments of the metropolitan Spanish government. South America's preeminent absolutist was in the extraordinary position of having to disobey or ignore many of the commands of the government he served. The struggle began on 4 July 1810, when Abascal published the first proclamation of the Council of Regency, dated 14 February 1810, in which the Regency announced its succession to power and its intention of calling the Cortes and, in an attempt to gain the support of colonials, resorted to the most extreme rhetorical promises. The Regency said it was aware of the long history of arbitrariness, greed, corruption, and hypocrisy from which Americans had suffered and declared that the old regime was over. In sending deputies to the Cortes, it promised, Americans would free themselves from three centuries of misgovernment. "Your destinies no longer depend upon ministers, viceroys or governors," the Regency declared; "they are in your own hands." The paradox is that the Regency was much more conservative than the Junta Central had been and even delayed the opening of the Cortes from March to September 1810. Yet it resorted to rhetoric that Abascal testified was a clarion call to rebellion. The viceroy's initial reaction to the order, though uneasy, was not actively hostile. He did nothing to obstruct the election of the first deputies or their travels to the peninsula; and he declared that the "glorious event of the installation of the Cortes . . . filled the loyal inhabitants of this capital with pleasure."[1] His *Memoria*, written years afterward, makes his initial reaction sound more hostile, but in fact that hostility arose only several months later, after the direction of the Cortes's legislation became clear to him.

Over the next few years the Cortes passed a series of sweeping reforms.[2] These included freedom of the press, abolition of the Indian tribute, abolition of the Inquisition, declaration of the equality of Americans and Europeans, and freedom of manufacture. Equally fundamental, of course, was the impact on the foundations of the regime caused by the Cortes's declaration that in the absence of the king it held sovereignty in the name of the Spanish nation. The principles of parliamentary responsibility and popular sovereignty mingled and, first implicitly, later explicitly, questioned the king's primacy and thereby the viceroy's authority. In 1812 these and many other fundamental reforms were incorporated into the Constitution of the Spanish Monarchy, the hallmark and ultimate expression of the liberal campaign to convert the empire into a parliamentary system with a limited monarchy. In almost every case it was not only the reform itself, but also the spirit behind the reform, that Abascal found dangerous. Indeed, a number of the reforms were never actually implemented in Peru, either because of Abascal's obstruction or because they were temporarily set aside in the interest of winning the war against the rebels. Nonetheless, the Peruvian national debate on the Cortes reforms revolved around five basic themes: free press, the status of the Indian and financial problems, institutional political reforms, elections, and subversion. The first two will be dealt with in this chapter.

The most salient effect of the Cortes was not that it provoked further support for independence, but rather that it exacerbated Peru's confusion of purpose and polarized political attitudes. And the polarization did not follow simple criteria such as whether one were a creole or a peninsular. There were creole conservatives whose opposition to the new forms of government and to independence itself was crystallized by the Cortes, just as there were creole liberals who were led by the Cortes to renounce a mother country that, even when it was controlled by liberals, could not or would not take serious steps to ameliorate the inequality of America's treatment within the empire. This polarization among politically active Peruvians was the first and most important step toward Peru's national paralysis in decision-making, which would play such an important role in 1820 and 1821. From 1810 to 1820, Peru was not moving toward a consensus, it was moving away from one.

No single act of the Cortes so clearly illustrates the incredible disruption that could be caused in the overseas territories by the well-intentioned but ill-informed determinations of the parliament as did the abolition of the Indian tribute, decreed on 13 March 1811. As a poor country, perpetually on the verge of financial collapse, Peru simply could not afford to lose the tribute, which accounted for approximately one-third of the viceregal treasury's income in the year of its abolition. Just as critically, abolition of the tribute provoked yet another round in the never-ending debate over the proper status and condition of the voiceless Indians who composed 60 percent of Peru's population. Although Abascal had no choice but to implement the decree, he made no secret of his outrage. His letters to the Cortes and the Regency protested the imminent bankruptcy of Peru and the harm that would be done to the Indians themselves by ending the tax that had, he insisted, been their primary motivation to work for a living. Abascal declared that abolition of the tribute was the product "either of the most incredible ignorance or of the bad faith of the government that decreed it."[3]

The loss of the tribute did, as Abascal said, deprive his government of the very means it required to preserve Spanish control in Peru. Although the Peruvian deputies to the Cortes, especially the Indian Dionisio Inca Yupanqui, had been among the chief initiators of the abolition, there is no indication that the Cortes was aware of how important the tribute revenues were to Peru. A report of the contador general of tribute, Juan José de Leuro, made clear what a serious blow it was. Of the total viceregal revenue, which in the year September 1810 to September 1811 was 3,659,000 pesos, tribute accounted for 1,235,781 pesos. Of that total sum, 763,197 pesos had been net income to the royal treasury, while the remaining 472,584 pesos had gone to cover various expenses permanently assigned to the tribute—including the payment of a yearly grant to priests in Indian parishes, a grant to subdelegates, a grant to primary school teachers in Indian districts, a grant to Indian hospitals, a grant to the Escorial monastery in Spain, and the salaries of medical doctors ministering to the Indians in several partidos. According to Leuro, in 1811 the viceroyalty of Peru—counting Guayaquil, Chiloé, and Quixos, but excepting Mainas, for which statistics were not available—counted a total tributary population of 909,228 persons. Of that number, 204,902 adult males—of whom 142,560 worked their own assigned plots of land and 62,342 had no land—were tribute-paying. The remainder of the tributary population consisted of women and children, men under age eighteen or over age fifty, and some few hundred nobles, alcaldes, and religious who were exempt from the tribute.[4] These figures reveal the relative poverty of the Indians—three-quarters of the national population had contributed only one-third of the national revenue. Leuro's figures also make it clear that many mestizos or castes were tributaries, since the 1795 census counted only 648,615 Indians as a racial category. When Leuro and others spoke of "Indians," therefore, they were referring both to true Indians and also to those castes who lived among them. Nevertheless, the startling fact is that abolition of the tribute exempted three-quarters of Peru's total population from paying their only state tax (existing laws exempted tributaries from paying other duties such as the sales tax).

Could any state, especially one engaged in warfare on its borders, survive the loss of income from such a large portion of its population? The city council of Lima, upon being asked by Abascal to propose new sources of revenue, replied in no uncertain terms that the burden must not be allowed to fall on the whites or on the citizens of Lima, since the capital city was already overburdened, nor should it be replaced by increased taxation on trade and luxuries, for the nation was already on the verge of commercial collapse. Abascal replied that he recognized the cabildo's zeal to defend the public, but he could not abandon his duty. Since every division of the government would say it was bankrupt, he repeated his request that the cabildo propose ways of making up the deficit.[5]

Acting on this urgent problem, Abascal convoked a Junta General de Tribunales, a general junta of representatives from all the major corporations in the capital, which first met on 22 November 1811 to propose methods of raising new revenues. This junta would eventually produce in 1815 perhaps the most comprehensive and professional general assessment of the economy that any colonial regime in America ever wrote (see chap. 5), but for the time being it succeeded in proposing only five methods of increasing revenue. It suggested increasing the price of tobacco, establishing lotteries in other intendancies modeled on the one that already existed in Lima, transferring income from the Indian Caja de Censos to the national treasury, increasing customs duties at the port of Guayaquil to make them as high as those at Callao, and distributing Indian lands in freehold. There were such critical political problems attached to each of these proposals that for the time being Abascal simply settled for ordering an increase in the price of tobacco.[6] Nevertheless, before the end of 1815 the government had begun to implement all the other proposals except the creation of new lotteries—which Abascal did not think would produce much revenue. The proposals of the revenue junta led to several years of sustained conflict between the viceroy and the Chilean-born fiscal de lo crímen of the Lima audiencia, Miguel de Eyzaguirre, which constituted the most serious political feud within Abascal's administration.

Eyzaguirre was probably the most popular man in all of Peru, after General Goyeneche. While the general was the token creole in a military position of great importance, Eyzaguirre was the leader of creole opinion in civilian politics and financial affairs. A convinced liberal, he also held the formal title of "defender of the Indians," a position attached to the job of fiscal de lo crímen. For years he had advocated abolition of the Indian tribute as part of his general campaign to alleviate the misery of the indigenous population. In all the many letters of denunciation that Lima creoles sent to Spain criticizing the audiencia members for their graft and corruption, Eyzaguirre was the only minister who was excepted. Everyone testified to his rectitude, honesty, and hard work. Everyone, that is, except Abascal. In 1811 Eyzaguirre became the leader of the creole faction that opposed an increase in taxes on trade and commerce. He was joined in this by the cabildo's syndic, Ignacio de Orue, who published in the liberal periodical *El Peruano* a denunciation of the junta's revenue proposals.

Abascal developed a fierce hatred of Eyzaguirre and wrote many pleas to the peninsula accusing him of being the chief enemy of the regime and demanding that he be transferred to Spain. He denounced him as a rebel, for Eyzaguirre's brother Agustín was a leader of the rebels in Santiago de Chile. He said the fiscal had opposed all the proposals raised in the revenue junta, arguing that the Indians should be exempt not only from tribute, but from any other contribution. In his role as defender of the Indians, Eyzaguirre had proposed abolition of the tribute as early as 1808. In this, Abascal claimed, the fiscal was ignorant and erroneous. Furthermore, as early as 1809 Eyzaguirre had complained to Spain of the audiencia's use of income from the Indian Caja de Censos—the major national annuity fund supported by Indian contributions and required by law to be spent only on such things as the building of schools, roads, and bridges in Indian communities, and the payment of tribute in times of famine. Eyzaguirre complained that in 1798 the audiencia had extracted a loan of 50,000 pesos from the fund; in 1799, another of 75,000 pesos; and in 1809, another of 25,000 pesos. In 1811 he charged again that the audiencia had taken another 40,000 pesos from the Caja. In every case the audiencia paid only 3 percent interest rather than the standard rate of 6 percent. The council of the Indies finally determined that this use of Caja funds was not illegal, as the money might be considered war loans. Nonetheless, in 1813 Eyzaguirre again complained that the audiencia had ordered the Lima city council to take a loan of 17,000 pesos from the Caja at only 3 percent interest, to help pay for the transportation of deputies to the Cortes.[7] Abascal also accused the fiscal of obstructing the prosecution of Indians accused of treason.

In the first constitutional elections, conducted in Lima in December 1812 and January 1813, Eyzaguirre and Abascal again clashed. The viceroy charged him with influencing the parish voting in order to get men of liberal and procreole persuasion elected. Abascal reported that the fiscal and his party excluded various honorable citizens from the voting, including Europeans who could not produce their passports authorizing them to come to America. In the parish elections for the new city council and in the separate parish elections for deputies to the Cortes, according to Abascal, Eyzaguirre got himself and his followers elected by conspiracy. The viceroy declared that "all those named as electors were distinguished by their adhesion to revolutionary maxims, including among them Eyzaguirre." When Eyzaguirre, who was chosen as the elector from the city and partido of Lima for the selection of Cortes deputies, went to join the electoral junta, Viceroy Abascal excluded him from participation on the grounds that ministers of justice were not allowed to serve in any elected capacity. Eyzaguirre protested strongly to Spain that the decree excluding magistrates had been received in Lima only after he had been chosen, and that as a result of the viceroy's arbitrary actions, more than 120,000 persons had not been represented in the elections. He further accused the viceroy of placing troops in the streets and plazas, and even on the stairs of the municipal palace, to intimidate the junta of electors, and of presiding over the final voting behind closed doors, which the Constitution prohibited. Eyzaguirre insisted that the viceroy accused him of treason merely because "with reason and justice I have contradicted his caprice and arbitrariness."[8]

In August 1812 Eyzaguirre wrote his strongest letter of defense to Spain. He charged that the viceroy was persecuting him merely because he had defended the Indians against illegal contributions imposed on them after the abolition of the tribute, because he had represented Indians accused of treason in various hearings, and because he had opposed the contract the viceroy gave to Xavier María Aguirre to sell tobacco at an excessively high price. He insisted that his only crime was to defend the weak against the despotism of the powerful, and he concluded, "I know that the viceroy . . . has sent you secret reports against me on grounds about which I am ignorant and which are false. . . . If I am guilty, why is there no public cause against me? If I am not guilty, why is one brought against me in secret?"[9]

This sort of reasonable attitude impressed the Council of the Indies when it finally attempted to reach a decision on the case. In a series of discussions, several members of the Council were willing to give Eyzaguirre the benefit of the doubt because it appeared the viceroy was too dependent on circumstantial evidence. The similarity of Eyzaguirre's case with that of the Mexican creole fiscal de lo crímen Jacobo de Villaurrutia—who had been ordered back to Spain on identical charges—was mentioned in several of the individual opinions. As late as December 1816, the Council's fiscal for Peru pointed out that every major group in Peru had testified on behalf of Eyzaguirre and suggested that only Viceroy Abascal thought him a rebel.[10]

In many ways the most impressive thing about the Eyza-guirre-Abascal conflict is that both were men of such forth-right rectitude. Only their priorities differed. Eyzaguirre was not a rebel, but he was totally committed to the improvement of the Indians' lot and to the advancement of the creoles. Abascal was totally dedicated to the preservation of Spanish rule, which under the conditions of the day required him to resist any opposition. Consequently the two men were locked in a head-on struggle, with Abascal convinced that Eyzaguirre must be expelled from Peru no matter what the grounds.

In 1812 the Regency, concerned merely to remove an impediment to the smooth running of the Peruvian government, offered Eyzaguirre the office of fiscal in the Supreme Tribunal of Justice in Spain. He declined on the grounds that he was going blind. After implementation of the Constitution, which declared that the Indians were now to be called Spaniards, the Lima audiencia took advantage of the supposed new protections it guaranteed and abolished the office of defender of the Indians. The final blow came when Ferdinand VII was restored to the throne and ordered Eyzaguirre transferred to the next vacancy in the audiencia of either Granada or Valladolid. José Irigoyen replaced him as Lima's fiscal de lo crímen. By that point, however, Eyzaguirre was too ill to travel. In some desperation to be rid of him, Viceroy Abascal sent Dr. Baltasar de Villalobos, a notorious quack, to examine Eyzaguirre. Villalobos pronounced him to be suffering from melancholy brought on by hypochondria. Villalobos was also engaged at the time in promoting a cure for leprosy which the Lima Protomedicato had already declared a fraud that hastened the death of most patients. Fortunately, Dr. Miguel Tafur, acting protomédico of Peru, also examined Eyzaguirre and found that he was not just a hypochondriac but had what sounds very much like heart disease, referring to his "spasms of the heart" and irregular pulse.[11] Consequently, a royal order permitted Eyzaguirre to delay his trip until he was able to travel. On 18 March 1816, Eyzaguirre requested restoration to office. The Council of the Indies again heard his case and in 1817 ordered the original command for his return to Spain carried out. Even so, Eyzaguirre lingered in Lima until 1818, when Viceroy Pezuela, who was apparently no better disposed toward him than Abascal had been, ordered him home to get him out of the way of General Mariano Osorio's campaign to reconquer Chile.[12]

The problem of the catastrophic loss of revenue after abolition of the tribute remained critical. By 1813 Abascal was prepared to report that Peru's total deficit would be 1,342,781 pesos that year, and he was obviously getting desperate. A year later he reported that "this kingdom's income has been reduced to less than is needed to cover ordinary expenses"; that he had suspended financial aid to Chile; that Lima's garrison was on half salary; and that he had granted credits of 300,000 pesos to the Army of Upper Peru with absolutely no funds to cover them. This particularly concerned him since he understood that "where funds do not exist it is necessary to maintain credit."[13] Consequently, he continued to beg for restoration of the tribute.

In this cause Abascal received powerful support from every level of government in Peru, with the notable exception of Eyzaguirre. In Spain, José Baquíjano urged the Regency to restore the tribute, if only on a temporary basis. In Lima, Lázaro de Rivera, the former intendant of Huancavelica, wrote a strong protest urging Spain not to be caught up in the "mania, or fad of reading and listening to nothing but the humbug of foreign writers" who accused Spain of mistreating the Indians.[14]

Provoked by the necessity of finding new revenue, Viceroy Abascal and his Junta General set out to replace the tribute with something else. In one letter to Spain he said in exasperation that if it were the word "tribute" that bothered the liberal Cortes delegates, then let the name of the thing be changed. He admitted that the tribute had been characterized by corruption and abuse, but all human things were susceptible to those vices. The first alternative Abascal and his advisers came up with was the establishment of "provisional contributions" from the Indian communities, which were simply the tribute by another name. There was considerable resistance, and Eyzaguirre complained about it in one of his letters. Abascal may have been attempting to cover up revenues from this contribution when he told Spain that some Indian communities continued to make tribute payments voluntarily. Nevertheless, to judge from a letter of Isidro Vilca, an Indian who held the largely honorific title of procurator of the Indians in the audiencia of Lima, collections from the new contribution must have been very sparse. Vilca informed the Regency that the provisional contribution was merely a return to the tribute under a different name. The tribute was a heavy burden, he said, not because it was too high, but because it put the Indian under the control of the hacendados. Under the provisional contribution, Vilca said, "the hacendados, miners, and other powerful men are preparing to reduce the Indians again to their ancient slavery."[15]

The most unusual of Abascal's proposals, however, and certainly the most significant—if it had ever been implemented—was to replace the tribute payments with direct taxation over freehold lands distributed among the Indians. He tentatively formulated this program throughout 1812, though in 1813 he told Spain that it had been suspended awaiting Cortes approval. It is more likely, however, that the sheer complexity of the plan was the major impediment. By August 1814 Abascal was prepared to explain his idea to the government. It consisted of a proposal to distribute the land occupied by Indian communities to the Indian families as individual freehold. They would then pay "a moderate yearly quota" to the state. This plan was made final by the Provincial Deputation of Lima in June 1814 and was made to appear like an attempt to conform to a Cortes law of 9 November 1812 that called for the distribution of land to the Indians *en dominio y propiedad*. The tax the Indians would pay would not be viewed "as an exaction or ignominious tribute, nor as a personal charge or pension, but as a contribution . . . that they are required to pay as a sign of their being Spaniards." The Indians would be given the same lands they now occupied, but as freehold, inheritable by their children. Each Indian head of a family was to receive four topos of first-class land (with water), or six topos of second-class (without water), or eight topos of third-class (rocky), while caciques would receive twelve topos (a topo measured 4,680 square varas, or 1.5 square leagues). Common pasturage and woods would not be affected. Cholos, mestizos, and sambaygos—various caste terms for mixed populations—would also participate in the program. Lands belonging to the community of Indians, the ayllu, would be set aside, and the properties would be distributed under the direction of the constitutional cabildos. The tax would be two pesos a year on each topo of first-class land, one peso on second-class, and four reales on third-class. [16]

Full implementation of this proposal would have constituted a revolutionary change in Peru's ancient system of communal land use, while the sheer task of distributing the properties would have required a resolve that many modern Latin American governments still have not been able to marshal. For these reasons, the program was never actually implemented. Abascal and his advisers appear to have given no thought whatsoever to the difficulty of the task, for in the viceroy's draft resolution he set a time limit of one month for local cabildos to complete the distribution. José Baquíjano, who wrote to the Regency enthusiastically supporting the program, recognized that it was an immensely laborious task and would take a long time, and in the interim he urged temporary restoration of the tribute. Baquíjano supported the principle, declaring that the Indians "want what everybody else wants—to have a little piece of land to call their own." [17] He also pointed out that whereas women, nobles, employees of the state and church, and men under eighteen and over fifty years of age had been exempted from the tribute, every Indian would be subject to the land tax.

Abascal's proposal thus brought together some very strange bedfellows with what can only be called mixed motives. Never was it more true that a man's individual politics and ideology determined his interpretation of the Indians. Abascal wanted agrarian reform because he strongly felt that if the Indians were to be called "Spaniards"—as the Constitution required—then they must also contribute to the state as other Spaniards did. Baquíjano, himself a former "protector of the Indians," favored the proposal because his paternalistic ideology convinced him Indians had the same aspirations that European yeoman farmers were thought to have. Both viewpoints merely reveal lamentable ignorance about the Indians.

Since it was never put into effect, it is impossible to tell exactly how this fundamental reform would have affected the Indians under the viceroyalty. Yet, when similar legislation was adopted in 1825 by Bolívar, it demonstrated that individual freehold did not improve the Indians' lot. Quite the contrary, it was a disaster, destroying the fabric of Indian social and economic life and forcing them to stand unprepared and defenseless against the assaults of rapacious landowners who coveted their properties. Even as the viceroy was formulating his proposal, for example, Isidro Vilca, the procurator of the Indians, was begging Spain to reestablish the office of defender of the Indians, citing the example of a land dispute currently under way between a village in the partido of Jauja and a landowner. The Indians would surely lose, he said, because they hardly understood the Castilian language and did not know the intricacies of the law. The Constitution might declare them Spaniards, Vilca said, but they were still not able to hold their land against estate owners equipped with money and power. Only a few months earlier Vilca had written the Regency thanking it for declaring the Indians to be "Spaniards" and asking that it substantiate its decree with an order that no political, ecclesiastical, or military office be closed to them in the future. The Cortes determined that such a decree would be superfluous, since the Constitution had already declared them equal. Only on paper were they so, and that of course was the basic fallacy in the liberals' handling of Indian problems in all parts of America. To declare them equal was merely to remove their legal and traditional defenses. In January 1814 Mariano de la Torre y Vera, vicar general of the army of Upper Peru, submitted a report to the Regency declaring that the Indians were little changed since the days of the Conquest, for they were still meek, mild, timid, starving, and, most of all, totally outside the white man's culture.[18] The state of the Peruvian Indian would not, therefore, be improved by either the paternalism of Baquíjano or the Machiavellian statecraft of Abascal.

The fundamental problem in the Cortes's dealings with the Peruvian Indian thus remained the almost universal belief of Europeans and creoles that the Indian was inferior. Even the impassioned speeches by the Peruvian substitute deputies, declaring that the Indians were civilized, were presented chiefly to convince the Cortes to count the vast indigenous population in apportioning Peru's representation. The prevailing view of the Indian, even at this late stage, probably more closely approximated the opinions of the former Huancavelica intendant Lázaro de Rivera than those of the upright Eyzaguirre. In February 1815 Rivera, an intimate adviser of both Abascal and Pezuela, wrote to Spain criticizing every aspect of the constitutional system, especially its abolition of the tribute, which he claimed had made the Indians more shiftless and lazy than ever. He summarized:

> The Indian is extremely diffident and malicious, he is timid and pacific, but haughty, cruel, and overbearing when he thinks he can get away with it. . . . He is ungrateful, thieving, and vengeful even when he receives the most notable favors. His inconstancy makes him a worshipper of anything new. Deceit, guile, and bad faith are the principles that guide his conduct. He is indifferent to everything; he would as soon be alcalde as cook. In their councils young boys of ten or twelve years of age are allowed to enter and are heard as oracles. The mothers wean their children on brandy, and by the age of ten they are professional drunkards; this is their dominant vice, for they drink themselves to death.[19]

This sort of attitude among royal administrators no doubt accounts for the failure of both the Cortes and the viceregal regime to do anything substantial to improve the lot of the Peruvian Indian. The peninsula did issue two orders in 1814 designed to preserve and defend Peru's rich Indian heritage, but neither was implemented. In April 1814 the Regency ordered the viceroy to appoint an official to tour the country, accompanied by an artist and a scribe, to "search for, observe, and copy the ancient historical and artistic monuments of Peru's inhabitants before their discovery." As this would require adding three more salaries to the payroll, it remained a dead letter. So did a Council order of 27 July 1814 that commanded the viceroy, on the advice of the former deputy from Puno, Tadeo Gárate, to establish a junta or society to preserve Peru's vicuña and alpaca populations, which were essential to the Indian economy. Particular care was to be given to an attempt to domesticate the vicuña, or at least to reduce it to controlled pasturage. The order also commanded the viceroy to see to the preservation of alpacas, guanacos, llamas, and chinchillas. The chinchilla population was so large that in 1818 Peru exported 66,000 skins.[20]

In the end, the brave words of Yupanqui, Feliú, Morales, and the other Peruvian Cortes delegates in defense of Indian civilization, and the braver acts of Eyzaguirre in defense of the Indians themselves, were wasted. The reformist Cortes remained imperialist for all its liberalism, and except for temporary abolition of the tribute and patently meaningless declarations of equality, did nothing for the Indian.

For all the frustration and anger his methods generated, it should be pointed out that Abascal was remarkably successful in increasing the revenue of the royal exchequer. Income for 1811 was only 3.6 million pesos, but in 1812 it rose to 5.2 million pesos.[21] The increase derived from heavy borrowing, a determined effort to collect old debts, and an increase in the price of tobacco. Other sweeping expedients were enacted in 1815.

After the problem of revenue and tribute, a second major concern of Abascal was the Cortes's declaration of freedom of the press on 10 November 1810. The decree was received in Peru in April 1811. Convinced from the outset of its danger, Abascal immediately adopted and consistently pursued the policy that would constitute his response to many other radical Cortes reforms. Technically Abascal adhered to the free press decree. He created the Provincial Censorship Board that the new law required in each capital to supervise the free press, and, indeed, some liberal and even antigovernment literature did appear in Lima. He was not so heavy-handed as simply to ignore the law. Rather, his policy consisted of appearing to adhere to the law, but personally intervening whenever he found a publication objectionable, and in that way he made the writing of dissenting opinions so risky that few would attempt it. In a sense, therefore, one can say that the free press existed in Peru from 1811 until 11 March 1815—when Abascal published the king's order annulling it—yet at the same time, it never really existed at all.[22]

It was public pressure that forced Abascal to initiate the formal institutions of free press in the first place. The Lima city council received the Cortes's decree on 19 April 1811. On 25 April it received a letter directly from the Peruvian Cortes deputies carrying news of the free press and of other reforms. Convinced that the viceroy was planning to withhold or delay announcement of this fundamental reform, the city councilors determined to print and distribute it themselves at their own expense. Sure enough, in May the viceroy confirmed their fears by announcing that he would suspend the publication of the free press decree until the Supreme Censorship Board in Spain had appointed the five members who were to compose the Lima board. By June the five appointees had been named, and Abascal could no longer delay. What recourse did he now have? He simply waited until writings he considered subversive began to appear, then exercised his particular and undoubted privilege of interpreting the law. In September 1811 he made his policy clear to the peninsula when he wrote that although he did not doubt the advantages this extension of freedom would bring to the peninsula itself, he would nonetheless preserve to himself the interpretation of the law in Peru, for a completely free press would spread creole-European rivalry and encourage the entry of Napoleonic propaganda by French agents.[23]

It was toward the famous periodicals *El Peruano* and *El Satélite del Peruano* that Abascal exhibited the greatest hostility. *El Peruano*, the first of the two periodicals and the more important, was published from 6 September 1811 to 9 June 1812 and was unabashedly the mouthpiece of the liberal creole intellectuals of Lima. But it was toward Gaspar Rico y Angulo, one of its principal contributors, that Abascal hurled his full anger. Rico himself was not a rebel. Indeed, he fled Lima in 1821 with the royal armies of Viceroy José de La Serna and functioned thereafter as the chief publicist of the royal cause. Rico became Abascal's main target chiefly because he let down his guard enough to become vulnerable. In the 18 February 1812 issue of *El Peruano*, Rico published a note asking if Pedro Abadia, one of Lima's leading merchants, were not in fact the son of a foreigner named Pedro Abadia who had been sought in Peru since 1788 as a criminal and heretic. Whether such a person even existed, and exactly what Rico thought he was doing in impugning the honor of one of Lima's most influential men, is not clear. Nonetheless, the censorship board condemned *El Peruano* for publishing Rico's note. Rico replied in the 25 February issue, repeating the charge that Abadia was not really a Spaniard, and Abascal took advantage of the quarrel to ask Spain to allow him to suspend the free press. With Rico playing the inept fly, Abascal did not have to be a very cunning spider. He wrote sweetly to the Regency, "I find myself in the unhappy position of having to speak to Your Highnesses about the abusive freedom of the press and the unspeakable evils it occasions in these dominions." He insisted that he was hampered in his life-or-death struggle with enemies of the regime by "dilatory and sluggish routines" imposed by the excessive scruple of the Cortes—such as the necessity of waiting upon a final decision from the Supreme Censorship Board before he could close down a subversive periodical.[24] For the moment, he said no more. But it was clear that he had declared war on both Rico and *El Peruano*.

The struggle was joined. Although the Lima city council wrote to Spain on 12 May 1812 complimenting Rico for his talent and merit, Abascal kept a sharp watch on *El Peruano*. Throughout the early months of 1812 the periodical annoyed him on several occasions—as when it charged mismanagement in the tobacco monopoly or when it published letters of Eyzaguirre and cabildo syndic Orue favoring free trade. Abascal even sent Spain a letter from the director of the tobacco monopoly denying the charges against his department. Meanwhile, seventy-seven leading citizens of Lima sent the viceroy a denunciation of *El Peruano*, which provided fuel for Abascal's actions. On 23 March the censorship board denounced yet another issue of *El Peruano*.[25] The final straw came in a patriotic discourse Rico published in the issue of 5 June 1812. Reflecting on the origin of authority, Rico declared: "The governors are not the origin of authority. . . . They are responsible to all whom they make unhappy; but the people do not answer except to God. . . . In them sovereignty resides originally." Viceroy Abascal denounced this essay in support of popular sovereignty as an incitement to rebellion, and the Lima censorship board agreed. Unable to resist such concerted pressure, *El Peruano* ceased to publish with its issue of 9 June 1812. This last issue consisted of the censorship board's 23 March denunciation and of Rico's editorial defense against all the charges. He insisted that the periodical had been destroyed by a cabal of "men not accustomed to hearing the truth." He charged that authority could be delegated in the great crisis currently facing the empire. And he repeated his charges that Peru's distance from the seat of power in Spain meant that justice was not accorded to her people in equal measure, supporting his contention by quoting from a commission of the Cortes that was then involved in drafting the new constitution.[26]

Now Abascal struck. First he asked the censorship board for another censure of *El Peruano*, this time against the 9 June issue, then on 23 June he and the audiencia arrested and deported Rico on the grounds that he was a subversive revolutionary. Rico went to Cádiz, where in March 1813 he was released from detention because Abascal had not sent enough evidence to bring charges against him. The Regency had received yet another testimony in

Rico's behalf from the Lima city council, this one from the city's agent in Cádiz, complimenting Rico on his role in the creation of the Concordia Regiment in Lima.[27]

In the last months of the struggle against *El Peruano*, a second and frankly more dissident periodical, written by Fernando López, began publication. Called *El Satélite del Peruano*, it averred that it was a satellite of *El Peruano* just as in the heavens planets of first magnitude had satellites. Its first issue, 1 March 1812, declared that it firmly rejected "the ancient colonial government" and that it supported the liberal revolution in Spain. It announced that the "iron bonds" that had tied Spain and the Indies together for three centuries were broken. *El Satélite* said that those persons who thought the periodical was subversive and revolutionary could leave Peru, taking their ill-gotten riches with them, and join their protector, the traitor Godoy.[28] With such provocative phrases, it is not surprising that Abascal opposed this journal too, and when *El Peruano* ceased to exist in June so did *El Satélite*.

Rico fired one more round in the battle against the viceroy before he finally subsided. In Cádiz, three days after his release from custody, he published an article in the liberal Cádiz journal *La Abeja Española*, defending his past actions and accusing the Lima censorship board of censuring him so often because "the censors feared or wanted something from the viceroy," and announcing to the world that in Peru "the law is null . . . when the will of the viceroy is contrary to it." Abascal responded forthrightly to this charge by sending letters to both the Regency and the minister of grace and justice, declaring that if his services in keeping Peru free of anarchy meant anything at all then the government must approve his actions in Rico's case and must also censure *La Abeja Española* for printing Rico's charges. The matter died there, for Abascal had accomplished what he wanted in destroying *El Peruano* and *El Satélite* and in sending Rico to Spain. In November 1812 the Spanish government had given Abascal permission to proceed within the law against publications he found subversive and to do in general whatever was necessary for the good of the state.[29] Although this did not actually constitute permission to abolish the free press, Abascal took it as permission to permit freedom of the press on a selective basis, and that is how he functioned until the end of the constitutional period. Thus he found it irrelevant when the Supreme Censorship Board in Cádiz cleared Rico of all charges and exonerated *El Peruano*.

There were two other cases of a suspect's being sent to Spain for trial on charges of subversive writing. One was a merchant named Tomás Menendez, who in 1814 published a paper accusing the prior of the Consulado, the conde de Villar de Fuente, and the consuls, Francisco Xavier Izcue and Faustino del Campo, of illegal commercial activities. He was sent to Spain for a hearing after the Lima audiencia found him guilty in 1816. The Council of the Indies and the king confirmed the decision in 1818.[30] The other was the rather pathetic case of a friar named Angel de Luque, whom the viceroy testified was mad. Overcome by an excess of fervor in support of the Constitution, in 1813 Luque published a statement addressed to the Cortes criticizing the bishop of Orense, Pedro Quevedo y Quintano, a former chairman of the Regency who had been exiled for failing to support the Constitution. Luque asserted that "sovereignty resides essentially in the nation" and called the bishop "a criminal of state whose head would have been removed already if he were not a bishop." In August 1814 the crown ordered Abascal to arrest Luque because by that time the king had been restored and the bishop of Orense was again a powerful personage. Luque therefore issued a contrite apology to the bishop, in light of which he was given a general pardon. The hapless friar then asked permission to come to court to kiss the king's hand, which was denied with an official note declaring curtly, "this presbyter is a bit touched in the head."[31]

It is a measure of Abascal's abilities that, in addition to merely resisting the publication of what he judged subversive literature, he also acted decisively to direct popular reading in Lima along channels he considered desirable. As the time drew near for the publication of the Constitution, he sponsored the publication of a progovernment periodical named the *Verdadero Peruano*—the "true Peruvian." It began publication on 22 September 1812 after the Constitution arrived but before its formal promulgation in Peru. Abascal informed Spain that he had sponsored this new publication "by a society of literati [who will] give the people all the information they need in order to know their legitimate rights."[32] In other words, it was designed to direct public thinking about the newly arrived Constitution, thereby preempting the opposition.

The list of editors and contributors to the *Verdadero Peruano* tells much about the thinking of liberal creoles in 1812. The chief literati who wrote for the new periodical were Lima's foremost creole progressives—including the group of medical doctors, José Pezet, Felix Devoti, Hipólito Unánue, and others. It includes the very group of men who are said by some historians to constitute the secret supporters of independence in Lima. And yet there they were in 1812 and 1813, writing for a publication the viceroy had secretly sponsored. In the first issue the editors declared that their periodical would "circulate whatever may be relevant to the public morals and politics of a Catholic people governed by a just Constitution." In its second issue Felix Devoti declared that the periodical's principles were "love of the nation, of the Constitution, and of the king."[33] Its appearance coincided with arrival of the Constitution—which was sworn to in Lima in the week of 1 October to 6 October 1812—and its chief focus remained its attempt to interpret and explain the Constitution. But always it advocated the Abascal line, which might briefly be described as "the Constitution is good for Peru, but only if its effects are contained within the limits of order and good government." Nowhere was this clearer, for example, than in the ode it published on the occasion of Lima's first constitutional elections, written by the mulatto physician José Manuel Valdés. Declaring he would always relish the memory of the first election, Valdés continued:

> O beloved country mine!
> Now you are free. Yes, free.
> O enchanting word!
> What joy
> You inspire for the treasures you contain!
> But if you be free, and not virtuous,
> Then liberty will be for you pernicious.[34]

By making it sound as if the Constitution were the fulfillment of every Peruvian's deepest wishes, Abascal hoped to put an end to underground political dissent. Hence the first major essay published in the *Verdadero Peruano* was an absurd paean of praise to the new order, composed by José Pezet, another medical man.

72

THE FALL OF THE ROYAL GOVERNMENT IN PERU

Pezet described how he had left the city on the morning of 21 September 1812—the day the Constitution arrived in Lima. Not bothering to explain why he had left, he proceeded to a breathless description of the brilliant sunrise that presaged the coming of the new order. Standing on a mountaintop, he heard the church bells of Lima pealing below. Returning to town he asked a stranger—who was described as "drunk with joy"—what the bells were for and was told, "Today the Political Constitution of the Spanish Monarchy arrived. Oh joy!"[35]

Oh joy, indeed. The message could not have been clearer if Abascal had signed the essay himself. And yet some historians continue to claim that the *Verdadero Peruano* was, in the words of one writer, "vanguardist and revolutionary."[36] It was no such thing—and that, in fact, is its most important characteristic. Reading the *Verdadero Peruano* is like listening to Abascal at a reception—coolly rational, but prepared to use the Constitution for whatever extra attractiveness it seemed to impart to the regime.

On some political issues the *Verdadero Peruano* was a direct but disguised mouthpiece for Abascal. From December 1812 to February 1813, for example, many letters and learned disquisitions appeared in the journal calling for the resignation of the priest Antonio José Buendía, who had been elected to the city council in the first constitutional elections. Abascal was the leader of the campaign against the priest. Finally Buendía was forced to tender his resignation as a result of public pressure and the arrival of the Cortes order prohibiting clerics from holding elective office.[37] The cabildo, however, refused to accept the resignation. On 13 April 1813 the journal published a long letter criticizing the election of Eyzaguirre as an elector—another of Abascal's favorite themes in this period. In many ways, then, it showed itself a mouthpiece for the viceroy, and while its contributors may not all have known that Abascal was its secret sponsor, it remains that the progressive doctors, entrepreneurs, and ecclesiastics who contributed articles were writing Abascal's party line in the journal he had founded and sponsored.

The only impartial periodical published in Lima in these years was *El Investigador*, a daily that first appeared on 1 July 1813 and that continued until the end of 1814. It was edited by Guillermo del Rio, Lima's only really professional journalist in these years, and it was chiefly a newspaper. Whereas the official *Gazeta del Gobierno de Lima*—in continuous publication during this period—was the viceregal government's organ for publication of decrees and orders, *El Investigador* published news, reprinted extracts from foreign journals, and carried announcements of interest to private citizens—sales of slaves and houses, weather reports, and news of what was being offered in the theater. Its only noticeable political view was its constant and rather heavy-handed opposition to the Inquisition and to certain aspects of clericalism. Almost every issue carried a letter, editorial, or poem criticizing the Holy Office. Since the Inquisition was abolished in 1813, *El Investigador* had a field day. Poking fun at ecclesiastical pretensions delighted Rio. On 3 September 1813 he editorialized about a sermon preached by Domingo López against *El Investigador* and concluded that only the censorship board could censure the newspaper, not a priest. On 7 September a letter appeared complaining that the convent bells in the city were too loud and concluding that if the friars would not stray so far the bells would not have to ring so loud to call them back. What kept Rio out of trouble was that Viceroy Abascal also disliked the Inquisition, and Rio exercised his editorial duties with scrupulous care. At one point he wrote that he had received many contributions to be printed in *El Investigador*, but some were acrimonious, some too long, and some purely self-serving. Their authors could publish them at their own expense and risk, "but there is no obligation on me to do so, because this periodical is mine, and I can put in it whatever I want. . . . I am an editor, not a printer."[38] *El Investigador* continued publishing, apparently unhindered, until the last day of 1814.

There were a number of other minor periodicals during this time in Lima—including the *Gaceta Ministerial de Lima*, *El Semanario*, and *El Peruano liberal*—none of which were of great importance.[39] The government published its annual *Guía de Forasteros*—an almanac and guide for visitors, listing names and addresses of government officials, temperatures, weights and measures—but it contained no editorial content.

Despite this narrative of Viceroy Abascal's avoidance of the free press and his persecution of Gaspar Rico, it is nonetheless impressive how little directly subversive propaganda there was during the period of the Cortes and Constitution—the one period in which dissident publications would be expected to appear in large numbers (as they did, for example, in Mexico City). One modern author, in an article dedicated to uncovering subversive propaganda in preindependence Lima, could find only two examples.[40] Even Rico, whom Abascal apparently assumed was the ultimate threat, was never a rebel; after his return to Peru he showed himself to be one of the last royalists. Indeed, true insurgent publications, except for those imported from outside the country, did not appear in any significant numbers until after the arrival in 1820 of San Martín's expedition, which carried a printing press with it.

The explanation for the absence of subversive propaganda lies partly in Abascal's preventive policy. Clearly his treatment of Rico was an overreaction designed to quash press dissent before it could spread. At any rate, it certainly had that effect. Nonetheless, the fundamental explanation is that Lima simply was not revolutionary. Its creoles felt a vast number of grievances, most of which revolved around their desire for position, status, and income or around their perception that the imperial system blocked them from fulfillment and acquisition. At all times, however, their enthusiasm for independence was tempered by their awareness that the imperial regime's social and racial constraints protected them from being engulfed by the nonwhite, non-Spanish population and culture that predominated in Peru. It is chiefly only at the level of innuendo, therefore, that political dissent in the press is to be found. One has to guess the meaning of individual essays and notations. Clearly *El Investigador* wished to convey something when on 9 July 1813 it reprinted a plan for the reform of the regular religious orders that had been written in 1713 by a fiscal of the Council of the Indies, or when it announced on 10 July 1813 that North American merchants in Havana were happy to hear of Spain's neutrality in the War of 1812, since it allowed both British and American shipping to continue using Havana, with great advantage to Spanish America. Obviously the city council of Lima was overreacting when on 19 October 1813 it wrote a formal denunciation to the viceroy of *El Investigador*'s several essays and letters criticizing municipal street cleaning and night patrols.[41] But as examples of the struggle of a courageous and outspoken press against royal authoritarianism these are rather insipid.

While there was little contest involved in Viceroy Abascal's attempts to prevent widespread subversive propaganda, he faced a far more serious challenge when it came to resisting the disruption caused by the political reforms of the Cortes and Constitution.

Chapter 4

# Political Disruption under the Cortes
# and Constitution

THE PERUVIAN VICEREGAL REGIME survived the political reforms of
the Cortes and Constitution just as it survived the tribute and
press reforms, but it came out badly damaged. The damage
occurred at two levels. One, the level Viceroy Abascal and his
fellow absolutists recognized, was the damage done to the authority of the viceregal regime, the crown, and the political institutions of the state by the confused tinkering of the Cortes and
Constitution, by the establishment of elective bodies to share
power with royal appointees, by the diminution of the powers of
the viceroy and audiencia, and by the unabashed attempt to
lessen the power of the sovereign. But more important and
longer-lasting damage was done to royal authority at the level of
what might be called indirect effect. Abascal's frequent attempts
to obstruct full implementation of reforms played a role, but even
more central was the hypocrisy of the Cortes on certain issues. It
eventually became clear to some Peruvians that the Cortes, for all
its enlightened liberalism, was just as imperialistic as the old
regime. To Americans, the experiment in Cortes government was
a giant breach of promise. The net effect was that Peruvians who
started out deeply conservative or who had vested interests in
maintaining the old regime were offended, frightened, or
angered by the Cortes, responding finally with enthusiasm upon
hearing of the restoration of the king in 1814 and his annulment of
the Constitution. On the other hand, Peru's liberals emerged

76

from the constitutional era disabused of their hopes of a brighter tomorrow, convinced that Spain would never grant America political or commercial equality. In general, therefore, the era of the Cortes and Constitution weakened Spanish authority. But authority and power are not the same thing. Though intimately related, power may continue to exist for some time even where authority has disappeared.[1] And Peruvians, aware of the narrow margin that separated them from being overwhelmed by the Indian and caste masses, could not give up the protective might of Spain. Consequently, even further initiating causes would be required before the Spanish regime would fall. Peru inched closer to the agonizing dilemma of 1821.

Even before publication of the Constitution in 1812, the Cortes, the Council of the Regency, and the Junta Central caused serious administrative disruption in Peru by their decisions involving incumbent royal officials there. In the period 1809–11, Spain's administrative confusion following the capture of Ferdinand VII was directly reflected in Peru by actual or contemplated changes of personnel in the intendancies and audiencia. In this period, for example, every intendant, except the one for Trujillo, either was removed from office or had his removal recommended and later countermanded.[2] In every case these administrative changes, reflecting the peninsula's concern to take account of the complaints of Americans, caused serious political disruption in the affected intendancies. And yet most of the individual complaints were not valid and could not be substantiated.

Even farther reaching, however, were the multitude of upsets in the prestigious audiencia of Lima in this period. Here the story is less one of Cortes or peninsular arbitrariness than of well-deserved but ineffectual attempts to discipline the Lima audiencia members for their scandalous public conduct. Between 1808 and 1815 both Viceroy Abascal and the peninsular government made repeated attempts to discipline the audiencia. Ultimately the king himself intervened. All their efforts were ineffective, and as a consequence Viceroy Abascal was forced to rule Peru virtually single-handed, without the advice and consent of an audiencia he distrusted and disliked.

The universal public discontent against the audiencia members matched Abascal's feelings. On 23 May 1808 the viceroy wrote to Spain complaining that the majority of Lima's audiencia members were engaged in private business or were operating haciendas, both of which were strictly prohibited by law. Acquisition of property through marriage or in the name of minor children was not prohibited, but management of such property was. The viceroy charged that the positions in the Lima audiencia were so lucrative that not one of the oidors would accept appointment even to the Council of the Indies, for it would require him to leave Lima. The Council of the Regency acted on these charges in 1810, expressing its royal disapproval of the oidors' contravention of the law and ordering them to cease renting and leasing haciendas, to sell any property they owned outright, and to rent out any land they might have inherited or acquired through marriage.[3] These warnings had no effect whatsoever.

Provoked by the continued complaints of the viceroy and many private citizens as well, the Regency began to solicit secret reports about the conduct of the audiencia members from various prominent residents of Lima. From 1810 to 1812 it received testimony from the former commandant of Callao and president of Quito Joaquín de Molina, and from the marqués de Torre Tagle, Archbishop Las Heras, the Peruvian Cortes deputies, the bishop-elect of Huamanga, the inquisitor general, the subinspector general, two Lima city councilors, and two merchants.[4] After weighing the contradictory evidence, the Regency was able to piece together a damning bill of particulars against the audiencia members. Manuel de Arredondo, the regent, was over seventy years of age and owned two large haciendas inherited from his two wives. Manuel García de la Plata rented three haciendas, was reputed to be carrying on a long-standing love affair, and had refused appointments to both Buenos Aires and Bogotá. Juan del Pino Manrique ran an hacienda. Domingo Arnaiz de las Revillas had abandoned his wife and six children and lived with a lower-class woman in a bread shop he owned. Francisco Xavier Moreno y Escandón, formerly an oidor in Manila, was reputed to be engaged in commerce with the Philippines. Manuel del Valle y Postigo owned three haciendas. Tomás Ignacio Palomeque was said to be a gambler and to own haciendas. Francisco Xavier Esterripa was deaf. Gaspar Antonio de Osma was thought to be too inexperienced and was active in the grain trade (as he made clear in 1813 when he complained to the city council about its regulations for wheat sales). Juan Bazo y Berri was said to be ignorant, corrupt, and venal. José Pareja, the fiscal, administered estates belonging to absentee owners and was involved in a milk shop, but the informants disagreed as to whether he was faithful to his wife, the viceroy charging that he lived with another woman. José Muñoz, the assessor, was particularly unpopular, and everyone agreed was a drunkard, corrupt, and the father of several illegitimate children. Muñoz, incidentally, defended himself against the specific charge that he was living with a concubine by submitting the testimony of thirty-two witnesses, including the woman he was accused of living with and her husband, proving that the lady in question was then seventy-seven years old. The other charges against him, however, were never refuted. Even the fiscal Eyzaguirre by this time was accused of treason by the viceroy. So sweeping and public was the scandalous behavior of the audiencia members that even Archbishop Las Heras, though being careful, he said, "not to incur the sin of the Pharisees," repeated allegations that Manuel del Valle had stolen an hacienda from the Dominicans and testified from firsthand information how Domingo Arnaiz had treated his wife (since she had sought the archbishop's intervention).[5]

The Council of the Regency determined to take more drastic measures against the audiencia since its first warning had gone unheeded. On 31 January 1812 it ordered Viceroy Abascal to suspend from the audiencia and bring charges against García de la Plata, Arnaiz, Valle y Postigo, Palomeque, the fiscal Pareja, the alcalde de lo crímen Bazo y Berri, and the assessor Muñoz. In addition, Abascal was ordered to reprimand Pino Manrique for sleeping in court and Baquíjano for gambling and to chastise all the members for their poor attendance and neglect of duty. However, since Peru was surrounded by rebellion, the Regency gave Abascal the option of suspending action against the oidors if he thought the political situation warranted it. And on 8 August 1812 that is the decision Abascal made. He told the Regency that the war did not permit him to take so drastic a measure as the suspension of seven members of the audiencia.[6] Nor could the viceroy ignore the effect that action against the oidors might have upon the elite families of Lima; for almost every oidor had married in Lima or had family contacts at the highest level of local society.

Although Abascal took no action against the oidors at this

point, it is clear that the audiencia had lost not only his confidence, but that of the public as well. It was certainly this public lack of confidence (as well as an expression of southern Peruvian regionalism) that led the cabildo of Arequipa in 1812 to order its Cortes deputy to request that cases from its jurisdiction be referred to the audiencia of Cuzco rather than of Lima.[7]

By 1814 Abascal could no longer restrain himself. On 2 August he sent the Regency a stinging letter of indictment against the audiencia, accusing it of delay and sloppiness in handling the cases of alleged rebels. Intensely angry, he declared "I could write a book about it." He referred especially to the accused leaders of an uprising in Tacna and Arica, claiming that the audiencia took three years to consider the charges and ended up releasing the rebels. He was even angrier about the audiencia's releasing Manuel Rivero, an accused rebel from Arequipa.[8]

This letter arrived in Spain just as the restored Council of the Indies was setting to work. It reopened the case, reviewed the mounds of documentation and testimony already collected by the Regency, and in 1815 recommended that cases be brought against Pino Manrique, García de la Plata, Arnaiz, Valle y Postigo, Palomeque, Bazo y Berri, Pareja, Eyzaguirre, and Muñoz, and that the regent, Arredondo, be retired. Since this had turned into the sort of dilemma that only the king himself could resolve, the matter awaited Ferdinand's disposition. Sometime in August 1815 the king wrote in his own hand on the folder enclosing the documentation:

> I am resolved: I retire Regent Arredondo at full salary; García de la Plata at 2/3 salary; and Pino Manrique at full salary. . . . The new Regent will form a case against Arnaiz de las Revillas, suspending him from office, making him leave Lima to a certain distance, and having him retain 2/3 salary for the support of himself and his virtuous wife and family. The same for Valle y Postigo and Fiscal Pareja. In regard to Palomeque and Bazo y Berri, I agree with the decision of the Fiscal [to issue them warnings of the king's displeasure]. The Fiscal Eyzaguirre I order to Spain to the first opening that comes vacant in either of the two chancelleries of Valladolid or Granada . . . .I retire the assessor Muñoz on 2/3 salary. And I order the viceroy secretly to keep watch on the conduct of Moreno y Escandón.[9]

The king thus ordered the retirement of four ministers, the suspension and trial of three, the transfer of one, and warnings for two others. The audiencia was to lose eight of its sixteen members. Francisco Tomás de Anzotegui, formerly regent of Charcas, became the new regent, and several emigrant oidors from Chile, Cuzco, and Quito who were then in Lima as refugees from the rebellions raging in their jurisdictions were appointed substitute oidors pending selection of permanent ones.[10]

Ferdinand's handwriting is easy to identify, his rubric is clear, and nowhere else in the palace documents is the first person ever employed. There is no question that these were the king's personal commands. It is all the more astounding, therefore, to discover that they were never carried out. The four audiencia members who were granted retirement left office, as did Eyzaguirre. But none of the others ever did—including the three who were ordered suspended. Arnaiz eventually died, leaving Palomeque, Bazo y Berri, Valle y Postigo, and Pareja still members of the audiencia, even though the last two were among the three to be suspended. Their cases were simply listed as "pending." At the moment of independence in July 1821, these four were still members. Indeed, Valle y Postigo signed the Declaration of Independence, and Palomeque was one of the six oidors who asked San Martín to allow them to remain in Lima. The king did, however, take a type of vengeance on Valle y Postigo when in 1817 he rejected the recommendation of the Cámara de Indias to allow the oidor's six daughters to marry in Lima. Pareja was particularly elusive in avoiding a hearing. In 1818 the Council of the Indies ordered Regent Anzotegui to proceed with the case against Pareja. But Anzotegui replied that he had been regent too short a time to undertake so delicate a commission. The Council then assigned the job to Viceroy Pezuela, who by then was too preoccupied with the war effort to do anything about it.[11] In 1822, after Pareja had fled back to Granada, the Council was still wondering how to proceed. Meanwhile, Valle y Postigo coasted placidly along, untouched by the royal command. Incidentally, there is no indication that either the oidors who retired or those who remained in office ever divested themselves of their property. On the contrary, Arredondo and Valle y Postigo were noted as major landowners at the time of independence. Nowhere in the independence era is the gap that separated command in Spain from implementation in Peru so clearly exemplified.

During most of his administration, therefore, Abascal had to function with a deeply divided and practically incompetent audiencia in which neither he nor the people had confidence. That might have been tolerable, for no one needed to know how rarely he consulted the audiencia, and the public was never aware of his distaste for the oidors. The regime could present the appearance of solidarity even if it had no relation to fact. But from 1813 to 1815 Abascal also had to function with elected municipal and provincial officals, and that greatly compounded his troubles.

The Constitution of the Spanish Monarchy, which was written by the Cortes, was promulgated and sworn to in Lima in the first week of October 1812. It constituted, at least in theory, a genuine political revolution, for it converted the empire into a parliamentary state with a limited monarchy. The king was effectively downgraded to the status of constitutional head of state, and legislative initiative was vested in the Cortes. The royal family was placed on a yearly pension, and Ferdinand VII was required to accept the Constitution upon his release from French captivity before he would be recognized. The viceroy was downgraded to the status of "superior political chief" (jefe político superior), and was required to share power with an elected Provincial Deputation, whose jurisdiction encompassed most of Peru except Cuzco. The territory of the Provincial Deputation was the same as the audiencia's and comprised the provinces of Lima, Tarma, Trujillo, Arequipa, Huamanga, Huancavelica, and Guayaquil. The territory of Chiloé with Valdivia fell under its jurisdiction but had no representative. One representative from each of the seven provinces, plus the viceroy, made up the deputation.[12] The Provincial Deputation was meant to function as something of a mini-Cortes, although it was not autonomous and did not possess initiative. The jefe político superior was chairman of the Provincial Deputation. Intendants of the provinces became jefe político of their territories. At the local level, the city councils were made elective, the proprietary regidors losing their offices. Duties and responsibilities of cabildos, provincial deputations, and political chiefs were all theoretically rationalized, though in most cases they were no improvement, except on paper, over the long-standing traditions based on cédula and the Laws of the Indies.

Indeed, the most important, though rarely mentioned, characteristic of the Constitution may well be that it was not much of an improvement in administration, at least not for Peru—a country permanently isolated from Spain by geography. For all its appearance of rationality, and despite its length, the Constitution was neither all-encompassing nor truly rational. It possessed some remarkable gaps. For example, city councils, Provincial Deputations, and Cortes deputies were to be elected by an extraordinarily complex series of indirect votes. Months before the final selection of the Provincial Deputation and Cortes delegates, voters were to meet in their home parishes to choose a list of "electors." These electors then met at a scheduled time in each province to select that province's "junta of electors." The junta of electors—consisting of one member from each partido—then met to choose the Cortes deputies and the Provincial Deputation member to represent that province. There were seven provinces in the jurisdiction of Peru—Cuzco was considered separate, since it had its own audiencia—and each province chose one member of the Provincial Deputation and one or more Cortes delegates depending on population. Distinct but less complicated voting was held for the city councils. The voting citizens met in their parish to select electors, who later met to select the city council. In neither case could the electors themselves be chosen to fill the offices. But in the middle of this whole marvelous construct was the most remarkable oversight. The Constitution itself never clearly specified who possessed the vote. Consequently, each viceroyalty, and in truth probably each locality, set its own standards. The Constitution did, however, exclude certain inhabitants from the suffrage—women, minors, mestizos, castes (or people of African background), and servants. Apparently the Cortes simply assumed that white adult male heads of households and permanent residents of an area—vecinos—would be as easily defined everywhere as they were in the peninsula. But in Peru it was not automatically clear who was a vecino. The Constitution declared Indians to be "Spaniards," but were they to be "citizens with the vote"? How old did a man have to be in order to vote? Were celibates considered heads of households? Were the peninsular members of royal garrisons vecinos? The Constitution answered none of these questions and set no specific age or income requirement. Even its literacy requirement was set aside until 1830.

What seems to have happened, therefore, is that the right to

TABLE 4
POPULATION OF LIMA BY CONSTITUTIONAL CATEGORY, 1813,
STILL IN USE FOR 1821

| Category | Total |
|---|---|
| Ciudadanos con ejercicio | 5,243 |
| Ciudadanos sin ejercicio | 6,670 |
| Ciudadanas | 11,460 |
| Espãnoles | 7,871 |
| Españolas | 11,239 |
| Religiosos | 959 |
| Religiosas | 473 |
| Esclavos | 6,400 |
| Esclavas | 5,863 |
| Extrangeros | 106 |
| Total | 56,284 |

SOURCE: "Censo general de la población de Lima hecho a fines del año de 1812," AGI, Lima 747.

NOTE: This census is only for the six parishes that made up the city, not for the Partido del Cercado (one of the eight constitutional districts represented in the Diputación Provincial and which together made up the province of Lima).

vote was defined by local mores and tradition. Lima, for example, recognized 5,243 men as "citizens with the vote" (see table 4). These were probably white, adult male heads of households of some standing in the community, and they were probably literate or semiliterate. A total of 6,670 men were listed as "citizens without the vote." These were probably white and mestizo males who fell short of full citizenship because of age, occupation, income, or illiteracy. Ciudadanas, confusingly, were the wives and daughters of both these categories. "Spaniards" now included Indians and castes, and it was clear that no Indians except caciques could vote. The status of the 959 male religious was also confusing. Some ecclesiastics did vote, and some were even elected to office, which caused great controversy, but the decision whether members of regular orders voted was no doubt left up to the individual monastery. An additional 2,652 soldiers and 1,715 members of the Navy were "citizens without the vote," certainly a serious discrimination. Later Cortes decisions did not clarify eligibility to vote. The Cortes did allow people of African background to apply for citizenship if they were recognized as of high character, were legitimate, and were married. But apparently they still could not vote. The option was exercised in Lima by Ramón Castro, an español pardo, who in 1813 applied for and was granted naturalization.[13] Viceroy Abascal, for his part, repeated on many occasions his charge that the Constitution's confusion in granting suffrage led to the common people, the pleve as he called them, taking over the elections, while the "true citizens" preferred to retire from the "tumultuous babble" to the "silence of their homes."[14]

A second major fault of the Constitution was that it specifically removed the jefes políticos—the intendants, governors, and viceroys—from military command over their jurisdiction unless a direct and specific grant of military command was issued. For a country involved in suppressing rebellion, this was obviously an absurd technicality. Viceroy Abascal seems to have ignored it, as did his Mexican counterpart Viceroy Félix María Calleja.

As with the earlier Cortes reforms, therefore, Abascal's chief defense against what he considered the dangerous reforms of the Constitution and the administrative instability it provoked was merely to intervene personally in the operation of constitutional processes. There was not a single election in Lima in which he did not intervene. The first election ever held in the capital was the parish voting for electors to choose the new cabildo. It occurred on 9 December 1812 under supervision of the perpetual cabildo and of the viceroy himself. The twenty-five parish electors included Eyzaguirre, Segundo Carrión, Diego de Aliaga, Francisco Xavier de Echagüe, Toribio Rodríguez de Mendoza, Francisco Colmenares, and Agustín Velarde y Tagle, all among Lima's leading liberals. As distinguished and competent a group of men as Lima ever boasted, the electors included seven clerics, five lawyers, four militia officers, one professor, two titled nobles, one magistrate, three men whose occupations were not identified, and even two men officially described as "Indians." Originally, indeed, two magistrates had been chosen as electors. In addition to Eyzaguirre, the alcalde de corte of the audiencia, Joaquín Fernandez de Leyva, had been chosen, but he excused himself on the grounds that he was a magistrate, and his place was taken by José de la Riva Agüero. Nonetheless, for this first cabildo election the viceroy proposed absolutely no objection to Eyzaguirre's being an elector. On 13 December 1812 the twenty-five electors met in the city palace, where Viceroy Abascal pre-

sided, delivering a homily and scrutinizing each elector's creden-
tials. In rapid order the new cabildo of two alcaldes, sixteen
aldermen, and two syndics was elected. It consisted of: as alcaldes, José Cabero y Salazar and José Ignacio Palacios; as regidors, the conde de San Isidro, the conde de Torre Velarde,
Antonio José Buendía, Antonio Saénz de Tejada, Santiago
Manco, the conde de la Vega del Ren, Francisco Alvarez Calderón, the marqués de Casa Boza, José Manuel Blanco, Manuel
Santiago Rotalde, Juan Bautista Gárate, Juan de Berindoaga,
Manuel Alvarado, Francisco Carrillo y Mudarra, José María Galdiano, and the marqués de Conga; and as syndics, Francisco
Arrere and José Geronimo Vivar.[15]

Abascal was personally hostile toward the new cabildo. Even
before the elections he had endorsed an appeal of the proprietary
aldermen that they be allowed to keep the honors and uniforms
of the cabildo, and he complimented the old members on their
help in various essential projects. In a letter of 27 February 1813
Abascal informed Spain that Eyzaguirre and his faction had controlled the parish elections, choosing the winners beforehand,
and that Eyzaguirre personally "had been the oracle that decided
all doubts and dispensed all benefactions."[16]

The viceroy's anger, however, was even greater at the second
set of elections—the ones for Cortes delegates and the Provincial
Deputation—in March 1813. Eyzaguirre was elected a member of
the junta of electors, representing the entire city and partido of
Lima. Abascal charged that "the voting for electors for Deputies
was even more scandalous, and Eyzaguirre controlled it just as he
had the ayuntamiento voting, and he came out named an elector
by his partisans." As a consequence, Abascal refused to allow
Eyzaguirre to attend the electoral junta, charging that magistrates
were barred by law from being chosen to any elective office.
Indeed, just such a decree had been received in Lima after the
parish elections but before the selection of the junta of electors.
Thus the entire capital city and its environs were not represented
in the election that chose the marqués de Torre Tagle and Francisco Valdivieso as the deputies to the Cortes ordinarias. Some
months later the city council, on the motion of its most outspoken
dissident, the young conde de la Vega del Ren, determined to
lodge a formal protest with the Cortes about Abascal's act.[17]

The real importance of Abascal's exclusion of Eyzaguirre goes far beyond a personal vendetta. Having gotten away with such a blatant intervention in the constitutional process, Abascal now had the measure of the liberals. He knew there was nothing they could do to block his interference, and he knew that a Cortes censure of him was unlikely and in any case would be ineffective. The path was open for a series of personal interventions over the next two years that nearly made the Constitution a dead issue in Peru.

For example, Abascal constantly interfered with the Lima city council. He was not happy about the election of the priest Antonio José Buendía as a regidor, and he immediately launched, through the *Verdadero Peruano*, a campaign to force him to resign. Almost every issue of the periodical carried an editorial insisting that an ecclesiastic could not hold elective office. On 18 February 1813 the editors published the newly arrived Cortes order that ecclesiastics could not be elected city councilors. On 18 February Buendía resigned from the cabildo.[18] This remarkable harassment of Buendía has no explanation but that Abascal and the periodical he sponsored did not want priests involved in constitutional affairs.

The matter did not end there, however. An angry and aggressive city council refused to allow Buendía to resign. The two syndics were asked to interpret whether an ecclesiastic could remain in office. José Geronimo Vivar said that the Cortes decision could not be retroactive since Buendía was elected before its arrival. The other syndic, Francisco de Arrere, disagreed, saying that the cabildo must observe the Cortes order, which was not a new law but simply a clarification of an existing understanding that clerics could not serve on councils. The ayuntamiento took Vivar's advice, determining that Buendía must remain in office until the Cortes could be consulted. Shortly thereafter it wrote to the viceroy, demanding that he make some public statement in the cabildo's behalf to put an end to the defamatory rumors running through the city that the electoral junta had been a scene of great confusion and that Eyzaguirre and others had rigged the election.[19]

Since Abascal was the instigator of these rumors, his reply was quick. He informed the city council that he would not publish any statement in its defense, because he had no information with which to defend the elections. Furthermore, since equally disturbing and seditious elections for city councils had occurred in Cuzco, Puno, and Arequipa, he forbade the Lima city council to defend itself publicly because the Constitution did not authorize it. On the Buendía matter he was adamant. He replied to the city council's insubordination with an opinion of the audiencia fiscal, Pareja, that Buendía could not remain in office, and he ordered "that in the future, when [the cabildo] wishes to deal with such grave matters outside the realm of the purely economic, it must inform me, so that I can preside over the cabildo; and, finally, it must abstain from sending any report to the Cortes without my signature." For good measure he added that the city's syndic, Vivar, was "a native of Chile and one of the rebels of this city." The cabildo stood its ground, replying in turn that it had never considered any subject to be outside its proper jurisdiction and that the precedent of centuries allowed cabildos to write directly to the sovereign. In a final summary of all these problems to the government in Spain, Abascal urged the government "to keep in mind the criminal abuse with which some malcontents wish to adapt the sacred maxims of the Constitution to their sinister designs." Eventually the Regency decided that Abascal and Pareja were correct about whether a cleric could sit on the city council, but the decision arrived too late, and Buendía remained on the cabildo until the end of 1813.[20] With such notable bad feeling on all sides, it is not surprising that the cabildo did not effect any lasting reform in municipal life.

Lima's second city council election was held in proper order in December 1813. According to the Constitution, the two alcaldes, one syndic, and half the aldermen were to be replaced. The cabildo decided that the eight youngest regidors would leave office, and that Buendía, who had been anxiously requesting to resign all year, would be replaced. Newly elected were the alcaldes, Juan Baustista Lavalle and the marqués de Casa Davila; the regidors, the marqués de Santa María, Juan Pentica, Pedro Antonio Arguedas, Ignacio Cabero, Mariano Carranza, Ignacio Prio, Francisco Colmenares, Agustín Vivanco, and Miguel Fernando Ruiz; and the procurator, Manuel Villarán. But, in what may well be the most petty act of viceregal vindictiveness in the entire era, Abascal refused to allow the new city council to take the traditional paseo through the streets on the day of its inauguration, insisting that "it is not necessary for the newly elected gentlemen to give themselves to be known by the people who elected them."[21] The year before, he had not only allowed the paseo but had participated in it himself.

Abascal's relations with the Cortes deputies were no more cordial than those with the Lima city council. He viewed the deputies as interlopers who carried the creole point of view to the center of political power itself, either ignoring or bypassing vice-regal authority. In August 1811 he complained to the Cortes about the direct communication that was going on between the deputies and the Peruvian cabildos, insisting that all correspondence must pass through his hands. He was spurred on in this thinking by the intendant of Huancavelica, Lázaro de Rivera, who claimed that letters from the deputies to the cabildo of Huancavelica caused political dissension.[22] Abascal was extremely unhappy with some of the deputies chosen, including the former intendant of La Paz, Domingo Tristán, who was chosen in 1813 to represent Arequipa. Abascal claimed he was elected by extremists who controlled the voting and that he was "perhaps the most immoral, corrupt, and wicked" citizen in Arequipa. However, the viceroy reserved his greatest anger for the previous Arequipa deputy, Mariano Rivero. In March 1813 Rivero told the Cortes that the viceroy's despotic rule was preventing the reform of government in Peru. In retaliation, Abascal arrested the deputy's father, Manuel Rivero, a regidor of Arequipa, on charges of being the leader of a revolutionary plot in that city. He also arrested the deputy's brother-in-law, Estanislao de Aranibar, and removed from office his brother, Antonio Rivero, who was subdelegate of Arica.[23] It was the failure of the Lima audiencia to convict Manuel Rivero for treason that motivated the viceroy in 1814 to accuse the oidors of dereliction of duty.

There was also one case in which Abascal, in his role as chairman of the electoral junta of Lima province, intervened personally in the choice of a Cortes deputy. Three electors in the last Cortes election held in Lima wrote in May 1814 to protest that when they had first cast their votes Tomás de la Casa y Piedra had received four and the conde de Villar de Fuente had received three. There should therefore have been a run-off between these two candidates, but the viceroy, as chairman of the junta, determined that the conde de Villar de Fuente was not elegible because he was prior of the Consulado. The electors protested on the grounds that a position in the Consulado was not a royal appointment, but Abascal was firm and excluded the count's name.[24]

In the realm of justice, Abascal thought the Constitution's reforms were just as dangerous as those relating to administration. Just as the Constitution and Cortes instituted all sorts of legal protections for civil crimes and misdemeanors, and abolished torture and hanging, so too they attempted to reduce the plethora of magistracies that had been built up over the centuries. As a result, most of the existing courts of first instance were abolished, leaving only the magistrates called jueces de letras. As it happened, Lima ended up with only three of these magistrates—the former cabildo assessors José Irigoyen and Cayetano Belon, whom Abascal had appointed when the position of city assessor was abolished, and one alcalde in turn. Before the reforms, however, Lima had possessed fourteen courts of first instance. The new legislation was not meant to impose a serious privation—the Constitution had ordered the establishment of one juez de letras for every five thousand inhabitants—but the Cortes simply never got around to appointing the new magistrates. Here is an excellent example of the sort of confusion the Cortes caused, for Abascal, the audiencia, and the city council all testified that Lima suffered a crime wave because of this. The periodicals referred to it constantly, calling on the cabildo to take corrective measures. Abascal testified that "crimes of theft, assault, and homicide are very frequent. . . . And it is physically impossible for the three courts to keep up, even though they take not a moment's rest."[25]

In the entire constitutional period there was only one reform about which Abascal had no objection, and that was the suppression of the Tribunal of the Inquisition, ordered by the Cortes in early 1813. News of the impending abolition provoked nearly unanimous approval in Lima. The periodical El Investigator published everything from learned essays to satirical poems directed against the Inquisition. The Lima city council issued a letter on 31 July congratulating the Cortes on the abolition, and in September it thanked the Regency for ridding the world of an instrument of oppression whose mere existence provoked "limitless indignation."[26] Excitement reached such a pitch that on 3 September 1813 a mob of two thousand attacked and looted the Inquisition building. They stormed the torture room, carrying off the instruments they found there. They then looted the offices and archives, perhaps searching for the records the Inquisition kept on the ancestry of leading personages. The viceroy was obliged to call troops to clear the building, and the next day the archbishop issued an order excommunicating any person who failed to return the papers and other articles that were taken. Two years later, Intendant Juan María de Gálvez defended himself against Abascal's charges that he had not been effective in resisting the mob by saying that the viceroy should have foreseen the people's anger and given appropriate orders. It is possible, therefore, that the viceroy did not object to this demonstration of popular anger against what he viewed as Peru's most outdated and wasteful institution. The Englishman William B. Stevenson, who had himself been hauled before the Inquisition a few years earlier, participated in the sacking of the building as the invited guest of a group of distinguished persons who had the viceroy's special permission to enter.[27]

Enough of the Inquisition's papers were returned to Archbishop Las Heras to give an idea of how ineffective the Holy Office had been. The archbishop reported, for example, that the Inquisition's papers were in such disorder that it would take years to catalog them and that it would be pointless in any case, and he asked permission to burn them. He requested special direction concerning what to do with the famous book called the *Tizón de España*—the secret list of families who had some blood relation to heretics or Jews. The archbishop listed the contents of the Inquisition's library, which contained 287 entries, some of many volumes, and included histories, dictionaries, pious works, and classics—Dr. Johnson, Milton, Lucan, Diderot, Montesquieu, Voltaire, Raynal, Pombal, Millot, Pascal, Condillac, copies of the New Testament and lives of famous leaders, most of them in French or English.[28]

More important to the viceroy was the disposition of the Inquisition's considerable assets, which Intendant Gálvez valued at 1,508,518 pesos, most of it not suitable to amortization, since it consisted of properties and endowments. Gálvez recommended the appointment of a general administrator who would report to the Provincial Deputation, and pending royal approval he himself functioned as administrator. He also recommended that the

Inquisition's employees—consisting of three inquisitors, an alguacil, a presbyter, two secretaries, a treasurer, two administrators of confiscated goods, a lawyer, a jailer, a porter, and a nuncio—should all be given other appointments in church or state. Meanwhile, the audiencia—which had no building of its own and had to meet in four small rooms in the viceregal palace—requested that it be given the Inquisition building.[29]

Unfortunately, no permanent disposition of the Inquisition's assets was made because, after Ferdinand VII's restoration to the throne in 1814, the Holy Office was reestablished.[30] In response to the order to restore the Inquisition's property Abascal gave the clearest indication of his own feelings toward the institution. On 29 March 1815 he wrote: "From time immemorial . . . the Tribunal of the Faith in this capital has been a rock of scandal for the inhabitants of the three kingdoms that form the Holy Office's jurisdiction." Because it was constantly involved in internal feuding, he attested that the Inquisition was "not only useless, but damaging." His chief complaint, however, was that the inquisitors, upon hearing of the restoration of their tribunal, had hounded him publicly to return every bit of its assets—some of which could not be returned, having been spent on the urgent necessities of the government. In making public their campaign for complete restitution, Abascal insisted that the inquisitors had insulted him and denigrated his personal authority. He took a hard line against their pretenses because "I know that nothing has so damaged the cause of the King as the lack of resolution, or imbecility, of those who have held power" in America. He further demanded the resignation of the inquisitor José Ruiz Sobrino, the leading factionalist, who was also involved in commerce and farming.[31] The Spanish government took Abascal's advice and in 1818 ordered the retirement of two inquisitors—Sobrino and Francisco Abarca—replacing them with José Anselmo Pérez de la Canal, curate of the parish of San Lázaro in Lima, and José Mariano Larrea, a parish priest from Vizcaya.[32] As of January 1819 Larrea was still trying to finance his passage to Lima, and if he arrived in Peru at all it must have been only a few months before the Constitution was restored in 1820 and the Inquisition again abolished.

In the midst of this constitutional period of revolutionary upset and abortive reform, Peru at last experienced serious internal rebellion and subversion. It is difficult, however, to assess the extent of Peruvian internal subversion because the testimony of royal officials was frequently contradictory. For example, Felix de la Roza, director of the mails in Peru (who was later removed from office for corruption), reported in 1813, in a letter referring to the conduct of the war in Upper Peru, that "the political situation in this part of South America is more critical every day, because the majority of its [people] favors Buenos Aires." He pointed out that Peru was attempting to fight a suicidal "war of opinion" with creole troops. In another letter Roza expressed his opinion that the "germ of independence" was implanted in most people's hearts, "and some day force will not be able to contain it, and there will be a chaos of horror and confusion, a volcano in which all will be reduced to nothing." In the very same letter, however, Roza testified that Lima itself had remained immune to the rebellious spirit "because most people are frightened of the horrors they would experience in case of a revolution . . . and of what the immorality and barbarism of the castes—who surround us—would cause."[33] In 1815 Viceroy Abascal reported that the "party of opposition to the Spanish government" in Lima was "so small in number, weak, and non-representative, that it should be a matter of no concern in the eyes of the government." Nonetheless, he insisted that "sad experience has confirmed in similar cases that apathy is the worst of evils, and that the wayward take advantage of it to increase their power," so that he had to maintain constant vigilance.[34] Within Peru itself there was every hope, even in 1814 and 1815, that class conflicts would serve to sustain the royal regime. The most serious uprising before 1820—the Pumacahua uprising—only intensified the creoles' fears and tied them more firmly to the regime.

The Pumacahua uprising broke out in the city and province of Cuzco on 2 August 1814 as a direct result of the refusal of the royal authorities there to implement fully the constitutional reforms. It was also the major expression of the regional identity and of grievances against Lima felt by white, mestizo, and Indian residents of Cuzco and southern Peru. Political leadership of the uprising consisted of several creole members of the city council of Cuzco, who had been arrested in 1812 and 1813 for opposition to the heavy-handed policies of the president and audiencia of Cuzco. They overthrew the audiencia and established a triumvi-

rate, led by the former interim president, the mestizo brigadier
Mateo García Pumacahua, with military leadership of the largely
Indian forces vested in José Angulo. A minority of the rebels
favored independence, but most simply wished to obtain governmental reforms within the framework of the Constitution.
When Abascal refused to listen to their demands, the rebels sent
their Indian forces into the neighboring provinces of Huamanga,
Puno, Huancavelica, La Paz, and Arequipa. For a brief period the
rebels controlled nearly half the viceroyalty. As fighting esca-
lated, moderate reformers withdrew their support of the rebels,
and the movement took on more the look of an Indian uprising
for independence from both Madrid and Lima and for the establishment of a romanticized Incaic empire. The rebels managed for
a while to hold the city of Arequipa, but by the first months of
1815 royalist forces from Upper Peru (under command of General
Juan Ramírez) and from Lima managed to inflict serious defeats
on the rebel masses. In March 1815 Ramírez won a decisive
victory against Pumacahua's army, and the rebellion collapsed.
The leading rebels in Cuzco were executed.[35]

Apart from this very real military threat, Peruvian insurrection
scarcely passed the level of half-formed conspiracies and loose
talk during this Cortes era. Although it is not possible or necessary to review every case of conspiracy or suspected treason, I
will mention some of the more illustrative, especially of those
related to Lima. In 1810, for example, Viceroy Abascal's government broke up a conspiracy of supporters of the revolutionary
government of Buenos Aires, which met in the house of the
sacristan of the parish of San Lázaro, Ramón Anchoris and was
headed by spies from Buenos Aires, chiefly the lawyer Mariano
Sarabia. Most of the conspirators escaped, other were exiled, and
Anchoris, who had served as the archbishop's mayordomo, was
sent to Cádiz. After being held there in various convents, he was
released in 1811. A short time later he fled to the United States,
where he became a Mason, and by 1818 he was back in his
hometown of Buenos Aires, a member of the revolutionary government. Other cases of this sort included that of Friar Marcos
Duran Martel, condemned to ten years' imprisonment in the
presidio of Ceuta for attempting to organize a provisional junta in
Huanuco in 1810, and that of the young naval lieutenant Eugenio
Cortes, relative of leaders of the revolutions in Caracas and Chile,

who was held in suspicion by the viceroy for being "too free in talking, untruthful in conversation, and in the opinion of some, addicted to the ideas of the revolutionaries."[36]

At the level of individuals, the royal regime's fullest attention was devoted to surveillance of the men of foreign birth who lived in Lima. There had been at least a few foreigners living in Peru ever since the sixteenth century. Leon G. Campbell estimates that most were originally sailors who deserted in Peru.[37] In response to a secret order from the peninsula in 1809 to expel all suspicious foreigners from the capital, Abascal appointed Juan Bazo y Berri to conduct the investigation. In May 1810 he reported there were forty-six foreign-born men living in Lima whose expulsion he recommended because they either were unmarried or had come to Lima without a license. These included nineteen Genoans, fourteen Frenchmen, and thirteen others who were Milanese, Roman, Coriscan, Venetian, Portuguese, Swiss, German, or English. Another fifty-eight foreigners, however, he recommended should stay, because they were married or were engaged in essential trades. They included twenty-three Genoans, six Frenchmen, six Milanese, and twenty-three others from Gibraltar, Naples, Rome, Ireland, England, Portugal, Germany, and other Italian states. The viceroy narrowed down the list of men to be expelled by excusing nine Genoans. The unlucky others were sent to Cádiz aboard the *San Pedro Alcántara*. Once in Spain, the government did not know what to do with them and ended up allowing eight of the Frenchmen to proceed to North Africa.[38]

The closest thing to a genuine conspiracy of rebels in Lima in this period was a plot of 12 July 1812, and according to the defense of the accused, there was no plot at all. On the night of 11 July a group of alleged conspirators was arrested in Callao. The viceroy charged them with plotting an uprising, scheduled for 12 July, that would include the murder of the viceroy, the sacking of the houses of wealthy Europeans in Lima, the overthrow of royal officials, and an attack on the artillery base by 1,600 Negro slaves from outlying haciendas. According to the government, there were seventeen conspirators, of whom three escaped. All were from the lower classes—there was a Negro surgeon, an Indian tailor, a cleric, two sergeants of the Regiment of Lima, one volunteer from the Concordia Regiment, and others from the pleve. They were supposed to have received letters from the revolutionaries in Chile. The plot was denounced by one José Planas—described by the defendants as a murderer and a "drunkard by profession." Announcement of this conspiracy caused widespread excitement and tension in Lima, and the *Gaceta* of 22 July carried news of it together with a letter from the city council congratulating the viceroy on his escape. Abascal immediately ordered the suspects tried by a military commission, which provoked an outcry from Fiscal Miguel Eyzaguirre, who insisted that the trials must be turned over to civil authorities on the grounds that all the suspects were "Spaniards" according to the Constitution. It was feared that the city's Pardo Militia might be involved in the conspiracy, and there was widespread fear of slave unrest. The guards at the city gates were reinforced. By 30 September eight of the defendants had been found not guilty— including one Hilario Vial, whom the government had claimed was a spy from Chile, or at least the intermediary between the Chilean rebels and Lima. The viceroy is supposed to have ordered the remaining six—Bernardo Herrera, José Merida, Apolinario Cartagena, Miguel Bados, José Vargas, and Eusebio Mosquera—to be convicted immediately. The military commission condemned each to ten years' imprisonment. Once they had been convicted, a friend of the six men sent a violently worded protest to the Cortes accusing not only Abascal but even Eyzaguirre of injustice and begging the Spanish government to intervene in the case because no one in Lima could stand up to the viceroy.[39]

On those rare occasions when the Spanish government did intervene in Abascal's prosecution of suspected rebels it had no impact whatsoever. The best example of this is the case of the young conde de la Vega del Ren, the highest-ranking Peruvian to fall under suspicion of treason in the constitutional period. Abascal had his mind made up about Vega del Ren as early as 1810, when the count served as alcalde of Lima. Abascal described him as "a young man . . . who, because of his minimal education, lack of intelligence and excessive self esteem, was the man [the rebels] needed to attract the people." As the conde was motivated by "the supposed right of certain houses who are said to be descendants of the Incas," he led the aristocratic faction in favor of Peruvian autonomy. In 1810 the conde attempted to arrange an open city council meeting—a cabildo abierto—to read and discuss letters received by the council from the rebels in Upper Peru. This suggestion, which Abascal refused, "since [a cabildo abierto] was the beginning of the tragedies of Buenos Aires, Montevideo, Santa Fé and others," confirmed Vega del Ren's leadership over the faction of autonomists and rebels in the city as far as Abascal was concerned. Upon arrival of the Constitution, the conde became a leader of the conspiracies to elect creole liberals to city and provincial office and was himself elected to the city council. Abascal intensified his gathering of intelligence about the conde, but he was constantly frustrated by his failure to find enough evidence to convict him. His council of war urged him to act decisively to stop the drift toward popular disorder. "Although the risk was undeniable," Abascal explained, "I lacked sufficient data to proceed judicially against anybody."[40]

In order to acquire the necessary evidence, in April 1813 Abascal sent secret letters to a selected group of trusted citizens asking their opinions about a number of people he suspected, most of whom were involved in the elections. It provides a clear idea of who Abascal and his council of war found suspicious. They asked opinions about Miguel Eyzaguirre; the lawyers Francisco Paula Quiroz and Santiago Manco; Fernando López, editor of the *Satélite del Peruano*; the lawyer Manuel Pérez Tudela; Manuel García, substitute agent for Eyzaguirre; José Geronimo Vivar and Ignacio Prio, from the city council; the escribano Manuel Malarin; Domingo Sánchez Revata, the "penman"; the friars of the Oratory of San Felipe Neri, Segundo Carrión, Tomás Méndez and Bernable Tagle; other lesser figures; and of course, the conde de la Vega del Ren. The replies provided Abascal grounds enough to act. A number of nobles, prelates, and officers, including José Baquíjano, the marqués de Valleumbroso, Francisco Abarca, Friar Juan Gabriel Bracho, Francisco Xavier de Izcue, and others, replied that all the suspects named were notorious as instigators of the current political discord.

Only four of the witnesses refused to testify against the suspects. Friar José Gabriel Echeverria answered that he had nothing to say because he never left his convent. Archbishop Las Heras and the bishop-elect of Huamanga replied that they were not permitted to give testimony in matters potentially involving corporal punishment. Most strikingly, the marqués de Montemira showed himself, even in this confidential communication, to be the man of utmost honor and rectitude that Lima reputed him to be. He replied that the viceroy should not make decisions on the basis of hearsay. While all the suspects might have been involved in the elections, he thought the peacefulness of the elections should be emphasized. It was such a potentially disruptive affair that he was surprised it had come off so quietly in such a populous city, "which has confirmed the concept I have always held that this capital is incapable of revolution against its legitimate government."[41] The viceroy was outraged at Montemira's reply, since the marqués was a member of the council of war that had unanimously urged him to investigate the danger posed by the election and the apparent spread of revolutionary sentiment.

In the particular case of the conde de la Vega del Ren, Abascal was finally able to act against him after he received, in October 1814, an anonymous letter accusing an unnamed group of Limeños of supporting the Pumacahua rebels and of planning an uprising in the capital. A second anonymous letter named three individuals involved in the plot, one of whom was vaguely associated with the conde.[42] Abascal claimed to have received information from several priests, obtained in the confessional, that such a plot was afoot.

From this complex of vague and contradictory hearsay evidence, the viceroy, who admitted he was prejudiced, concluded that Vega del Ren must be arrested. The arrest was accomplished in the predawn hours of 29 October 1814 by the Concordia Regiment in a slapstick episode. The troop detachment besieged in turn the houses of the count's mother and his wife, terrifying the peaceful inhabitants by climbing ladders into the courtyards, sending the family and servants fleeing to the streets crying that they were being attacked. Apparently to their surprise, the troops found the conde sleeping in his wife's house.[43] Abascal claimed that the anonymous pasquinades that had been appearing in the city ceased from the night of the arrest.

It seems to have taken the conde's family about a week to recover from their consternation, for not until 7 November did the condesa de la Vega del Ren write to ask the city council to intercede in her husband's behalf and to ascertain the charges against him. After three more such letters, the cabildo sent a request to the viceroy, with a testimonial to the conde's loyalty. The viceroy nonetheless tried with great energy to find enough evidence to prosecute him. His most promising lead was a letter sent to the conde from Arequipa on 18 November 1814 by the Cuzco rebels then occupying that city. After investigating the matter, however, the intendant of Arequipa replied that the letter was sent to Vega del Ren simply because his name was picked out of the newly arrived *Guía de Forasteros*, and that it had no greater significance. This was a telling blow to Abascal's case, and in some distemper he agreed to let the conde go for lack of evidence, ordering him to remain within the city limits of Lima and submitting all the evidence to Spain. The Council of the Indies finally took cognizance of the case in 1819. It was particularly concerned that the only evidence against Vega del Ren came from hearsay testimonies. Abascal refused to reveal his sources even to his own audiencia in order to preserve "the sacred law of secrecy." Thus Vega del Ren was cleared of all charges, and his agent in Spain asked that his innocence be published officially in Lima.[44]

The young conde de la Vega del Ren is characteristic of other political dissenters drawn from the Lima aristocracy in these years. He differed from others only in being more outspoken and, as the viceroy correctly said, foolishly unconcerned about the effect of his conversation and associations. Others, such as the young José de la Riva Agüero or Manuel Salazar y Baquíjano (conde de Vista Florida after 1818), were more circumspect in their conspiracies, and most would not be a serious concern to the government until about 1817, when the rebel victories in Chile again provoked support for independence in Lima. Even so, the conduct of Vega del Ren is the first sign of the growing political confusion of the Lima elite that would become manifest in 1821. Vaguely discontented with the restrictions imposed upon their political power by the imperial system, they chiefly sought an increase in their own powers and fortunes. Yet they were deeply troubled by the conflict between their loyalties to Spain and their loyalties to Peru. The ultimate example of this conflict of loyalties is the case of Manuel Lorenzo Vidaurre.

Vidaurre was a man of extraordinary intellectual powers. He was at once an ardent reformer and a supporter of Ferdinand VII and is thus the very symbol of Peru's inability to decide.[45] Born in Lima, he was educated in the college of San Carlos and was deeply imbued with the Enlightenment principles taught there. In 1810 he went to Spain, where the government asked him to

give a report on the situation in Peru. In his famous "Plan del
Perú," Vidaurre commented on many things—government, justice, the economy, social organization—but his two chief points,
repeated throughout his career, concerned the corruption of government functionaries in Peru and the necessity of reestablishing
respect for the law together with public austerity. He advocated
few changes, insisting that if the existing laws were properly
practiced they would be sufficient to restore loyalty. The Regency
named Vidaurre to the Cuzco audiencia in 1810, a position he
held until 1814. As the only creole on the Cuzco audiencia, and
the only oidor who favored the Constitution, Vidaurre was in
constant trouble with his colleagues. He considered the Constitution the source of Peru's redemption and urged the Cuzco audiencia to take the lead in implementing it. His colleagues, however, were evasive and considered the Constitution an attack on
the king's authority and a threat to their own positions. Vidaurre,
in his many letters and reports to Spain, accused the other oidors
of being corrupt and lazy. In 1813 Manuel Pardo, the regent of
Cuzco, described Vidaurre as imprudent and violent and asked
for his transfer to another audiencia. The Council of the Indies
decided that although there was no solid accusation against Vidaurre, he should be transferred to avoid further upset within the
Cuzco court, and it expressed its disapproval of his conduct.[46]
When the order, dated 4 October 1814, reached Cuzco, Vidaurre
had already been engulfed in the wake of the Pumacahua
rebellion.

In early 1814 Vidaurre had sent the Regency a long report about
the political tension then prevailing in Cuzco. He ascribed the
deterioration in creole loyalty to the arbitrariness and despotism
of the audiencia and warned that if the crown did not stop the
royal officials' flagrant misuse of power, America would be lost.
Vidaurre bluntly said that the uprisings could not be contained by
arms, for Spain did not have the material force to dominate
America; rather, Spain ruled through the loyalty her American
subjects felt. He repeated that the laws, including now the Constitution, must be scrupulously enforced, and that the failure of
Spanish magistrates and officials to obey Spanish law was the
source of the rebellions.[47] This attitude made Vidaurre a favorite
with the creole city councilors and other rebels who rose up and
imprisoned the royal authorities in Cuzco in August 1814. When

all the high-ranking officials of Cuzco were imprisoned, only Vidaurre was allowed to remain free. Indeed, the rebels offered him political command of the uprising. He refused, and it is clear he opposed the rebellion, insisting that violence was harmful to the cause of redressing creole grievances. In late August 1814, Vidaurre fled to Arequipa with a passport given him by José Angulo, military leader of the uprising. He eventually made his way back to Lima.

Vidaurre was deeply compromised because he remained free while the rest of the Cuzco audiencia was imprisoned by the rebels. Abascal began an investigation to discover the extent of his complicity, finally reporting in October 1815 that not only had Vidaurre taken no part in the uprising, but he had strongly opposed it. Yet the viceroy still hated him, for Vidaurre had aimed his strongest remarks, after those directed against his Cuzco colleagues, against Abascal himself. The viceroy told Spain that "although Vidaurre is not a rebel, he is animated by an evil and seditious spirit, and his continuation in the magistracy would be harmful to the peace of America." Thus Vidaurre spent the years from 1815 to 1820 living in Lima and defending himself against the accusations of other royal officials, making himself even more of a thorn in Abascal's flesh. The viceroy insisted that Vidaurre spent his years in Lima doing nothing but complaining of tyranny and telling everyone how powerful the rebels were and how they were fighting to be free.[48] In a letter to Spain Vidaurre advocated what he thought was the correct way to end the rebellions: "Gentleness in government, good political and civil laws, choice magistrates. Of all these things there has been a defect since the Conquest, and these vices have prepared our ruin." The greatest paradox, however, was that—as he told Spain in 1815—it was just as impossible for America to be independent as it was for it to be entirely subjected by force of arms, for America lacked the people, the civic virtue, and the cohesion to make a success out of independence, while Spain lacked the arms and resources to reconquer it.[49] Thus Vidaurre foretold the great dilemma that soon faced Peru.

Neither a rebel nor an absolutist, Vidaurre remained suspended between two worlds. In 1817 he wrote the king one of his eloquent testimonials. After so many years of warfare, he said, Peru was dying. "America is depopulated, but not subjected."

The soldiers came, and died, and "every dead soldier of Spain leaves two children in the women of the country. These same children twenty years later are soldiers fighting their father's country." Meanwhile, Peru was starving. "There are not enough people to do the work needed in the war, and those who remain do not want to work, knowing that their products will not be theirs." In despair he reminded the king that "he who can die, can never be enslaved." The only hope was to reform the administration, lessen the oppression, and give all Americans a stake in the preservation of royal government.[50]

At his best, then, Vidaurre was the eloquent voice of a troubled people who had no alternatives, who did not know what they wanted, and who had nowhere to turn. At his worst he was simply maudlin, as in a letter of 17 March 1817 to Viceroy Pezuela, in which he offered a regular contribution to the king and quoted his three-year-old daughter. When asked, "What will you give up each day to your Father, the King?" she replied, "I will give Padre Rey half my cookies and my sweet pickles." His wife vowed to buy no more jewels, his daughters to wear no more silk blouses, and his sons to forego milk at tea and butter at breakfast. He urged the viceroy to carry his little daughter's sacrifice to the king, who was said to be bathed in tears, and to tell him, "Do not believe that Americans abhor thee; receive the votes of a poor but loyal family . . . who know that there are many decided in favor of thy just cause."[51] Thus Vidaurre was himself a paradox, for he remained a defender of the Spanish monarchy even as he wrote to the king with accusations that no one else dared make. He was, in the words of one historian, "a bourgeois viceregal courtier with revolutionary aspirations, and a republican with viceregal nostalgia."[52]

The most striking fact of all is that Vidaurre remained unable to decide between his loyalty to the crown and his desire for reform. At the insistence of Viceroy Pezuela, who charged him with being a fanatical rebel, he finally left for Spain in November 1818. He was in Spain in 1819–20, agitating for a position and for restoration of his salaries, and also pressing for full implementation of the Constitution. In August 1820 he was named a member of the audiencia of Puerto Príncipe, Cuba. In Cuba he continued his insubordination to what he considered arbitrary local authority. Taking his seat in June 1822, he was ordered back to Spain almost immediately, on the request of the captain general of Cuba, for having opposed the sending of a garrison of troops to Puerto Príncipe. He left Cuba in November 1822, bound for Spain via Philadelphia. On reaching Philadelphia, however, his long struggle of conscience was at last decided. For reasons he never made clear, he determined to seek refuge in the United States. His long duality was finally over, and after years of advocating union with Spain and constitutionalism at home he became a supporter of independence. He returned to Peru in 1824, where Bolívar made him president of the Supreme Court of Trujillo, then of the Superior Tribunal of Justice in 1826. He was a deputy to Congress, twice a minister of government, and a deputy to the Panama conference.

Vidaurre is thus the very symbol of the Peruvian creole in these years. He was not a rebel, but rather was a monarchist, a reformer, and a liberal.[53] He risked his career, and even his life, to protest the abuses of the royal regime—no one in Peru did so as fervently or as brilliantly—yet he could not break the intellectual and psychological bonds that tied him to Spain. While protesting the abuse of the Indians in Cuzco, he also opposed abolition of the tribute. Though offered the political command of the Pumacahua uprising, he refused to cast his lot with independence until 1822. These were the same agonies of conscience other Peruvians faced, and their inconsistency, if less spectacular, was no less thorough.

At any rate, on 4 May 1814 the king, recently freed from his captivity in France, issued at Valencia a proclamation annulling the Cortes and the Constitution. In the months ahead, he proceeded to annul all the acts and legislation of the Cortes, and by the end of the year the empire had returned to absolutist government. Abascal greeted news of the king's restoration with unrestrained joy; at long last his resistance to the Constitution was over. On 6 October 1814 he published the royal decree annulling the Constitution.[54] The Provincial Deputation was immediately dissolved. Lima gave itself over to several months of celebrations and fiestas.

A peculiar anomaly of the annulment, however, was that the king did not at first disband the elected city councils. Indeed, a decree published in Lima on 25 October 1814 ordered the elected cabildos to remain in office pending further instructions. With an air of unreality, therefore, the regularly scheduled parish voting for the third elected city council took place on 6 November, even though the Constitution had already ceased to exist. In this election serious irregularities did occur and were for the first time substantiated not by the viceroy but by private citizens. According to a letter sent to the alcalde by Gaspar Vargas y Aliaga, the election in Lima's chief parish, the Sagrario, was controlled by a conspiracy. Very few ranking citizens of honor had voted, he said, while the people who did vote were "indecent." As a consequence, the viceroy annulled the election in the Sagrario and called for a new one on 20 November.[55]

All problems notwithstanding, the electors gathered to choose the new cabildo on 18 December. The viceroy did not preside over the meeting, declaring he was too busy with other duties. They proceeded to choose two alcaldes, one syndic, and eight regidors. Alcaldes were José Antonio Errea and Francisco Moreyra; regidors were the marqués de Lara, Pedro Abadia, Joaquín Manuel Cobo, Diego de Aliaga, José Sarnia, Tomás de la Casa, Francisco Vallés and the marqués de Montealegre; the syndic was Antonio Padilla. In a remarkable act of interference that no one seems to have objected to, the viceroy, after being informed that a ninth regidor wished to resign, personally chose his replacement, José Matías Elizalde, from among the unsuccessful candidates who had ranked high in the voting. But, even as the new aldermen were being chosen, rumors ran through the city that the king had abolished the constitutional cabildos. The city council had even received letters to that effect, and several proprietary regidors had already applied to have their seats restored. On 30 December, the day before the new council was to take office, formal certification arrived. Thus none of the newly elected members ever took their seats. The next day the perpetual city council was seated "with transports of joy."[56]

Abascal was wrong, however, if he expected the restored cabildo to disallow the authority of the former elected one. So great was the feeling of creole identity among the proprietary regidors that they immediately chose as alcaldes for 1815 the very same men who had been elected alcaldes by popular vote a few days earlier—José Antonio Errea and Francisco Moreyra. This was, as Fisher points out, "a clear demonstration of creole solidarity and of the cabildo's determination to press for the redress of creole grievances."[57] In the next two years the proprietary cabildo accepted the claims for proprietary seats of no less than six gentlemen who had been elected during the constitutional era— Manuel Blanco y Ascona, the marqués de Casa Boza, Juan Bautista Lavalle, the marqués de Casa Davila, Errea, and Moreyra. In 1816 the cabildo recognized several precedents set by the constitutional city council and declared that it "differed from this cabildo only by being elected and in its membership, [for the cabildo] is one, . . . and therefore [the elected cabildo] should be and is considered to have been the proper cabildo."[58]

Four years of government by the Cortes and two years of a written constitution had accomplished remarkably little in the way of substantive reforms. Just how little can best be judged by considering the recommendations submitted in June and July 1814 by the former Cortes deputies of Peru in response to an invitation from the king that they, and all the other American ex-deputies, should inform him of the reforms they thought necessary to restore peace and prosperity in their homelands. Of the sixteen Peruvian ex-deputies to both the extraordinary and the ordinary Cortes who were invited to submit recommendations, nine did so.[59] Most of the suggestions were for purely local reforms, but several dealt with more important matters.

Mariano Rivero, ex-deputy of Arequipa, listed the reforms he had advocated on instructions from the cabildo of Arequipa: free trade for Peru, internally and externally; equality of Peruvians in job appointments; the establishment of a university at Arequipa; the transfer to Arequipa of the Cuzco audiencia or, failing that, the establishment in Arequipa of a branch of the Cuzco audiencia; abolition of the sales tax on brandy; and reduction of the property tax established by Abascal. None of the demands had been granted. Tadeo Gárate of Puno requested the creation of regular sources of income for royal subdelegates in order to prevent corruption, and he particularly urged the creation of a state bullion bank in Puno, managed locally rather than from Lima. The proposal, rejected by the Cortes in 1813, was again rejected by the Ministry of the Indies in 1814. Pedro García Coronel of Trujillo also asked for reduction of Abascal's property tax, but the Council of the Indies replied that this matter would require much further discussion before it could be considered. Martín José de Múxica, representing Huamanga, advocated increased political participation for Indians, particularly that at least one Indian should be on the city council of Huamanga as a sign of the king's regard for the native people. The Council seems never to have debated this proposal. Two of Lima's ex-deputies—the marqués de Torre Tagle and Francisco Valdivieso—submitted a detailed list of demands representing the wishes of the capital's inhabitants. They asked that there be genuine implementation of the Cortes decree that America was free to produce any natural or manufactured product; that Lima be given permission to mint 20 million pesos of silver money in small denominations over the next forty years as a provincial currency; that the office of escribano de gobierno in Peru be abolished; that the price of official paper be lowered; that new sources of revenue be found for the University of San Marcos and the cathedral chapter; and that the mail system be reformed. All these demands were either denied or shunted aside.[60] Thus the constitutional era ended with the creoles' grievances as great as ever, their hopes for a measure of equality within the empire dashed.

The royalists, on the other hand, breathed a sigh of relief upon the restoration of absolutism. Lázaro de Rivera, former intendant of Huancavelica, expressed the most outspoken absolutist view of the Constitution and Cortes when he wrote in February 1815 to declare that the Cortes had been an abomination, vomiting out oppressive decrees, destroying the sovereign's and the clergy's authority, exposing the royal governors to attacks from the common people, and in general encouraging the bloodshed and terror that now reigned in America. For his constancy in supporting Abascal, the viceroy asked Spain to grant Rivera, who had served as administrator of Temporalidades in Lima since 1812, a salary increase from 3,200 pesos a year to 6,000. The Council of the Indies compromised by raising his salary to 4,000 pesos.[61]

But the real impact of the Cortes and Constitution in Peru was deeper than Rivera recognized. If the authority of royal officials had declined, it was the result not of the Constitution but of their open disobedience to it, and if some creoles had been disabused of their faith in the regime it was because after so many promises and so many years of expectation, nothing substantive had been accomplished. If the Peruvian regime had been arbitrary before 1810, its treatment of liberals like Eyzaguirre and Vidaurre and its general attitude toward the reforms only made its arbitrariness all the more obvious. The regime's authority was badly weakened by the internal inconsistency it had revealed—professing loyalty to the Cortes and Constitution but refusing to implement the really critical reforms, dispatching armies to uphold the monarchy while simultaneously disobeying the duly constituted royal power. Yet the most critical element was that the Cortes itself had failed to solve the major complaints of Americans; the liberal experiment rocked the empire to its foundations but accomplished nothing. The failure of such a massive reform program appeared to leave no options for redress of grievances, and the Peruvians' ability to decide was paralyzed. The absolutist option had already caused widespread dissent; the liberal option now collapsed. Where was Peru to turn?

On 31 August 1814 José Baquíjano, conde de Vistaflorida, submitted to the Ministry of the Indies a long memorial on the pacification of America that made specific the point about the failure of the Cortes. His statement constituted a scathing indictment of what he called Spain's "antipolitical" conduct in the suppression of the revolts. Most important, he pointed out the real damage the Cortes experiment had done to imperial governance. The fault lay not so much in misgovernment (though he cited several detailed examples of loyal Americans whose sacrifices were not rewarded by the Cortes) as in promises not kept. The guarantee of the Cortes, he insisted, had been that it would institute massive reforms, and it had promised, explicitly or implicitly, to solve the fundamental grievances of creoles and Indians alike. Citing the Spanish proclamation of American equality, he reduced the multitude of American complaints to two chief insults perpetrated by the Cortes: its refusal to grant equal representation and its refusal to establish free commerce. The proposal of equal representation, he said, had been defeated because the peninsular deputies refused to recognize the Indian as an equal. The proposition of free trade had failed because of the interference of the Consulado of Cádiz, "the absolute dictator of the resolutions of the Regency and the Cortes." The eleven demands that the entire American delegation presented on 16 December 1810 had been ignored or voted down by the peninsular delegates. Baquíjano declared that "this antipolitical conduct has been the true origin of the desperation of the American peoples; [the Cortes] never wanted to hear their complaints, nor to listen to their propositions." The Indians, too, had been promised land in freehold (a cause Baquíjano particularly supported), but, although the Peruvian viceroy actually drew up a plan to distribute freehold land to the Indians, the Cortes delayed and accomplished nothing. More than any other commentator, Baquíjano articulated America's complaint against the imperial regime when he concluded by declaring that both the creole and the Indian had long memories; neither of them would forget unkept promises or broken guarantees.[62] Although Baquíjano was a former councilor of state, his memorial received no more of a hearing than did those of the ex-deputies. Spain was not listening, and the Americans knew it.

After several years of warfare, nothing had really changed: creole grievances were as numerous as before, the threat of rebellion was as great as before, the regime was as absolutist as before. There was only one significant difference: Peru was poorer and more confused, its resources further stretched. Could Abascal restore confidence in the regime before Peru went bankrupt?

Chapter 5

# Foreshadowings of Economic Collapse

THE ROYAL REGIME IN PERU had proved itself capable of resisting and defeating its enemies in the military and political realms. It was economic collapse, however, that eventually destroyed the regime, and as early as 1814 that collapse could be anticipated. The period from the annulment of the Constitution to Abascal's retirement from office in July 1816 was largely devoted to attempts to restore the viceregal economy. In the face of the regime's deteriorating financial situation—provoked by the massive destruction in the interior caused by the war, by the disruption of normal shipping, and by the costs of a government that was greatly overextended—Abascal instituted an extensive program of emergency taxation, which in itself represented a more herculean task than launching armies.

By the end of 1814 the royal treasury in Peru was in serious trouble. Contador Joaquín Bonet reported that the total income of the treasury amounted to less than half of total expenses each month. In the last four months of 1814 alone, the deficit for upkeep of the army, the navy, and the artillery was 150,000 pesos; deficits to various monasteries and other creditors were 45,000 pesos; and a total of 200,000 pesos in grants to Concepción, Chiloé, Valdivia, and Upper Peru remained uncovered. Bonet stated that the government urgently required an increase of at least 50,000 pesos a month. In terms of actual operating expenses, therefore, the viceroyalty was in serious difficulty, although the overall gross report of the central treasury (Caja Matriz) for 1814—characterized as usual by carryovers from past years—showed a favorable balance between income (2,635,942 pesos) and expenses (2,561,718 pesos). The problem, of course, was that uncovered drafts were simply not shown in the formal reports. With income of the Caja Matriz in 1814 at a mere 2,635,942 pesos, Peru was failing fast, for in 1813 total income in that account had been 3,396,200 pesos. These figures represent the income from all government sources of revenue except the customs, which was kept in a separate account and, to judge from the total for 1816, produced about a million pesos a year.[1] Félix de la Roza, director of the mail system, wrote Spain in 1813 to report that "I have frequent and close dealings with the first chief of this vast kingdom and I assure you that in spite of the fact that he possesses a great spirit and presence of mind in the greatest conflicts, today I see him almost desperate—not for lack of expedients, but because he finds himself without any recourse to money, having drained all imaginable ones and discovering no others to use."[2]

Abascal was forced to turn frequently to the Consulado for help. In September 1814, for example, he asked the Consulado to collect a loan from its members to support his plans to send 1,500 men from Arequipa to Cuzco to put down the Pumacahua uprising. In late 1814 and early 1815 he turned to it for grants of 120,000 pesos to help pay for sending the warships *Asia* and *Descubierta* from Cádiz with peninsular troops bound for Peru. When the Consulado replied that it could not raise the necessary money, Abascal worked out a special arrangement exempting it from the usual duties on the export of gold and silver that had been sent to Spain the year before on the same ship *Asia*, if it in return would apply the duties collected on arrival of that ship at Cádiz toward refitting it for return to Peru. In June 1815 he demanded half a million pesos from the Consulado as a loan to the government. A few months later he demanded 20,000 pesos as a loan against income from the sales tax on wheat and cereals. Then, upon receiving word that the reinforcements had been dispatched from Cádiz, he demanded from the Consulado a further 8,000 pesos to pay for supplies aboard the ship *Casadora* sent by the government of Panama to carry the troops down to Peru.[3]

Nor was Abascal slow to demand money or services from other corporations. In June 1815, for example, he ordered the Company of the Philippines—the private corporation granted by the crown the right to undertake a yearly shipment of goods between Lima and Manila—to dispatch its ship, the frigate *Príncipe de Asturias*, to Panama to transport troops that were expected to arrive there from Spain. The directors of the company later complained bitterly that the frigate had arrived in Panama at the end of July only to discover that the troops were not expected until October, which meant it missed the winds it needed to return to Manila.[4]

When Abascal turned to the Lima city council for special donations, he found it was no longer able to sustain the sort of grants it had made during the reign of Charles IV. As of 1812, the city council—although it was making donations of approximately 17,000 pesos a year to the army—was more than 700,000 pesos in debt. Of that total debt, more than 300,000 pesos came from its donations toward rebuilding the walls and fortresses of Lima, grants to Buenos Aires, and a grant to the crown in return for restoration of the municipal tax over goods entering the city—the bodegaje. In 1814 the contador, Fernando Zambrano, reported that the municipality's total debt was "the astounding sum" of 745,238 pesos, and that it was absolutely impossible to mortgage further any of its regular sources of revenue.[5]

Finding the usual sources of credit dried up, therefore, Abascal launched a thorough reorganization of the plethora of taxes and duties that existed in the viceroyalty. A Junta de Arbitrios—composed of the viceroy, archbishop, intendant, prior of the Consulado, two merchants, alcalde, syndic, director of the mining guild, factor of the Company of the Philippines, maestreescuela (chancelor) of the cathedral, and the directors of the tobacco monopoly and the customs—began meeting on 18 February 1815. It chose a smaller commission to report on methods of raising new revenue. The commission was composed of the conde de Villar de Fuente, prior of the Consulado; José Antonio Errea, Lima's alcalde; Matías Querejazu, maestreescuela of the cathedral; Valentín Huidobro, municipal syndic; Pedro Abadia, factor of the Company of the Philippines; and Joaquín María Ferrer, a leading importer.

At its meeting of 28 April the Junta de Arbitrios read and approved the commission's *Plan General de Arbitrios* and, in addition, its recommendation for the collection of a patriotic loan of half a million pesos. The General Plan was as sweeping and as thorough an assessment of the economy as was ever produced in the colonial era. The commission, after reviewing Peru's financial records, found "that its poverty is very ancient." Although Peru's war expenses were "insignificant for the smallest of the independent states of Europe, they are insupportable for a young country like this one which lacks the foundation of wealth, which is population." Insisting that Peru was actually a poor country, the commissioners pointed out that the millions it had sent to Spain in bullion over the years had no relevance, for bullion and wealth were not the same things. To prove that contention, the commission said, "it is sufficient to point out that the annual income of the royal treasury of Peru has always been equal to the annual coinage," almost the entirety of which, having passed from private hands back to the government to cover purchases from the state monopolies and taxes, was remitted to Spain. In short, little of Peru's annual coinage remained in the country to stimulate true wealth. The royal treasury of Peru actually kept only about 500,000 pesos of the total each year. Add to that the loss of much of Peru's population in the past decades through the transfer of Upper Peru, and the additional expenses of the war, and Peru found itself "in the most deplorable situation, without means to exist, with a debt so heavy that it has reduced it to the verge of dissolution."[6] In 1812 Peru's yearly deficit was 485,083 pesos, and its accumulated deficit was 8,088,212 pesos. As of 1813 and 1814, the annual deficit was estimated at 1.5 million pesos, and the accumulated total was more than 12 million. Taking as its fundamental principles the ideas that any new taxes on consumer goods should not hurt the poor, that any new taxes on luxury goods should not damage domestic industry, and that taxes should be against production rather than capital, the commission proposed a sweeping series of nine tax reforms, all of which were immediately implemented.

The reforms consisted, first, of increases in the three basic royal taxes: the alcabala, the almojarifazgo, and the quinto de la plata. The alcabala—a 6 percent tax on all sales and resales—produced 611,928 pesos in 1812. The commission called for it to be increased by 1 percent, which would allow a net increase of 101,988 pesos. The almojarifazgo—a 3 percent tax on goods introduced into the country by sea, which in 1812 produced 181,708 pesos—was increased to 4 percent, allowing a net gain of 60,566 pesos. The

TABLE 5
LIMA URBAN PROPERTIES, 1815,
CLASSED BY ESTIMATED RENT VALUE

| Number and Type of Property | Estimated Annual Rent Value (in Pesos) |
| --- | --- |
| 500 large houses, 600–1,000 pesos yearly rent | 400,000 |
| 1,200 large houses, 300–500 pesos yearly rent | 480,000 |
| 2,000 small houses, 150–300 pesos yearly rent | 450,000 |
| 3,000 shops occupied by employees and owners, 36–130 pesos yearly rent | 249,000 |
| 100 multidwelling houses (callejones de quartos), 200–400 pesos yearly rent | 30,000 |
| 250 bodegas, pulperías, and chinganas, 200 pesos yearly rent | 50,000 |
| 100 general merchandise shops, 180–260 pesos yearly rent | 24,000 |
| 150 small shops (caxones), 96–180 pesos yearly rent | 20,700 |
| 72 small riverside shops, 108 pesos yearly rent | 7,776 |
| Total of 7,372 properties, with total annual rent value of | 1,711,476 |

SOURCE: "Memoria, Plan General de Arbitrios," Lima, 28 April 1815, AGI, Lima 751.

royal fifth taken on silver mined in the country produced in 1812 a total of 383,216 pesos. Increased by one real on each mark of silver, it added a net gain of 55,000 pesos. Second, the commission called for the equalization of customs duties paid in the province of Guayaquil, where the alcabala was only 3 percent. Raising it to 7 percent, as in Lima, produced a gain of 51,242 pesos. Third, the commission instituted a tax on urban and rural properties. Rural property was to be taxed at 5 percent of its annual rent value, allowing an increase to the state of 175,000 pesos a year. Urban property was to be taxed at 5 percent also. "Rent value" meant either what the renter paid or an estimate of what the owner-occupant would pay if he were renting. In 1791 the *Mercurio Peruano* had estimated there were 3,941 houses in Lima. Allowing for an estimated increase, and adding shops and stores, the commission estimated there were now 7,372 urban properties, distributed in nine categories depending on their yearly rent value. These figures, though only estimates, provide valuable information on the cost of living in Lima (see table 5). In all, the urban properties accounted for an annual rent of 1,711,476

TABLE 6
CAPITAL INVESTMENT FUNDS IN LIMA, 1815:
CAPITAL VALUE AND ANNUAL INTEREST INCOME

| Fund | Total Capital (in Pesos) | Annual Interest Income (in Pesos) |
|---|---|---|
| Consulado | 4,716,956 | 203,909 |
| Caja de Censos | 2,041,355 | 62,869 |
| Tobacco monopoly | 1,891,102 | 57,865 |
| Caja Real | 1,647,562 | 49,705 |
| Inquisition | 1,508,518 | 70,211 |
| City council | 698,930 | 35,224 |
| Casa de Moneda | 76,000 | 2,420 |
| Temporalidades | 69,938 | 2,914 |
| Total | 12,650,361 | 485,117 (to be taxed) |

SOURCE: "Memoria, Plan General de Arbitrios," Lima, 28 April 1815, AGI, Lima 751.

pesos. The tax on this would produce an estimated minimum of 76,682 pesos a year. The commission called for the appointment of regidors to draw up a census of properties in each barrio of the city. Collection of the tax was to be in the hands of a special commissioner. If the tax was paid by a renter, the owner of the property was required to reduce the rent by 5 percent.

Since a tax was levied on rental income, the commission determined that unearned income from investments should also pay a 5 percent tax. There were eight fundamental capital funds in Lima—or agencies that administered capital investment funds (see table 6)—but the commission intended that other agencies that possessed annuity funds—such as the university—should also be taxed. On the basis of the total capitalization of these eight funds, the commission determined that a 5 percent tax would produce 24,255 pesos. It is not clear how the tax was to be collected, though presumably it was to be withheld by the investment agency administering the fund.

Furthermore, a whole new series of "extraordinary" taxes were levied on consumer goods, both imports and exports, in the Lima region. The commission presented the most complete list to date of the quantities or values of certain basic imports and exports (see table 7). Some items, such as Indian goods made in Trujillo or domestic rice from the valleys near Lima, had never paid any tax

TABLE 7

"EXTRAORDINARY" TAXES ON SELECTED IMPORTS AND
EXPORTS IN LIMA, 1815

| Product | Yearly Trade in Quantity or Value | Increase of Tax | Expected New Revenue (in Pesos) |
|---|---|---|---|
| | IMPORTS | | |
| Chilean wheat | 180,000 fanegas (2.5 pesos per fanega) | 1 peso per fanega | 180,000 |
| Chilean and Mexican tallow | 36,000 quintals (13 pesos per quintal) | 1 peso per quintal | 36,000 |
| Trujillo Indian goods (soap, woolens, textiles) | 47,000 pesos | 7% | 3,290 |
| Domestic rice | 96,000 pesos | 7% | 6,720 |
| Salt from Huacho | 6,000 blocks | 2 reales per block | 1,500 |
| Wine by sea | 6,300 botijas | 1 peso per botija | 6,300 |
| Wine by land | 1,350 botijas | 1 peso per botija | 1,350 |
| | EXPORTS | | |
| Cacao | 100,000 cargas (60,000 to Europe, 40,000 to Mexico) | 2 reales per carga | 28,125 |
| Cascarilla | 800,000 pounds | 5% | 10,000 |
| Sugar | 160,000 arrobas | 2 reales per arroba | 40,000 |
| Chilean copper | 15,000 quintals | 1 peso per quintal | 15,000 |
| Tin | 2,000 quintals | 1 peso per quintal | 2,000 |
| Salt from Huacho | 32,000 blocks | 2 reales per block | 8,000 |

SOURCE: "Memoria, Plan General de Arbitrios," Lima, 28 April 1815, AGI, Lima 751.

(the first because Indian goods were exempt from taxation, the second because of a special privilege granted by Godoy), and these were now required to pay the standard 7 percent sales tax. Other products simply suffered an increase in their existing tax. Note that Lima's major import by far was Chilean wheat, while its major exports (excluding bullion) were cacao, cascarilla, and sugar. While deciding against increases in the taxation of aguardiente—which was already heavily taxed and was subject to widespread contrabanding—the commission did increase the taxes on imported and domestic wines. Finally, the commission determined to increase the tax called the sisa—a tax on the slaughter of livestock entering Lima, the revenue from which went to the municipality—and to turn the additional 10,000 pesos over to the royal treasury.

A totally new tax was also created over public houses of recreation and amusement. The Coliseo Cómico—which already paid 7,000 pesos annually to the Hospital of San Andrés—was to be taxed an additional 1,000 pesos a year for the royal treasury. Lima had eight inns (fondas)—five large ones, called Animas, Mantas, Merced, Caballo Blanco, and Petateros—which were assigned a tax of 140 pesos a year, and three small ones, assigned 100 pesos a year. The city's eight cafés—Mercaderes, Bodegones, Santo Domingo, Puente, San Agustín, Abajo del Puente, Merced, and Inquisición—were assigned a collective contribution of 1,000 pesos a year. And the city's twenty-seven tambos (or inns for travelers and for the lower classes) were assigned a total tax of 1,200 pesos. Finally, a tax was imposed on both public and private coaches. The commission had no exact count of the numbers, but it expected the tax to produce 14,300 pesos of revenue.

Continuing with its resume, the commission urged that several separate royally sponsored funds existing in Peru should be turned over to the viceregal treasury's administration. For example, it urged that the Indian Caja de Censos—which possessed a capitalization of 2,491,328 pesos and a net income from interest of 52,384 pesos a year—should be administered provisionally by the royal treasury, pending the sovereign's approval for its direct confiscation. Meanwhile, any other special Indian funds throughout the country were to be considered possible sources of state revenue. Similarly, the Temporalidades—the fund administering the properties of the suppressed Jesuit order—should also be turned over to viceregal administration. The commission decided not to set a quota for the clergy to contribute yearly, but it urged the archbishop and bishops to establish such a quota in consultation among themselves, stating as the fundamental principle to be borne in mind that: "Generally speaking the quiet and conservation of the state is a good which interests all citizens, but particularly those classes elevated and constituted in dignity, for they have the most to lose when the established order is overturned and the government upset." In summary, the commission urged that its recommendations be adopted on a yearly basis and insisted that all the taxes created for collection in Lima should be applied to other parts of the country as conditions warranted. The anticipated revenue increase would amount to 1,003,497 pesos in the first year.

Having concluded the report, the commission added its observations on four other major sources of state income. Commenting on the still-abolished tribute, the commission asserted that it was an entirely humane and necessary tax, deeply ingrained in the history of the indigenous people. Spain's Indian policy had erred, it suggested, only on the side of leniency, for it had assiduously and wisely saved the Indian population and culture by allowing the native people to live in separate communities. The commission compared Peru's history with that of Brazil, where many Indian cultures had entirely disappeared because they had not been protected. Nor had the Indians been oppressively taxed, for while they formed a majority of Peru's population, they had paid only one-quarter of what other classes in society contributed.

Second, the commission rejected the suggestion made by some citizens that the capital city's gremios—trade associations or guilds—should have their annual capitation taxes increased. As it currently stood, Lima's five gremios mayores—merchants, hacendados, shopkeepers, diarymen, and tallowers—contributed 42,430 pesos a year in capitation tax. Lima's sixteen gremios menores contributed minimal sums (see table 8). The commission felt the gremios mayores were already overtaxed, while the menores were "composed, for the greater part, of the most indigent class." The commission also rejected the suggestion of

TABLE 8
LIMA TRADE GUILDS AND ANNUAL TAX, 1815

| Guild | Tax (in Pesos) |
|---|---:|
| MAJOR GUILDS (GREMIOS MAYORES) | |
| Merchants, Consulado | 12,000 |
| Hacendados | 10,000 |
| Pulperos (grocers) | 10,930 |
| Mantequeros (dairymen) | 7,500 |
| Veleros (tallow chandlers) | 2,000 |
| Total | 42,430 |
| MINOR GUILDS (GREMIOS MENORES) | |
| Shoemakers (zapateros) | 590 |
| Potters (alfareros) | 91 |
| Leather, wool, and rope makers (zurradores, curtidores, laneros y cuerderos) | 233 |
| Used iron mongers (caxones de fierro viejo) | 287 |
| Blacksmiths (herradores) | 10 |
| Caxones de ribera (shopkeepers in the viceregal palace) | 439 |
| Pharmacists (boticarios) | 225 |
| Chocolate makers (chocolateros) | 240 |
| Silversmiths (plateros) | 500 |
| Candlemakers (cereros) | 425 |
| Metalworkers (herreros, bronceros, y ojalateros) | 306 |
| Coachmakers (carroceros) | 200 |
| Bedding makers (manteros y colchoneros) | 107 |
| Printers (tiradores) | 100 |
| Hatmakers (sombreros) | 226 |
| Carpenters (carpinteros) | 352 |
| Total | 4,331 |

SOURCE: "Memoria, Plan General de Arbitrios," Lima, 28 April 1815, AGI, Lima 751.

organizing the tobacco sellers into a gremio, because it would only increase the price of tobacco products, which had last been raised in 1812.

Third, the commission rejected the popular cry for the reduction of official salaries, on the grounds that it would impoverish the state service and lead to corruption. Besides, by a decree of the Junta Central dated in Seville on 1 January 1810, state employees were already paying a salary discount of between 2 percent and 25 percent, graduated according to income. The commission said it would prefer that, instead of reducing salaries, the government make some serious attempt to limit the number of its employees.

Fourth, the commission made a number of comments on the highly controversial commerce in English cotton goods that came to Peru from Jamaica via Panama, denouncing it as a ruinous trade and a source of the treasury's present shortages. The commission recommended a radical and complete closing of this trade in British cotton, for it was thought to be destroying the interior South American markets for Peruvian textiles while it drained Peru of vast amounts of bullion. Of course, Panama might then go bankrupt, but the commission declared that if that territory had had the foresight to charge duties on the "millions and millions of pesos that in the last four years have passed back and forth from there to Jamaica in money, precious metals and goods," then it would have no problem. There was a hint of desperation in the commission's recommendation, however, for in 1812 the Junta de Arbitrios had recommended the same thing in even more dramatic terms—asking the government to close all Peruvian ports except Callao to Panamanian trade—but the plea was never acted upon.

As its last recommendation, the commission called for the establishment of a short-term loan of half a million pesos to meet the uncovered expenses of military salaries and grants to the armies in Upper Peru. The money was to be raised by selling bonds of 500 pesos each, payable in a year at 5 percent interest (rather than the usual rate of 6 percent). It was to be financed by the income from the other new taxes and guaranteed by two types of security. First, the holders of the bonds would be allowed to use them "as if they were silver" to pay any debt they owed to the government or any of its departments. Second, the bonds would be paid off out of the new taxes as a first priority before any other state purposes. The commission specified, however, that these bonds were not in any way to be considered paper money, because while they were declared acceptable by the government for purchases, private individuals were not required to accept them as payment. Further, holders of the drafts could also use them to purchase goods from any royal monopoly and were guaranteed a 1 percent reduction in the price of tobacco, ices, mercury, and other monopolized products.[7]

The plenary meeting of the Junta de Arbitrios accepted and approved all these proposals, making only a few changes. The Casa de Gallos—cockfight arena—was added to the list of recreational establishments and taxed at 500 pesos. The Caja de Censos was left as it was, but its income for 1815 was applied to the royal treasury. The question of a special contribution from the clergy was postponed for another year. The new taxes were made applicable to Upper Peru. And, finally, the long-debated "special Indian contribution" was instituted once and for all.[8] The last decision, as it turned out, was unnecessary, for on 1 March 1815, the crown ordered the reestablishment of the Indian tribute in America. In June 1817 the Council of the Indies reviewed and discussed Peru's new taxes and contributions, and while it did not specifically endorse them, it did not disapprove of them either.[9]

Abascal's new taxes thus remained in effect until the beginning of the final chaos in 1821. When combined with restoration of the tribute, they did stave off collapse of the viceregal regime. It was never financially secure, however, and after the loss of Chile in 1817 it began a rapid financial disintegration. The regime remained desperately poor. Although income of the Caja Matriz was never again as low as the 1814 figure of 2.6 million pesos, neither did it ever again achieve the levels of the first decade of the 1800s. By 1817 its revenue was up to 3,522,833 pesos, an increase of almost exactly the million pesos the special commission had predicted.[10]

Yet the real significance of Abascal's tax changes is that they point out the level of diminishing returns now reached by the regime. It now required the most extraordinary efforts to obtain a modicum of increased revenue. Abascal's successor would find every potential source of new revenue closed to him. The regime was straining to its limits. Guayaquil complained bitterly about the imposition of a 7 percent alcabala and the extension of the 5 percent tax on urban and rural properties to its jurisdiction, as its deputy to the restored Cortes in 1820 pointed out.[11] In Lima itself money was now so restricted, and faith in the government's economic measures so limited, that Abascal's attempt to issue government notes at 5 percent interest to be used as currency in transactions with the government was a total failure. Public suspicion of the government's financial promises caused these notes to lose their credit instantly. It is not known how much of the total issue of half a million pesos was purchased, but those few capitalists with money to spare who did take the gamble found that the government turned out to be unable to honor its own notes.[12] And if the regime was so hard pressed in 1815 as to initiate such a pathbreaking financial technique, it was no less hard pressed a year later when the bonds fell due. The regime's credit—which, as Abascal knew, was more important than its actual cash flow—was rapidly deteriorating.

A further effect of the increased taxation was to initiate a rush at the level of local administration to increase revenues and to raise consumer prices. When the price of the Chilean wheat imports was raised owing to increase in the alcabala and almojarifazgo, hacendados in the valleys of Chancay, Huaura, Pativilca, Cañete, and Chincha, who produced wheat for the capital's consumption, demanded that their prices be raised to par. But wholesalers and bakers opposed the increase. The city council held stormy debates on the issue, but the price rose anyway, from its earlier 2.5 pesos per fanega (about 1.5 bushels) to 4 pesos. The trend from 1816 onward was a steady rise in the price of almost all basic necessities, which by 1817 reduced some of the provinces to near starvation and by 1821 caused considerable privation in Lima. Furthermore, local jurisdictions, excessively hard pressed by the increased expenses of the war, joined the scramble for new taxes. Lima, unable to pay even the daily expenses of its municipal jail, imposed a tax of 2 reales on each jug of chicha (a local fermented drink) consumed in the capital. But the regidor in charge of the collection reported that although he expected a large income, it was producing only 25 to 27 pesos a week, a sum not even adequate to pay for the administration of the tax. Lima also imposed its own tax on tallow to help pay for the upkeep of jails and prisoners, but it produced disappointing results. Consequently, by early 1816 the cabildo ordered the rationing of clothes, lights, and medicines in the jails, limiting the total yearly budget for the jails to a mere 10,000 pesos. These economies soon took their inevitable toll. On the night of 16 August 1816, eight prisoners from the city jail took advantage of the lack of guards to escape over the wall and across the rooftops of nearby houses, wounding several citizens and throwing the neighborhood into turmoil.[13] Incidents of assault and robbery became so common that Viceroy Pezuela, as one of his first acts, was required to take extraordinary measures to stop them.

Meanwhile, complaints about low salaries and high prices were universal. In early 1815, both the members of the Lima audiencia and the chief officers of the royal treasury wrote to Spain pleading for the abolition of the discounts on their salaries. The audiencia pointed out that the cost of living in Lima was so great that royal officials were being forced into commerce and land transactions in order to survive. Although the fiscal of the Council of the Indies thought the salary discounts should be maintained, the king, on 10 August 1815, conceded the oidors' request and canceled them. [14]

The fundamental fact of the matter was that the royal regime of Peru was being strangled, and because of the country's inelastic economy the noose continued slowly to tighten even in the 1815–16 period when the threat of outright armed rebellion was absent. The two lifelines upon which the prosperity of Peru and the success of its regime depended—maritime shipping and domestic mining—were fatally stricken.

Shipping, which had been badly disrupted in the long years of war with the English and French, did not recover after 1815, because just as the war against Napoleon was coming to an end, the rebels in South America, starting with those of Buenos Aires, began taking to the sea to harass Spanish merchant and naval vessels. In January 1816 the first of several rebel naval expeditions drew up before Lima's port of Callao. It consisted of four corsairs in the service of Buenos Aires, under the command of William Brown. Brown and his "pirates," as Lima dubbed them, cannonaded Callao at irregular intervals and intercepted two small merchant ships caught by surprise in making for the port. The response of the Lima merchant community to this threat was rapid. On 19 January the viceroy asked the Consulado to arm two or three boats to defend the port and pursue the rebels. Appointing a commission composed of five merchants, the Consulado agreed to arm six ships, at a cost of nearly 160,000 pesos. [15] The task was massive, and the energy and efficiency of the Consulado were impressive. On 20 January Brown instituted a blockade of Callao, which made it necessary to repair and refit several armed launches that had been stripped of their sails and other fittings during the past years. The Consulado claimed it refitted these battery launches in four days, together with the frigate *Piedad*, which was to serve as a floating battery, all at a cost of 16,256 pesos. Now that the port was defended, the Consulado turned its attention to arming the six merchant ships. In less than a month these ships—three of which were already loaded and ready to sail to Cádiz—had to be unloaded of their civilian cargo, armed with cannon carried out from the forts of Callao, and manned. This massive job brought a complete halt to normal commerce. In the midst of the outfitting, the enemy began nighttime sorties against Callao, causing considerable delay and confusion in the job. Despite these dangers, the Consulado armed and outfitted the merchant frigates *Palafox, Tagle, Reyna de los Angeles, Minerva, Comercio*, and the brigantine *Europa* with a total of 122 cannon and 1,021 men. The squadron sailed on 16 February supplied with food and water for two months and manned by sailors who were paid a salary of 25 pesos a month. After this effort, the Consulado turned its attention to outfitting and dispatching the mail boat *Abascal* to sail the coast warning ships arriving from Spain and Chile of the presence of the enemy fleet. The Company of the Philippines dispatched warnings by land and sea to Guayaquil, saving four Spanish ships from surprise encounters with Brown's expedition. The six armed merchantmen and their upkeep cost the Consulado 383,293 pesos. The frigate *Palafox* was kept in service on orders of the viceroy when the other five were returned to commerce.[16]

Nor was this the end of the Consulado's expenditure for naval protection in 1816. At the end of the year the new viceroy, Joaquín de la Pezuela, fearing that the revolutionaries of Buenos Aires intended to land an expedition on the coast of Chile, asked the Consulado to arm two more ships—the frigate *Veloz Pasagera* and the brigantine *Pezuela*—which were added to the royal squadron. In its first year of support, the Consulado spent 243,177 pesos on maintaining the two ships.[17] All this activity exhausted the Consulado before the rebel invasion of Chile in 1817, which was the beginning of the final crisis.

These disruptions and expenditures virtually paralyzed commercial shipping in 1816. Vessels diverted for armed service could not carry goods to Europe even though they did succeed in defending Lima from Brown's squadron. Add to this the fact that in 1816 Viceroy Abascal renewed for a second year all the special taxes and donations of his Junta de Arbitrios, while he simultaneously renewed the sale of government notes but asked the Consulado to underwrite their amortization, and it is clear that the merchant community was severely disrupted. Between 1804 and 1815, the Consulado had already contributed nearly 6 million pesos to the government in loans and grants, and the contributions of 1816 alone ran to nearly a million pesos.[18] At the time of Abascal's retirement, civilian commerce was on the verge of breakdown.

Mining, too, was entering a period of stagnation and disintegration, the effects of which would be felt as much by the first independent regimes as by the last royal regime. The fundamental causes of the disintegration of the mines included flooding, the disruption in the supply of mercury for processing silver, and a shortage of labor. The Napoleonic war virtually ended Peru's supply of mercury from the peninsular mines at Almadén. By the beginning of 1814, the Tribunal of Mining had on hand only 651 quintals, and it asked the Regency to dispatch a minimum of 21,000 quintals—enough for the next four years. Viceroy Abascal endorsed the request, warning that mining was the "unique and productive" activity that sustained the viceroyalty, and that without new supplies of mercury the country would be ruined. Only a year later, however, Abascal again pleaded for mercury, this time asking for 25,000 to 30,000 quintals, adding that a number of the richest mines in the country had entirely ceased production.[19] What little mercury did get to Peru came in private shipments, under license of a royal order dated 30 December 1815, which allowed private merchants, whether members of the Mining Tribunal or not, to come to Seville in person and purchase mercury at the very moderate price of 38 pesos a quintal, to be resold in Peru at the set price of 50 pesos a quintal. The problem with free trade in mercury, as both Abascal and the tribunal pointed out, was that there were no merchants in Peru wealthy enough to buy Spanish mercury in sufficient quantities (since the purchase price of a shipment of 20,000 quintals was 760,000 pesos) and what little mercury did go on sale from private importers was priced far above 50 pesos a quintal. The Mining Tribunal testified that private sales fetched 150 to 200 pesos a quintal and urged that the official price in Peru be set at no more than 25 pesos.[20] Despite such unequivocal demands, Spain could do nothing to increase the mercury supply for Peru. In 1817 Viceroy Pezuela repeated Abascal's request for up to 30,000 quintals. In 1819 he again repeated the request and enclosed a statement of the Mining Tribunal that Peru was lost if mercury could not be provided. Pezuela endorsed this pessimistic view, saying that only with mercury would it be possible "to sustain this miserable political machine."[21] In 1820 the peninsula finally agreed to permit mercury to be transported to Peru on military vessels, but the decision was useless because no Spanish warships were being sent to Peru by that time.

The mining industry also suffered from a shortage of labor, and this became particularly acute after abolition of the Indian tribute and mita—a forced labor draft—and the imposition of constitutional protections for the Indian. In most cases the labor shortage arose because the mineowners were either unable or unwilling to pay high enough wages to attract workers. There was no group in all of Peru as dependent upon Indian labor, or as callous in its attitude toward the native people, as the miners. On repeated occasions they demanded the establishment of presidios—forced labor camps—to put vagrants and criminals, as well as Indians, to work in the mines. In 1813 the Tribunal of Mining discussed the labor situation at great length, pointing out that, with the suspension of the tribute, "there is no way to reduce the Indians to work in the mines." The tribunal proceeded to a long defense of the Indian tribute, and of the mita, by which Peruvian mines had long been manned. Insisting that the Indian conscripts had never been mistreated or forcibly taken from their homes, the tribunal asserted that the Indians had been well paid, had worked voluntarily, and had been well clothed and housed during the period of labor. They also defended themselves against the claim that mineowners lured Indians to work by offers of liquor, insisting that "if the Indians spent their income on liquor, it was to satisfy their own inclination, or vice, and not because the miner tricked them or paid them in liquor." Furthermore, the tribunal insisted that if the mines were bonanzas, the workers were often joined by their women and families, anxious to pick up whatever leavings of the silver there might be, "so that many of them remain in the mines, not from misery or necessity, but in order to acquire more; and those who return to their Pueblos . . . have enough to support themselves for the rest of their lives." Admitting that there were some cruel miners, the tribunal said that most viewed their Indians as "children, that is to say, that the miners would first care for the needs of their workers before the expenses of their own houses." In a remarkable long digression, the Mining Tribunal also defended the existence of the agricultural mita, making it clear that many prominent members of the Lima Mining Tribunal were also engaged in agriculture. The use of mita labor was largely restricted to cattle estancias, since the coastal haciendas were manned chiefly by slaves. In these cattle ranches, the Mining Tribunal insisted, the forced Indian laborers were just as well treated as those in the mines. They earned 12 pesos a month for doing no more work, said the tribunal, than taking the herds out in the morning and bringing them back in at night. "All the rest of the day they employ themselves in their own business, leaving the herd in the field under the care of a young boy or a relative. The men, meanwhile, go about more useful business, and their women weave and sew."[22] In reply to the tribunal's demand, the Regency agreed in general to the establishment of presidios near the rich Peruvian mines of Yauricocha but reminded the tribunal that paying good wages was the best guarantee of having adequate labor.[23] The labor situation was so severe that Viceroy Abascal once went so far as to propose that the government take over abandoned mines, establishing presidios of slave labor to work them.[24]

A further fundamental reason for the abandonment of many Peruvian mines was flooding, which in 1812 caused the collapse of production at Cerro de Pasco. Throughout his administration Abascal supported the campaign to import English steam-powered pumps. In this he was joined by Peru's most important importers—Pedro Abadia and José Arizmendi—who, in company with a Swiss watchmaker named Francisco Uville, formed a company to buy and import pumps for the mines of Cerro de Pasco. Uville carried 40,000 pesos in cash to England and spent two years having the steam engines built. Amid great rejoicing, he arrived in Lima in early 1815, bringing nine steam engines— four of thirty-three horsepower each to be used for drainage, four ten-horsepower winding engines to be used for extracting metal, and one engine of six horsepower to be used in minting at the Casa de Moneda. The engines were laboriously carried to the mines and installed, and they met with considerable success. By

1819, three pumping engines were working successfully, leading to a dramatic increase in silver production at Cerro de Pasco. During 1820 the silver registrations at Pasco increased 350 percent. The boom was short-lived, however, for in November 1820 rebel and royalist armies swept through Cerro de Pasco, and it remained a center of warfare for four more years.[25]

Other entrepreneurs quickly became involved when the steam-engine craze swept Peru. Agustín de Arpide, a native of Guipuzcoa, spent years trying to build a domestic steam engine from a model Uville had brought from England. In 1812 Arpide claimed to have four engines under construction and asked for the exclusive privilege to manufacture and sell them. But he was apparently never able to perfect his machines. Meanwhile, a third proposal for exclusive rights came from one Samuel Curzon, a North American, who asked permission to form a company capitalized at 50,000 pesos to import foreign steam engines on Spanish vessels and to bring into Peru four mineralogists, four mechanics, and four foreign artisans with their families. The Council of the Indies decided to grant exclusive privileges to none of the companies, but it encouraged all three to proceed. Curzon was given permission to bring foreign specialists and machinery into Peru, under the careful scrutiny of the viceroy, while Abadia was given further encouragement and royal thanks but was denied the royal order he had requested requiring the Lima Consulado to help finance his company.[26]

Of the three proposals, however, only the Abadia-Arizmendi-Uville consortium succeeded in importing machines and installing them in the mines. Arpide's endeavor apparently came to nothing. Curzon's broke up on the rocks of official suspicion of all foreigners. Viceroy Abascal, intensely suspicious of Curzon's traveling from mine to mine, ordered him to leave Peru, for he suspected him of being an insurrectionist and of being in league with foreign merchants to smuggle contraband silver out of Peru. Curzon left the country sometime in 1816. In 1819 the retired Viceroy Abascal testified that Samuel Curzon, who came to Lima in about 1810, was the same person who was in Lima in 1806 under the name Samuel Burling claiming to be a creditor of the North American merchantman *Washington* that had been captured by the Peruvian government some years earlier. Abascal had expelled him on charges of contraband and suspicious conduct.[27] In short, although the steam engines had the potential of revolutionizing Peruvian mining, and although the Spaniards were by no means slow in recognizing and attempting to employ the new technology, wartime conditions made any further exploitation impossible.

Although mining continued to deteriorate, there was no lack of intelligent suggestions on how to salvage the industry. Martín José de Múxica, deputy to the Cortes for Huamanga, suggested in late 1814 that, to repair the widespread collapse of mining in his province, mercury should be offered for sale in quantities smaller than a quintal, so poor miners could purchase it; that the taxes derived from silver mined in Huamanga should be returned to the province rather than being spent in Lima; that a special tax should be instituted on all silver to create a school of mining; that discoverers of new veins of silver should be given land grants smaller than the present 800 varas, thus preventing them from preempting too much territory; that miners should be decorated for special discoveries and investments; and that vagrants and malcontents should be sent as forced labor to the mines and processing facilities.[28] And in 1814 the Regency authorized the Peruvian viceroy to establish finance banks for the silver industry (bancos de rescate) "as circumstances permit." In 1813 the Mining Tribunal reported that the current method of financing was for miners to sell their silver to private financiers (rescatadores) who then transported it to Lima for sale to the Casa de Moneda. This private exchange allowed the financiers tremendous profits. For example, private dealers bought silver for as little as 6 pesos 6 reales a mark in mines that were 200 or 400 leagues away from Lima and sold it in the capital at a profit of 40 percent. Dealers who bought from mines within 50 leagues of the capital gained an average of 30 percent. More serious, it was not possible to prevent private financiers from selling contraband silver to English and North American ships on the coast. The Regency delayed the Peruvian request to create a mining college in Lima and instead ordered the Lima Mining Tribunal to send six young sons of poor miners to the Mexican Mining College.[29]

It is clear that Peru's economy was rapidly declining. In a general summary report about the economy, Abascal admitted that "in spite of everything, the actual state of the kingdom is deplorable." The roads were deteriorating both on the coast and in the mountains, making travel dangerous and trade abnormal. He spoke of the general poverty of the nation and its role in the spread of crime. The privation caused by the war in Upper Peru was, he thought, the cause of continued creole unrest and insurrection. The productive coastal lands, he reported, were entirely under the control of a few great proprietors, whose labor supply consisted of miserably clothed and poorly fed slaves. He broached the question whether it was desirable to allow continued import of African slaves into America, but he refused to state his own opinion. The decadence of the mining industry was caused by the poverty of the mineworkers, the failure of the Nordenflicht expedition, the lack of skilled technicians, and the collapse of many mines. He recommended the foundation of a mining college, the repair of disused mines by the state or the Tribunal of Mining, and the formation of new regulations for the care of the workers. He reminded Spain that the shortage of mercury was the fundamental weakness of the mining industry. Baron Nordenflicht had estimated that to reopen the old mercury mine at Huancavelica would cost a minimum of 2 million pesos. It was also necessary, Abascal reported, to revitalize the paralyzed commerce of the nation. The complaints of maritime merchants centered on high taxes, navigation and customs regulations, and the extensive contrabanding, which together had ruined the market for domestic manufactures and drained bullion from the marketplace. His suggested solution was an absolute prohibition on all foreign trade, forcing Peruvian consumers to buy domestic goods, even though he recognized they did not want them. Unless this were done, Abascal predicted, the Spanish flag would disappear from Pacific waters. Agriculture was also decadent and unproductive. Hunting was restricted to sporadic vicuña hunts. Fishing was a major unexploited industry both in lakes and on the coast. The natives who did fish were not industrious and supplied only their own needs. He pointed out the untold riches that Peru's teeming coastal waters could produce, specifying sperm whales particularly. But the only commercial fishing going on was in the hands of foreigners. He estimated that there were thirty to forty British and North American whaling ships in Peruvian waters each year each taking a catch worth about 100,000 pesos, adding up to 4 million pesos a year—equal to the value of Peru's bullion production. Yet Spanish and Spanish American ships were nowhere to be seen. In addition, he suggested that Peru had untold mineral deposits that were not yet exploited, and he cited—in addition to the obvious gold and silver—platinum, mercury, copper, iron, zinc, arsenic, cobalt, nickel, manganese, and salts. Finally, Abascal testified that Peruvian industry, largely in the hands of the lower classes, was entirely decadent, with even the notorious textile obrajes entirely ruined.[30] Abascal thus retired from a Peru that was still in Spanish hands, but on the verge of economic ruin. During the administration of General Pezuela the whole flimsy structure would come crashing down.

Viceroy Abascal governed Peru for ten years—an unusually long term of office. After the king's restoration, however, it was clear that he would eventually be replaced, and he himself requested it. Consequently, although he did not actually leave office until July 1816, his impending retirement was publicly known by October 1815. Tributes and compliments were showered upon him. The city council of Lima—which had already honored him in many ways, including proposing his title of marqués de la Concordia and voting a lifetime annuity to his daughter Ramona—wrote the king in October 1815 to declare that Abascal was "a viceroy who has given great and continuous proofs of his integrity, purity, and constant dedication to the well-being of this capital, and in whose memory the city will remain perpetually indebted."[31] The Consulado, meanwhile, requested that the viceroy be exempted from the residencia, or trial of office, and offered to post his bond if a residencia were conducted. The Council of the Indies agreed to exempt Abascal from the residencia. In addition, the Consulado also published a pamphlet containing formal letters to Abascal congratulating him on his administration and the viceroy's reply thanking the Consulado for its fidelity during the long war.[32] Isidro Vilca, procurator of the Indians, wrote an extravagant account of the loyalty the Indians felt for Abascal.[33]

Yet Abascal had so dominated Peru that even as he retired the complaints against his arbitrary use of power continued. The foremost witness against him was the intendant of Lima, Juan María Gálvez, who frequently complained that Abascal absorbed all powers to himself, including even those of the intendancy. During the constitutional era, when the viceroy's power was supposed to be limited, Gálvez reported that "the viceroy not only gave up none of the attributes that belong to his office according to the Laws of the Indies, but he extended his absolute power to an extraordinary degree." He even asked Spain not to let the viceroy know he had testified against him "because he will view as a crime [the fact that] I have proceeded against the authority, powers and faculties of his person." Even after Abascal was gone, Gálvez kept up his lament. In 1817 he complained that the viceroy had reappointed Antonio María Bazo as subdelegate of Cañete even though subdelegates were not supposed to be reappointed and though Bazo was the son of the audiencia's Juan Bazo y Berri (only the king had the power to grant office to sons of audiencia members in the district of their fathers' magistracy).[34]

Other complaints against Abascal were motivated by the grievances of the creoles. One outspoken correspondent, who signed a false name in his denunciation, accused Abascal of being a Bonapartist and a warmonger. Another, the Limeño Antonio Arroniz y Lainfiesta, reviewed the fall of Miguel Eyzaguirre—"the first victim sacrificed to the vile resentments of our viceroy." Abascal, "an object of execration among all the people," had pushed Peru to the brink of extermination. Concluding with the warning that Ferdinand VII might well be the last king of Spain to rule the Indies, Arroniz urged amnesty for dissenters and a residencia for Abascal.[35] Thus Abascal, old, tired, and ill, left office amid the same controversy that had always surrounded him. Pedro Trujillo, director of the tobacco monopoly, wrote that on the day Abascal turned command over to his successor he was "so ill that it was believed he would not live many days."[36] It is not clear what the illness was, but Abascal survived and, back in Spain, frequently advised the Council of the Indies on Peruvian affairs.

The new viceroy was Joaquín de la Pezuela, former subinspector general of artillery, currently serving as commander-in-chief of the army of Upper Peru; father-in-law of Mariano Osorio, the general who reconquered Chile in 1814; and brother of Ignacio de la Pezuela, the secretary of the Council of the Regency in the days of the Cortes. He was at first appointed "interim viceroy," probably because he was in active command of Upper Peru at the time and still faced some personal danger. The city council was much exercised in trying to determine whether this meant he should receive the same extravagant reception as regular viceroys, but in the end it spent as much on his reception (16,936 pesos) as on anybody else's, considerably exceeding the budgeted 12,000 pesos. Pezuela's formal reception occurred on 17 August 1816, although he took possession of the office on 7 July. As an "interim viceroy," the Council of the Indies wanted to pay him half the normal 60,500 pesos, but the king personally intervened to have him granted full salary. A number of institutions, including the Tribunal of Accounts, requested Spain to confirm him as proprietary viceroy, and that was done in early 1817.[37]

No one knew it at the time, but the royal regime was about to enter its death throes, over which Pezuela had the regrettable duty of presiding. It is clear that the royal regime needed two things to survive: a massive increase in Spanish shipping to rebuild commerce and industry and peace in South America to permit Peru's treasury to recover. It was denied both. Pezuela's diary, published under the title *Memoria de Gobierno*, records in his own starkly eloquent words the mounting anguish of this very good and humane man as he gradually became aware of the desperation of his government's position.

Chapter 6

# Disintegration under Pezuela

TWO FUNDAMENTAL ELEMENTS destroyed the government of Viceroy Joaquín de la Pezuela between 1816 and 1820: the regime's financial collapse, caused by the total cessation of Spanish shipping, and José de San Martín's brilliant strategy of crossing the Andes to attack not Upper Peru, as the Buenos Aires rebels had been doing for six years, but Chile—Peru's southern flank. Having served as commander of the Upper Peruvian provinces of Potosí, Chuquisaca, La Paz, and Cochabamba—where he won the important battles of Vilcapugio, Ayohuma, and Viluma—Pezuela was somewhat out of touch with the condition of the viceregal government. He was therefore shocked to discover the extent of the government's deficits. Furthermore, he had to contend with an army that was already restive over its lack of pay (the Extremadura regiment had staged a brief mutiny in the last days of Abascal's rule) and a Consulado that was unable to fulfill his first demand for a loan of half a million pesos.[1]

More critical, however, was the threatened attack on Chile by San Martín's army, which was being gathered and trained in Mendoza on the Argentine side of the Andes, directly opposite Santiago. Owing to his long preoccupation with the Upper Peruvian theater, Pezuela refused to believe that San Martín would attempt the impossible and try to cross the mountains to attack Chile. Instead, he believed the rebel commander's object was simply to employ the safety of Mendoza to prepare an army for

133

use against Upper Peru. Consequently, Pezuela concentrated on rushing fresh forces—3,300 men—to Upper Peru, even though his military advisers warned that San Martín's real target might be Chile. Only five months after taking power, however, Pezuela received letters intercepted from San Martín, making it clear that the rebels did plan to cross the Cordillera to attack Santiago.[2] Clearly, Pezuela cannot be faulted for failing to foresee an event never before thought possible, yet it remains that his failure to reinforce Chile in time permitted San Martín's victories at Chacabuco and Maypú. His tactical error in ignoring this possibility cost him the confidence of his chief commanders, who in January 1821, after Peru had suffered further disasters, removed him from office. The fall of Peru began with the fall of Chile in 1817.

Only seven months after Pezuela took office, the crisis began. The viceroy's diary entry for 27 February 1817 announced that San Martín had invaded Chile with a small army of 3,800 men. The first report was that a number of skirmishes had been fought and that 1,200 royal troops waited outside Santiago at a place called Chacabuco, twelve leagues from the city, to block the rebel advance. Within hours, however, other ships began to arrive in Callao, and Pezuela recorded the unfolding catastrophe. The royal army at Chacabuco was wiped out, with all but one hundred men taken prisoner. Large numbers of Chileans joined the rebels. Santiago was captured. Troops and officers fled Valparaíso in launches, fighting for places in the boats. The system of command disintegrated. The artillery section fled from Santiago to Valparaíso, but halfway there it became bogged down, and so the soldiers burned their munitions and fled toward the port. The Chilean government sent the treasury from the capital to Valparaíso, but on the road it was stolen by its own escort. The president of Chile, Francisco Casimiro Marcó del Pont, fled to Valparaíso, but, arriving after the ships were already under sail, he turned down a side road and was captured. The ships, without supplies, joined in a convoy off the coast, leaving half the royal troops on the quayside to be captured. From 27 February to 13 March, eleven of these ships arrived in Callao carrying the fleeing Chilean army—including 2 brigadiers, 7 colonels, 2 commandants, 23 captains, 94 subalterns, 58 sergeants, 443 soldiers, 2 oidors, and a number of civil servants and their families. The Chilean army of 5,267 men was in total disarray.[3]

In the wake of the catastrophe, Pezuela ordered General José de la Serna, the new commander of Upper Peru, to make a quick attack on Manuel Belgrano at Tucumán in order to weaken the Argentine flank. This order, which was quite inappropriate given the desperate need to prevent a total rout on the coast, provoked open disagreement between Pezuela and La Serna, for the commander was convinced that Chile was now the greater threat and refused to obey the viceroy's order to attack the Río de la Plata provinces. Meanwhile, the entire royal fleet was ordered to the coastal town of Talcahuano in southern Chile to help hold Concepción province, which was still in royal hands, and to divert the Chilean rebels from any contemplated action against Peru. Colonel Joaquín Primo de Rivera was ordered to Callao to begin organizing the refugee royal troops for their return to Chile, and also to keep them from coming to Lima, where public anger ran high over their precipitate retreat.[4]

Pezuela thus began the difficult task of gathering a new army composed of both Chilean and Peruvian troops to undertake a second expedition for the reconquest of Chile. He chose as its commander General Mariano Osorio, his son-in-law, who had led the successful first expedition to take Chile from the rebels in 1814. Despite some setbacks (anticipated reinforcements from Panama did not arrive), the expedition, consisting of ten ships and 3,607 men, gathered at a cost of over a million pesos, set sail on 9 December.[5] Pezuela ordered his son-in-law to secure Talcahuano and to join the 2,000 royal troops waiting there. Then he was to attack Bernardo O'Higgins, the Chilean rebel leader, in Concepción province. After driving him back, he was to reembark, land at Valparaíso, and attack San Martín's main army at Santiago.

Remembering Goyeneche's prophecy in 1808 that Chile would prove the jugular vein of Peru, the royalists understood that the stakes were high. If Chile were not retaken, Peru would lose not only its chief supplier of wheat and tallow, but also its chief market for sugar. Pezuela estimated that revenues of the Peruvian customs would be reduced by half a million pesos, while many hacendados and merchants whose trade depended on

Chile would be ruined. Peru's coasts would be open to Chilean corsairs and blockaders, while Chile would be able to trade on its own with foreign ships and buy the goods needed to make war on Peru. The Russian naval commander Vasilii M. Golovnin, who was in Peru early in 1818 while the Osorio expedition was in Chile, suggested that public opinion agreed with the viceroy regarding the importance of the reconquest of Chile. "It is said that sooner or later Peru will have to become independent of Spain, but that for now its destiny depends on the success of the royalist forces in Chile." It is not clear who influenced whom, but the opinion of another eyewitness, Commodore William Bowles, commander-in-chief of the British Royal Navy's South American station, was remarkably similar: "The situation of Lima . . . is in the highest degree critical, and from all the intelligence I could collect an insurrection against the Spanish authority may be looked forward to with almost absolute certainty. It will be accelerated by any decisive reverse which befalls the expedition against Chile."[6] Reversing his policy of the previous year, Pezuela now had to order 3,300 troops transferred from Upper Peru to the coast to protect Lima while the Osorio expedition was away. This again provoked a strong protest from the commander of Upper Peru, General La Serna, who was fast becoming Pezuela's chief opponent within the high command. La Serna told Pezuela that he doubted the wisdom of any attempt to reconquer Chile.[7]

Pezuela waited four long months to hear the success of his son-in-law's expedition. William Bennet Stevenson, who was in Lima at the time, described the mounting excitement of the royalists, who expected Osorio to repeat his exploits of 1814, defeat the Chilean rebels, and thereby guarantee Peru's security. Only news of royalist victories came from Chile, Stevenson said, and the bells of Lima never ceased to ring with the joyous tidings. After the royalist victory at Cancha Rayada, Osorio was viewed as a demigod who would destroy Chile, cross the Andes and take Buenos Aires with the reinforcements known to be coming from Spain, then return in triumph to Lima with the heads of San Martín and O'Higgins.[8]

These dreams were crushed at the Battle of Maypú. On 21 April 1818 the North American warship *Ontario* (which had broken the royal blockade at Valparaíso and sold 7,610 rifles to the Chileans) arrived in Callao carrying news of the royalists' disastrous defeat at Maypú on 5 April. General Osorio's army was devastated by a larger rebel army under San Martín. The royalists lost 70 officers, 1,500 men, and all their artillery. It was a crushing blow that guaranteed Chile's independence. Pezuela reported that the public did not at first believe the news of Maypú, "but I do not doubt it, . . . because I have always found the news that the enemy publish in their public journals to be true." The viceroy now became genuinely frightened by the combination of disasters that seemed to threaten him. His son-in-law's army was routed, Chile was definitely lost, Lima and Arequipa were left defenseless, and General La Serna continued to defy his direct orders to march against Tucumán. "In a word," he wrote, "the situation I find myself in is extraordinarily difficult."[9]

The defeated Osorio fell back on Talcahuano but, finding it too difficult to defend, returned to Callao on 22 September. Stevenson described how the haughty Spaniards were now dismayed. The great Osorio, the demigod, was now viewed as an ignorant coward who had sacrificed his men to save his own life. In December, overcome by disgrace and feeling the need to represent himself personally in Spain, Osorio left Lima bound for Spain via Panama. He and his wife traveled aboard the North American warship *Macedonian* rather than on the royal warship *Sebastiana*, which had been put at their disposal. Lima merchants had refused to ship their silver aboard the same vessel Osorio used, so unlucky had his name become, and public rumor had charged that the Spanish naval vessel was being used solely to evacuate Osorio and the viceroy's daughter.[10]

Now Pezuela began to suffer personal tragedies as well as official setbacks. On 4 October 1818 he received news that the reinforcements so long awaited and fervently prayed for had left Cádiz for Lima—2,500 men from the Cantabria regiment aboard a convoy of thirteen transports, with one frigate and two brigantines. One of the transports—the *Trinidad*, with 250 men aboard—mutinied and landed at Buenos Aires, giving the rebels the fleet's secret plans for reconnoitering at the Island of Santa María in the Pacific after rounding the Horn. Consequently, the newly formed and as yet untried navy of independent Chile set sail in hopes of intercepting the convoy. In October and November 1818, some of the troop transports began to arrive at

Callao and Talcahuano. Then on 28 November Pezuela learned that the frigate *María Isabel*, flagship of the reinforcement fleet, and five of the troop transports had been captured by the Chileans off the Island of Santa María. He noted: "This misfortune has changed all my plans. If [the reinforcements] had been able to join our maritime forces at Callao, we would have dominated the Pacific; . . . commerce would have recovered from its paralysis; and there would have been less work in maintaining the war effort." It was not until two days later, on 30 November, that Pezuela learned that his son Ramón was on board the *María Isabel* and had been captured or killed. On 10 December his daughter and his son-in-law General Osorio left Lima, taking with them the viceroy's two youngest sons. A year and a half later the viceroy learned that General Osorio had died from an epidemic in Havana on 19 July 1819. He had been sick only three days. Wild with fear for the safety of his widowed daughter and his two sons, who were now traveling on to plague-infested Cádiz, Pezuela also mourned his son-in-law, lamenting that "a man is not always able to enjoy the high opinion that he sought from his king and country."[11]

Thus Pezuela's reign was initiated with the loss of Chile, punctuated throughout by personal tragedy, and ended with his overthrow by the chief officers of the army in January 1821. The royal regime reeled from catastrophe to catastrophe, while signs of popular support for independence began to appear in Lima. Peru moved slowly toward the agonizing stalemate of 1821. The royal regime, desperately weakened, was no longer able to suppress the urge for independence. The Chilean rebels, flushed with victory but very limited in resources, launched their master plan for the liberation of Peru, though they were not yet strong enough to win total victory.

To Peruvians, the immediate implication of the loss of Chile was its impact on trade. In February 1817, as the news of the battle of Chacabuco was just arriving, the Lima city council turned its attention to the loss of the Chilean wheat supply. After extensive discussion, the regidors agreed to call on nearby hacendados to sow wheat, for the capital had on hand no more than 65,000 fanegas in the public storehouses and in private establishments. Since the city consumed 500 fanegas a day, the cabildo foresaw the threat of starvation. To encourage domestic production, the council agreed to lift all price controls—a necessary but disastrous decision that caused the price to skyrocket over the next two years. And, finally, because the loss of the Chilean supply cost the cabildo about 30,000 pesos a year in municipal duties, the city determined to add new charges against domestic wheat. In March the viceroy announced that in the future wheat would be free to find its own price. Bread producers soon were reporting that wheat dealers were charging ten to twelve pesos a fanega, three times the price of the year before. [12]

But if Chacabuco was a great worry to Peruvians, Maypú was more frightening, for it opened up two simultaneous threats: the clear danger that the Chilean rebels would now take to the sea to harass Peruvian shipping, and the ultimate threat that San Martín would make good his promise and attack Peru. On 4 May 1818, Pezuela made these implications clear in a long address to his Junta de Arbitrios. He also warned that there were Peruvians who would aid the Chileans and that large numbers of slaves on the coastal plantations might do so as well. Pezuela reported that in response to this threat the government was shifting troops from the interior to the coast and was proceeding with great haste to reequip the fleet. But all this would take money. He estimated that from May 1818 forward the government would need an additional 117,000 pesos each month, while 200,000 pesos was needed immediately to cover preparation of the fleet. The Junta de Arbitrios began a painstaking search for new sources of revenue. Even in its first meeting, someone mentioned free trade with foreign nations as one likely solution. [13] This would shortly become the central topic of debate, since by this time Spanish shipping was under constant attack from both Chilean and Argentine squadrons.

The Junta de Arbitrios's first money-raising scheme was for the viceregal government to collect in Lima the royal duties usually payable at Cádiz on the year's silver shipment to Spain. Admitting that in approving this plan he was making use of powers reserved to the sovereign alone, Pezuela nonetheless agreed. This produced the extra 200,000 pesos needed to finance the fleet. The remaining increase of 117,000 pesos a month that the viceroy demanded from the Consulado was more difficult to come by. As early as June 1818 Pezuela was complaining in his diary that no one was making any special effort in this regard. He was particularly critical of the city council, which he accused of refusing to make special contributions.[14]

After three months of debate, the Junta de Arbitrios was still unable to propose ways of raising the money. In response to the paralysis of commerce, in July 1818 the Junta de Arbitrios suggested that Lima be opened to foreign shipping, and Pezuela agreed to consider the idea. The Consulado, however, was so violently opposed to free trade that it promised to make up the 117,000 peso monthly deficit for five months if the government would postpone implementation.[15]

The viceroy was a major advocate of free trade, viewing it, as he wrote to Spain, as "the only method of saving the state." Nonetheless, he agreed to postpone implementation for five months to appease the Consulado. In the course of these five months Pezuela testified that he had discovered that the chief opponents of free trade among the Consulado's members were a group of leading merchants engaged in contraband trading with Panama and Jamaica. Perhaps the clearest indication of the viceroy's personal support for free trade, however, is that he was so hostile to the Consulado that he simply failed to tell Spain about the 117,000 peso a month contribution it was making. The Council of the Indies later realized that the viceroy had neglected to inform them of the Consulado's patriotic efforts and thought it not only very strange, but even "scandalous."[16]

Despite the Consulado's objections, therefore, Viceroy Pezuela began on his own initiative to grant individual licenses to foreign vessels to sell their cargoes in Lima. In 1817 the French merchantman *Bordelais*, which carried refugees from the battle of Chacabuco, was allowed to sell some of its cargo at Lima, as was the Portuguese *Brillante Magdalena*. The North American merchantman *Sydney* was allowed free entry, although this was part of an agreement negotiated between the crown and the United States government to make up for the loss of the *Warren*, which had been captured off Chile during the regime of Viceroy Aviles. The *Warren*, bound from Baltimore to Canton, was taken by royal troops in 1807 when it put in near Concepción. Its cargo was sold, and more than 300,000 pesos was deposited by the government. The Senate of the State of Maryland retaliated by attempting to seize all Spanish property in the state. Luis de Onís, Spanish minister to the United States, worked out an arrangement with

Smith and Company of Baltimore to send the *Sydney* to Lima as compensation for the losses sustained in the *Warren* incident. Both the Consulado and the Company of the Philippines protested, but the *Sydney* was allowed to enter Callao and sell tobacco, silks, ironware, and luxury goods, even though it unloaded a larger cargo than originally agreed. In December 1817 two ships of the Russo-American Company—the *Kutusov* and the *Suvarov*—which were en route up the Pacific, were allowed to drop anchor in Callao and sell some cargo. The Russians also landed at Túmbez and at the mouth of the Guayaquil channel, where they sold the rest of their cargo illegally. In May 1818 the North American ship *Governor Shelby* arrived in Callao and sold 3,344 rifles sent on consignment to José Arizmendi by Luis de Onís. In June 1818 the North American ship *Canton* entered, and in September the *Beaver*, which had helped evacuate troops from Concepción province. Perhaps the most unusual of Pezuela's arrangements with foreign ships was carried out when in July 1818 the North American frigate *Dos Catalinas* discharged 6,000 fanegas of wheat in Callao and carried Peruvian sugar destined for Hamburg to Valparaíso. Pezuela allowed these ships to enter Callao on his own initiative and in clear violation of existing law. He urged the crown to excuse his insubordination as being required by necessity.[17] As foreigners began to arrive on Peru's coasts, the naval commandant of Callao wrote to warn Spain that the North Americans, British, and French were helping to increase the partisans of rebellion.[18]

By November 1818 Pezuela found the Consulado no longer able to pay the 117,000 pesos a month. Consequently, he signed a contract with the commander of the English naval frigate *Andromache* to allow the free entry of English goods into Callao for two years. The commander of the *Andromache* agreed to urge other English ships then anchored in Valparaíso to continue on to Callao. Pezuela, greatly cheered by the possibility of opening trade with the British, reminded Spain that this would tie the powerful British merchants to the royal regime in the approaching battle for Peru, and that the British would not submit to any blockade by the Chileans, thus guaranteeing that Lima would not be totally without the commerce it depended upon. In January 1819 Gaspar Rico was commissioned to survey the foreign ships then in habor, and he reported six, all British and North American, carrying goods valued at 424,000 pesos, plus 2,700 fanegas of wheat. The Junta de Arbitrios allowed these ships to discharge their cargoes, levying a 50 percent customs on cotton goods and 36 percent on other goods.[19]

Pezuela's contract with the British merchants did not sit well with the Lima Consulado. A private correspondent, in a letter later copied by the conde de Casa Flores, Spanish ambassador to the Portuguese court at Rio de Janeiro, wrote: "You cannot imagine the commotion that this contract caused among the merchants." In February 1819 the Consulado again offered to make up the 117,000 pesos a month if Spain would repudiate Pezuela's actions and prohibit free trade. It asked the crown to order all foreign ships to leave Callao and all foreigners to withdraw to the nearby town of Bellavista. It warned that once the English were allowed in, it would be impossible to get them out, and that they would soon dominate Lima's commercial affairs. Finally, the Consulado insisted that free trade would not produce the revenues needed by the government but would ruin Peruvian capitalists. The crown responded by appointing a special committee to study the matter.[20]

In the midst of this controversy Lima suffered a major shock. Viceroy Pezuela spent the morning of 28 February 1819 reviewing the royal warships in the harbor of Callao. The royal fleet at anchor consisted of the two great frigates *Esmeralda* and *Venganza*, backbone of the Spanish fleet, the two brigantines *Pezuela* and *Maypú*, and seven gunboats. A dense fog had settled, making it necessary to illuminate the ships with torches. Pezuela and his entourage thought they saw a very large ship at the mouth of the harbor, but the fog was too thick to make out its identity. The viceroy returned to Lima at 1:30 that afternoon. At 3:00 he heard the beginning of a fierce cannonade in the harbor. Callao was under the first of many attacks it would suffer from the Chilean navy under command of Lord Thomas Cochrane.[21]

The beginning of sporadic blockades and attacks by the Chileans on Callao confirmed the viceroy in his opinion that free trade was essential, for under blockade conditions only neutral ships were safe. The first blockade lasted only from 28 February to 27 March 1819, and even at its height, two North American ships were allowed to leave harbor and a Portuguese ship was permitted to enter. In the months ahead the Chilean squadron re-

TABLE 9

SHIPS LANDING IN CALLAO IN 1819

| Date | Ship(s) | Nationality | Cargo |
|------|---------|-------------|-------|
| 14 January | *Boxer* | U.S. | Arms purchased by Onís |
| 10 February | 6 ships | U.S., British | Various |
| March | Unnamed | Portuguese | Not given |
| 3 May | *Vitoria* | Spanish | Mexican goods |
| 16 May | *Ballón* | U.S. | Arms from Onís |
| 18 May | *Palos* | U.S. | Arms and goods |
| 3 June | *Beaver* | U.S. | Wheat, rice |
| 2 July | *Spectator* | British | Wheat from Chile |
| 25 July | *Beaver* | U.S. | Wheat, aguardiente |
| 25 July | *Volador* | Spanish | Wheat, aguardiente |
| 6 August | *Amanda* | U.S. | Arms |
| 6 August | *Canton* | U.S. | Rice, wheat |
| 6 August | *Merope* | British | Clothes from Calcutta |
| 9 September | *Palos* | U.S. | Aguardiente from Pisco |
| 16 September | *Elena Maria* | ·U.S. | Aguardiente from Pisco |
| 21 September | *Inspector* | U.S. | Wheat, rice, flour from Huanchaco |
| 23 September | *Catalina* | British | Wheat from Huanchaco |
| 5 October | *Prueba* | Spanish warship | Driven off by blockade |
| 8 October | *Primarosa Mariana* | Spanish warship | Reinforcements from Cádiz |
| 9 November | *Macedonian* | U.S. warship | No cargo |
| 15 November | 3 ships | 2 of them British | Coastal trade, wheat |
| 28 December | *Gazelle* | French | Wheat from Valparaíso |
| 30 December | *Andromache* | British warship | No cargo |

SOURCE: Pezuela, *Memoria*, pp. 392–590 passim.

peatedly blockaded or harassed Callao, until finally Spanish
commercial shipping entirely disappeared. The Consulado defaulted on its promised loans to the government, and by May
1819 the treasury reported that it was short 110,000 pesos to pay
the Lima garrison, and that there was no money at all for June.[22]
By 1819, therefore, Lima had become entirely dependent on
foreign vessels to supply its needs. As table 9 shows, almost
every ship anchoring in Callao in 1819 was foreign. In July 1819
Pezuela even granted permission to eight foreign ships to engage
in the Peruvian coastal trade. The Spanish commander of the
*Primarosa Mariana*, returning to Cádiz at the beginning of 1820,

reported that Callao was filled with foreign ships and that they were carrying Chilean wheat to Lima and Peruvian sugar to Valparaíso. He testified that there was also a heavy traffic in rebel emissaries and propaganda.[23]

The significance of this debate over free trade is twofold. First, it illustrates the extent to which Peru's resources were overstrained, converting foreign trade—something that had been prohibited for three centuries—into an absolute necessity. As early as 1815, according to a letter from Lázaro de Rivera, more than 150,000 artisans in Peru were out of work. But the loss of Chile in 1817 greatly intensified Peru's economic troubles. Writing in 1817, Manuel Vidaurre, the former member of the Cuzco audiencia, pointed out the economic catastrophe that was sweeping the country. In Cuzco province wheat was then selling for 27 pesos a fanega, and at La Paz it cost 40. Entire towns were dying of hunger. In Moquegua war taxes on its chief product, brandy, had quadrupled the price; in La Paz war taxes on its chief product, coca, had quadrupled the price; in Lima war taxes on wheat and grains had the same effect. "When a man has nothing," concluded Vidaurre, "then he becomes a rebel, because in order to survive no other recourse remains to him but a resort to arms." Some indication of the widespread deterioration already occurring in Peru is that Lima's population, which in 1813 was 56,284, had fallen by 1818, according to a count taken by the oidor Juan Bazo y Berri, to 54,098.[24]

Second, Pezuela's decision to allow free trade alienated him from many of Lima's merchants and army officers, while it simultaneously created considerable suspicion against him among official circles in the peninsula. In the intransigent times of Ferdinand VII, viceroys were not expected to be innovative. Former Viceroy Abascal, who served as a major adviser to the Council of the Indies on Peruvian matters, testified that free trade would destroy Peru's industry and commerce and warned that the English presence was always "very dangerous." While he had no doubt that the Peruvian government's resources were badly strained, Abascal nonetheless thought it possible to make up the deficits by extraordinary loans and contributions. At any rate, just because Peru was in financial trouble was no reason, he thought, "to hasten the patient's death merely to free him from suffering, much less to apply remedies that are more analogous to the sickness." He concluded that free trade with the English should not be employed except as "the very last resort."[25] Some indication of the extent to which Pezuela's advocacy of free trade provoked suspicions against him in Spain is the fact that he was not granted a noble title until 1830. In early 1830, Pezuela himself complained that he was the only wartime viceroy in all of America who had not been granted a title, while even General La Serna, the man who overthrew him in 1821, had already received one. Pezuela was then granted the title marqués de Viluma.[26]

Free trade really was a vicious circle, and neither its advocates nor its opponents were totally right or totally wrong. Pezuela himself was no less suspicious of the English, both merchants and royal naval personnel. He frequently complained of the protection the English ships gave the insurgents and of the presence of British subjects in the Chilean forces. He even refused at one point to attend an official reception aboard H.M.S. *Andromache*, sending his wife to represent him instead. After San Martín's Liberating Army landed on the coast of Peru, the viceroy's anger against British interference became more intense. Yet, on the other hand, he was quite correct in predicting that free trade would help the government's revenue problems, for the administrator of the customs reported that in the two-year period 1819–20, even as the coasts were blockaded and Peru was invaded, the net revenue of the customs was an unparalleled 2,965,085 pesos, which constituted almost half a million pesos a year more than normal.[27]

On the other hand, opponents of free trade were equally correct in predicting that it would have a disastrous long-range effect on Peruvian trade and prices. The conde de Casa Flores, Spanish ambassador to Rio de Janeiro, submitted in June 1819 a devastating indictment of free trade in Peru. Casa Flores said that the free trade in foreign ships had the effect of raising prices in Lima to extraordinary heights. Foreign ships now carried supplies of wheat from Chile to Callao, but charged from 18 to 20 pesos a fanega for it. Compare this with the 1815 price of 2.5 pesos and the 1817 price of 4 pesos. Tallow was purchased in Chile for about a peso a unit and sold in Callao by foreigners for 20 pesos. The *Gazeta de Buenos Aires*, chief journal of the Argentine rebel government, gloated that Peru was now divided between Pezuela and the supporters of free trade on the one hand, and the

Consulado—whose members called the British "Jews, thieves, and enemies"—on the other.[28] In short, the debate was destroying any semblance of unity among the Peruvians.

Casa Flores pointed out that a chief reason British goods were taking over the Lima market, and at prices totally beyond official control, was that a handful of Lima merchants—men who were already actively involved in foreign trade and well situated to take advantage of its increase—were reaping large profits. Chief among these were Félix de Olabarriague y Blanco, José Arizmendi, and Pedro Abadia. One informant, Agustín Tavira y Acosta, told Spain that these men were the chief consignees of foreign shipments, and that Abadia was so prominent in the trade that the foreigners actually called him "the consul." Abadia was said to have gained the confidence of Pezuela and to be able to manage him, while the consortium of merchants was said to hold virtual control over Pezuela's government. One reason Abadia gained such prominence is that he spoke both English and French, a rare achievement in late colonial Lima. Frequently placed in charge of arrangements for visiting naval vessels, he had been given the order of Saint Anne by the Russian emperor for his service to Russian shipping.[29]

Contrabanding, particularly of gold and silver, was the inevitable concommitant of the foreign trade. Several sources testified that Abadia and his British cohorts exported more than 2 million pesos in gold and silver aboard the English warship *Blossom*, without paying any duties. Many government employees were actively involved in contrabanding. Indeed, Viceroy Pezuela testified that the employees of the Administration of Mails were so engaged. In 1819 a general investigation was conducted into the affairs of the mail system, and it was discovered that various officials, including the director, Félix de la Roza, were guilty of stealing funds. Viceroy Pezuela also admitted that 2 million pesos in silver had been illegally exported aboard the *Blossom*, and in May 1820 he ordered military boats to aid customs officers in patrolling the harbor at night, especially in the vicinity of British vessels.[30]

Even so, although he had not received royal approval for his actions, Pezuela continued to negotiate contracts with both foreigners and Peruvians for the introduction of foreign goods. With José Arizmendi, for example, he negotiated four special contracts permitting the import of 450,000 pesos worth of goods, including naval stores and arms, each shipment paying special government loans or contributions. Another contract allowed the North American Daniel Coigt to introduce European goods on the ship *Boxer*.[31] Pezuela had become so convinced of the advantages of free trade that he sent a personal representative, Francisco Xavier de Olarria, a relative of his wife, to Spain to urge open trade with British and North American merchants. The viceroy criticized Abascal's government for not having allowed it, pointing out that free trade would increase government income, allow for the purchase of ships, and permit the hiring of trained mariners, while also tying the two English-speaking powers to Peru and providing trade even during Chilean blockades. Pezuela also asked for two warships and 8,000 rifles. Olarria reported that the Lima troops had been on half salary since July 1819 and that the viceroy must be free to do whatever he could to raise money. He also asked that Spain send more priests, to be placed in various interior locations to help sustain popular loyalty to the regime. Precisely the same request for missionaries, arms, reinforcements, and ships was made by Domingo Espinosa, a Peruvian shipowner who had served as a spy for Pezuela in Chile and who, after a long imprisonment in Chile, fled to Spain.[32]

In the final analysis, the importance of the debate over free trade lies in the damage it did to Pezuela's personal authority, for the viceroy was accused of a variety of sins including open collusion in foreign meddling and direct encouragement of contrabanding. Yet on the basic question of whether free trade was necessary for Peruvian survival there could be no argument, for Spanish commercial shipping simply disappeared from Peruvian waters. At the end of May 1820 it was reported that in the last twenty-eight months only two Spanish merchant ships had arrived in Lima from the peninsula. In all of 1820, only two ships landed at Cádiz from Lima, compared, for example, with fifty-nine from Havana. The Consulado was simply deluding itself when it assumed there was any imperial trade left to protect. Yet the Consulado continued to resist free trade. It told the peninsula that it was Pezuela's granting of individual licenses to foreign ships, together with the widespread contraband in Panamanian goods and the massive expeditions of the Company of the Philippines that lay at the root of the decline in Peru's prosperity. The

Company of the Philippines replied to such charges by claiming that the decadence in Lima's commerce was the result not of its occasional shipments of Chinese goods but of the foreign contrabandists.[33]

There was also plenty of proof that when Pezuela let down the bar to foreign commerce he also opened the floodgates to contraband direct from England. In the past, most of the British goods entering the Peruvian market had come indirectly, from Panama and Buenos Aires. Now merchants in England began to outfit expeditions for the precise purpose of breaking into the Peruvian market, with no intermediate stopovers. The first warning was sounded in 1818 when the Spanish ambassador to London, the Lima-born duke of San Carlos, wrote Spain to report that various expeditions were being fitted in England for Chile, but that the real object was to land cargoes in Peru. By 1820 the British merchants, sensing that the entire western seaboard of South America was about to open to them, were blatantly advertising for investors in expeditions that were still technically illegal in the Spanish view. In September 1820 a private correspondent wrote that Spaniards living in London had been approached by British merchants asking them to invest in a shipment of a million pesos worth of cotton goods to be sold in Peru under permission of Viceroy Pezuela. Another expedition was being outfitted to carry goods from India to Peru, and yet another was being secretly prepared to unload contraband on the coasts. London insurance underwriters openly published the information that Pezuela permitted foreign ships to land. In 1821 the Spanish consul in London reported the departure of the *Euxine*, bound for Callao under direct permission of Pezuela with a cargo valued at 40,000 pounds sterling, while an unnamed young Limeño was busily negotiating a second, larger shipment. Meanwhile, the Spanish consul in Rio de Janeiro wrote to ask directions concerning what to do with the considerable number of Spanish merchants who, with permission of the Peruvian viceroy, were undertaking expeditions from Rio to Lima with their holds filled with British goods.[34] It appears, therefore, that the British takeover of Lima's international trade was well advanced in the last four years of Spanish control, and that it occurred almost entirely as a result of Pezuela's initiative.

Despite the increase in customs revenue caused by free trade, other aspects of Peru's economy continued to deteriorate, while the threat of Chilean invasion increased. By January 1820 Pezuela was beyond consolation. He had received a rather vague reply from Spain to his request to establish free trade. The crown urged him to make better use of the other sources of revenue available to him, especially the Consulado's funds. On 28 January 1820 he replied that the question of revenue was not a secondary matter but was the central consideration. "Since I took this office," he said, "I have known that the real difficulty in conserving these dominions consisted in being able to find the necessary means to sustain its large sea and land forces." With the loss of Chile and the rebel acquisition of naval superiority, Pezuela suggested, finding the means to defend Peru was becoming impossible. He recounted the measures he had attempted. After Consulado money ran out and a forced loan of a million pesos failed, Pezuela proceeded to reduce civil and military salaries. However, after only four months he was forced to suspend these salary reductions at the request of both the ecclesiastical and the municipal cabildos, because their members, who supported soldiers out of their incomes, had canceled their subscriptions. This, said the viceroy, proved once again that the private interests of the citizens of Lima were more important to them than their obligations to the sovereign. On 5 February 1820 the viceroy wrote in his diary: "At no time since the beginning of the revolution has this capital and the viceroyalty been in greater want."[35]

An attempt to raise funds by revising and expanding the lottery also failed. In 1818 the lottery, which had virtually ceased to function under the direction of the contaduría general of the treasury, was reorganized under the direction of Gaspar Rico— the same publicist Abascal arrested in 1812. Rico's plan consisted chiefly of expanding the lottery along the lines followed in Mexico, Havana, and Spain. The new lottery began operation in January 1819, and a heavy publicity campaign was carried out for the rest of the year. Even the Lima city council pledged to buy 1,150 pesos worth of tickets, with any winnings to be applied against its debt. But in March 1820 Rico announced that the lottery had failed and would cease operations. The audiencia voted to disband it in the same month.[36]

Even the government in Spain was finally willing to concede that Peru had reached its limit, though it never told the viceroy that. A report to the Ministry of Finance at the end of 1820 pointed out that Peru's situation "could not be more critical." The ten years of war had consumed all its resources, raising its debt from 8 million pesos in 1812 to nearly 20 million pesos in 1820. "Ordinary and extraordinary contributions have been collected in enormous sums, and now it is not possible to add to them." Industry and agriculture were wiped out and commerce was paralyzed by the lack of traffic and the heavy taxes. In short, Peru had reached the point "of not being able to supply the troops with even what is necessary for their daily subsistence." The fiscal of the Ministry of Finance actually recommended that Pezuela's free trade arrangements be approved, but no decision was ever made. In April 1820 Pezuela confided in his diary, "In the four years of my command, I have never seen myself in such great need."[37]

The viceregal regime's economic collapse was reflected in its plans for defending the country from the expected Chilean attack. In January 1819 the viceroy and cabildo worked out arrangements for supplying and defending the capital in case of invasion. The city council was ordered to make plans to collect livestock and grain, though no one knew where these supplies would come from. In the event of invasion, the city councilors were to arm themselves and go to guard the city's jails. Meanwhile, Lima's municipal finances were in such chaos that, after years of debate, the king—noting the "ruinous state" of the city's treasury, the "confused and arbitrary system" by which the cabildo managed its funds, and the fact that it had defaulted on its interest payments—ordered that the viceroy exercise direct supervision over city finances "without the ayuntamiento being permitted to hide in the shadow of its privileges." Meat supplies were so limited and prices so far exceeded the official level of two pesos an arroba that in May 1819 it was decided to nullify all legal restraints barring the sale of various types of meats in city markets. In May the city had on hand a wheat supply adequate for only a month and a half, and by October the shortages were critical, owing to the second Chilean blockade of Callao. Throughout November there was less than a month's supply on hand, but at the last moment three ships, two of them English, arrived in harbor with fresh quantities. These periodic alarms and shortages became a regular part of life in Lima, and as supplies dwindled prices rose steadily. On top of it all, in March 1819 Pezuela instituted a forced loan of a million pesos, 60 percent of which was to come from residents of Lima and 40 percent from the merchants. Although the government paid interest of 6 percent, and although Pezuela himself led the way with a pledge of 20,000 pesos, the total sum was not collected. Most contributions were as low as 500 pesos.[38]

After the battle of Maypú it was clear that San Martín would press his invasion of Peru as soon as he could. Pezuela hastened to recruit new troops and to restrain the independence fever that began to sweep Peru. In both efforts he met with little success. As early as November 1818, nearly two years before the Liberating Army finally landed, the viceroy began to despair of his ability to resist. He wrote the government in Spain that there was little confidence among the common people. The Indians and mestizos especially were not favorable to the royal cause. Neither were the slaves, who were "openly decided for the rebels, from whose hands they expect liberty." Within the army desertions were "scandalous, continuous, and inextinguishable" and so numerous that in a few days whole battalions were lost. In general, Lima was still loyal to the king, but conspiracies were becoming widespread.[39] Pezuela, while not exactly defeatist, was far too honest to be sanguine about the regime's chances of success. This constituted yet another bone of contention between him and his chief officers.

To prepare his army for the military contest that was sure to come, Pezuela took special care to maintain the morale of his officers. Since salary increases and special monetary rewards were out of the question, he adopted the expedient of giving certain retiring officers high appointments in the civil service. Several major appointments, including accountant of the Arequipa customs and treasurer of the Lima customs, went to officers rather than to the career bureaucrats who would normally have advanced to those positions. This naturally provoked the anger of the civil servants, and the Ministry of Finance, concerned with upsetting the bureaucrats, ordered the viceroy to stop the practice. Pezuela replied by asking his representative in Spain, Colonel Olarria, to remind the crown that retiring officers had no way of earning a living and that appointing them to civil

service positions made good sense.[40] In a highly persuasive letter
of 30 November 1818, Pezuela struck a chord that would become
increasingly evident in the next few years:

> The time has long since passed, if indeed it ever existed, when the love
> of glory alone inspired combat and overcame the natural solicitude a
> man feels for the preservation of his own life. Since love of the
> sovereign is so weakly founded in the hearts of most of the inhabit-
> ants, our cause, unfortunately, has no other inducement than the
> hope of reward. The dissidents, in order to acquire their followers,
> depend on a false civil liberty, on the promise of personal enrichment
> and prosperity for the country . . . and on other things that work
> powerfully in the human spirit to seduce the ignorance of the masses
> and to encourage self-interest among the upper classes. It is all the
> more indispensable, therefore, in order to retain the small number of
> loyal defenders who remain to us, . . . that at the end of their service
> we should grant them the situations and advantages that they ask
> for.[41]

When the case was presented in so forthright a manner, the
crown could not deny Pezuela's logic. The Council of State approved all his appointments.[42]

In this regard, the financial exigencies of the viceregal regime
assume an even greater importance. What worried Pezuela was
the "revolution of rising expectations" provoked among Peruvian office-seekers by the very idea of an independent state. It
was clear the Peruvian creoles did not want revolution. They had
never advocated it, and had united in opposition to the threat
posed by the Pumacahua rebellion. The alternative offered by the
unsuccessful armies of Buenos Aires was not sufficiently attractive either, since it implied outside domination by Río de la Plata.
But how many Peruvian aspirants to state employment would
begin to favor independence as a means of self-advancement?
The rebels were quick to seize on the promise implied in the term
"self-government" and were not embarrassed to make blatant
promises of creole advancement in the propaganda that began to
appear in Lima. To this threat the royal regime had no reply. Even
though he recognized the value of reward as an inducement to
loyalty, Pezuela lacked the resources to fulfill the aspirations of all
those Limeños who clamored for appointment, advancement,
and status.

Nothing so well illustrates the role played by the desire for advancement as the careers of the men who would serve as the first two presidents of the republic—José de la Riva Agüero and the marqués de Torre Tagle. Both men were eaten up with ambition, documented in the form of frequent requests for appointment to positions higher than their age or experience would normally merit. And both were frequently embarrassed or frustrated by official rebuffs. Riva Agüero, the more radical of the two and the more dedicated to independence, suffered the most serious personal and financial setbacks at the hands of the royal regime. In 1811, for example, he complained to the crown of the disproportion of offices granted to peninsulars. And yet Riva Agüero's criticism appeared in a letter in which he requested appointment as either director of the tobacco monopoly or contador mayor of Peru—two of the viceroyalty's highest offices. This was an absurdly pretentious request for a young man of twenty-seven, who had served only one year as a minor functionary in the Tribunal of Accounts and the lottery. Although he claimed in his letter to have been in royal service for eighteen years (which would have made him nine years old when he commenced service), all but one of those years had been spent as a special assistant to his father, who was director of the Lima mint. Indeed, even as a youth assisting his father, Riva Agüero's dedication to the service had been less than total, for in 1815 the crown ordered him to repay the 4,901 pesos in salary that he had received from his sinecure between 1805 and 1809—years he had spent traveling and studying in Europe. He protested the decision, but it was confirmed in 1817. He suffered a further personal setback in 1814 when he was forced to resign his position on the Tribunal of Accounts, which he claimed was the result of a conspiracy of Viceroy Abascal and contador mayor Antonio Chacón to free the position for Chacón's son-in-law. He described in great detail his excruciating public embarrassment when Chacón, during a formal visit to his office by Viceroy Abascal, accused Riva Agüero of laziness and insubordination, whereupon the viceroy refused to sign Riva Agüero's annual service report and proclaimed that Chacón was free to dismiss any employees who were insubordinate. For good measure, Riva Agüero accused Chacón of covering up deficits of 700,000 pesos from the national monopolies. After his resignation, Riva Agüero dictated a statement entitled *Exclamación*, in which he set forth many of the basic creole grievances about career advancement. Yet he himself admitted that it was written in the heat of anger and embarrassment and urged the Spanish government to take that into account.[43] Was Viceroy Abascal persecuting Riva Agüero merely because he was a creole? Not according to the viceroy. When he wrote to Spain on 2 June 1814 to tell of Riva Agüero's resignation, Abascal testified that his removal was "very convenient to the service, as much because Riva Agüero has a sick temperament as because he lacks the knowledge to fulfill the job exactly, and besides, he is too proud to dedicate himself to acquiring [the experience] and he would never serve any other purpose than burdening the treasury with the salary he enjoys and his colleagues with the work."[44]

Still further financial setbacks occurred to Riva Agüero in the very years when he was emerging as the leading rebel among the Lima elite. In 1810 Riva Agüero's mother was denied the full widow's pension of her second husband—his father—on the technicality that the royal cédula permitting them to marry had been lost at sea. After she protested the order, the fiscal of the Council of the Indies in 1818 decided that high birth and high office did not take the place of that little piece of paper a widow needed to collect her pension, and the Council agreed, saying it was a great pity, especially as she had been married to the elder Riva Agüero for thirty years, but only the king could excuse her from the requirement. She had to settle for the much smaller pension of her first husband. Meanwhile, in 1814 the younger Riva Agüero applied for compensation for the salary he lost when he was forced to resign from the Tribunal of Accounts. In 1818 the Council and king agreed to find him a new job, on the basis of his father's merits, but refused to pay him retroactively. And finally, in 1819, the Council of the Indies rejected Riva Agüero's appeal to be restored to his job as an official of the lottery—from which he was removed in 1812 because of his youth.[45]

It is obvious that much of Riva Agüero's complaint against "Spanish tyranny" was based on personal grievance, which he interpreted as creole political grievance. From about 1814 he was the leading conspirator among the Lima elite. Under constant watch by viceregal authorities, he was frequently jailed, although Mendiburu reports one case in which his brother-in-law, Juan María Gálvez, the intendant of Lima, saved him from jail. Riva Agüero remained a notorious plotter who, in Vicuña Mackenna's words, was "an agitator, not a leader, not a revolutionary, but a conspirator."[46] Vicuña Mackenna agrees that Riva Agüero's discontent was personal and that his famous pamphlet, popularly called the "28 Causes" and published in Buenos Aires in 1818, was based on his own grievances. It is often taken as the most significant statement of creole complaints against the imperial regime, replete as it is with criticisms of the authoritarianism of Abascal, of Spanish commercial monopoly, and of the exclusion of Americans from high offices.[47]

The marqués de Torre Tagle did not emerge as a rebel until December 1820 when, as intendant and governor of Trujillo, he rebelled against Spain and brought his province into independence under conditions that led him to expect, and get, high rewards from a grateful San Martín. It remains, however, that although his personal grievances were not as acute as Riva Agüero's, he too left behind him a long record of frustrated self-interest. Born into one of Lima's premier noble families, Torre Tagle was soon tired of the various positions and offices he inherited—which included the commissariat of war and navy, a colonelcy of the Concordia regiment, and a proprietary seat on the city council. He sought political power, and in 1811 and 1812 he was elected alcalde of Lima, then in 1813 was elected one of Lima's deputies to the Cortes. After dissolution of the Cortes he remained in Spain until 1817, keeping up a constant barrage of requests for appointment. In 1816 he asked the Council of the Indies to order the Lima audiencia to hurry up its decision in a case concerning his succession to his father's mayorazgo. The Council decided that his case was not sufficiently strong to warrant its intervention but did agree to ask the audiencia to explain its delay. Finally having been appointed governor and intendant of La Paz, Torre Tagle demanded before he left Spain that he should be granted a supernumerary position on the Council of the Indies. The Council rebuffed his pretensions, determining that "his merits are sufficiently repaid with the governorship and intendancy of La Paz, and with the ranks of Colonel and Brigadier that have been conceded him. . . . Places on the Council should be reserved for subjects . . . with knowledge and merits greater than those the marqués alleges to possess." In reply, Torre Tagle again insisted on a position in the council, but without salary. After his return to Peru, Torre Tagle remained in Lima because La

Paz was under military rule. For an extended period he served as interim intendant of Lima, without salary, during the fatal illness of the incumbent Juan María Gálvez. After Gálvez's death on 15 March 1820 Torre Tagle applied for the Lima position, but Viceroy Pezuela transferred him to the intendancy of Trujillo instead. Since he was always unpopular with the peninsulars, after his subsequent rebellion his appointment to Trujillo came to be considered yet another critical error in judgment on Pezuela's part. Robert Proctor, an English commercial agent who lived in Lima in 1823 and 1824, alleged that Torre Tagle's motivation for accepting independence was simply that he had dissipated his family's fortune and that all his remaining property was mortgaged to Spaniards. Proctor also alleged that Torre Tagle was addicted to gambling and alcohol.[48]

Countless other Peruvian supporters of independence arrived at their convictions by roughly the same path as these two men, and although there is no doubt that many rebels were deeply dedicated and fervently patriotic in their support of the cause, there can also be no doubt that in the administration of Pezuela, seeing the imperial regime about to falter, the political opportunists began to gather.

In the wake of the battle of Maypú and the reopening of rebel hostilities the supporters of independence in Lima were galvanized into activity. Plots and conspiracies became frequent. The most significant of them was the uprising in July 1818 of political prisoners in Callao and Lima. Led by José Gómez, a dedicated rebel who had already been sentenced to execution but then was granted amnesty, the conspirators had the assistance of many persons from the community at large, including farmers, merchants, friars, imprisoned officers, and subalterns from the guard of the jails. The plan was to take over the chief fortress at Callao, the Real Felipe, free the prisoners, seize the Spanish warship *Venganza* in the straits, and, ultimately, kidnap the viceroy. Vicuña Mackenna thinks it was a hopeless plan.[49] The plot was exposed by one of the conspirators, and its participants fled in various directions. Among those captured, Gómez, José Casimiro Espejo, and Nicolás Alcázar were executed in December 1818. A second major conspiracy, which also proved abortive, was planned for October 1818 by a group of Chileans who had been captured by Osorio in 1814. They had escaped from jail and

were given refuge by José Flores, the Chilean owner of a cof-
feehouse. The plan was to attack Viceroy Pezuela in the theater
on 14 October, the king's ceremonial birthday. When the plot was
discovered, Flores and others went into hiding.[50]  After 1818 the
activities of the city's various conspirators changed in the direction of preparing the way for the planned invasion by San Martín.
This was the period when some members of the upper classes
became involved. Chief among them was Riva Agüero. Other
supporters included the young professor of mathematics,
Eduardo Carrasco; the pastor of San Sebastian, Cecilio Tagle; the
Chilean merchant Jerónimo Espinoza; the brothers José Man-
sueto and Joaquín José Mansilla, who were known as the "bank-
ers of the revolution"; the professor and republican theorist José
Faustino Sánchez Carrión and his disciple and confidant Francisco Xavier Mariátegui and other teachers and students of San
Carlos; the nobles Diego de Aliaga, son of the conde de San Juan
de Lurigancho; the conde de la Vega del Ren; the marqués de
Montealegre, uncle of Riva Agüero; Francisco de Zárate y Manrique de Lara, eldest son of the marqués de Montemira; the
marqués de San Miguel, "first volunteer of Peru," who joined
San Martín in 1820; and the new conde de Vista Florida, Dr.
Manuel Salazar y Baquíjano. Prominent ladies active in the conspiracies included the wife of Diego de Aliaga, who was herself
marquesa de Castellón; the condesa de la Vega del Ren; and her
mother, the marquesa de San Miguel. Many women took part in
support of their husbands, including Baltasara Flores, the wife of
Dr. José Gregorio Paredes, and María Cabrera, wife of Dr. José
Pezet and mother of the future president Juan Antonio Pezet. The
well-known medical doctors were again active, as were the prominent lawyers—including Manuel Pérez de Tudela, who defended many Peruvians on trial for treason; Nicolás Aranívar;
Jerónimo Vivar; and José de Arriz.[51]

The first Chilean blockade of Callao in March 1819 marked the
beginning of more active and outright subversive activities.
Emissaries from San Martín landed on the Peruvian coasts to
begin distributing propaganda and to carry correspondence between the rebel leader and Peruvian partisans. Pezuela noted in
his diary that among the spies were some who planned to assas-
sinate him. In May 1819 a rebel courier was captured, carrying
letters destined for Riva Agüero. Regent Anzotegui, Regent

Pardo of Cuzco, and subinspector general José Domingo La Mar discussed with the viceroy what measures should be taken against secret partisans in Lima, and for the time being they decided to institute surveillance over the conde de la Vega del Ren, Segundo Carrión, Cecilio Tagle, the marqués de Montealegre, Francisco Colmenares, Manuel Pérez de Tudela, José Pezet, Francisco Campino, and several others. Among the secret spies landed on the coast by Lord Cochrane's fleet was José García, who eventually turned himself in and denounced many of the partisans. Thus on 26 March 1820, Viceroy Pezuela felt he had enough evidence to arrest Riva Agüero, Cecilio Tagle, Segundo Carrión, Joaquín José Mansilla, Pezet, Carrasco, and about twenty other prominent citizens. Since the group included ecclesiastics and persons of distinction, Pezuela ordered them jailed separately and without communication in the Inquisition prison. They were all held for a number of months, but nothing could be proved against them, and all were eventually released.[52]

Along with the spread of political subversion, Peru experienced an outbreak of brigandage and highway robbery, certain symptoms of increasing civil unrest. Pezuela testified that the countryside around Lima was alive with bandits—mostly free blacks and escaped slaves—and that they were even active inside the city. The transport of silver by private individuals became impossible without military escort, no one was safe after dark in Lima, and merchants refused to use the Callao road except in broad daylight. Especially notorious was a bandit group that attacked and killed travelers and even committed robberies inside the walls of Lima, under the leadership of a mulatto popularly dubbed "the King of the Mountain." Abascal had earlier created two special patrols—one of infantry and one of cavalry—to defend the Lima-Callao road. In October 1816 Viceroy Pezuela, finding these troops insufficient, established a special military tribunal called the Permanent Council of War to have jurisdiction over robbery, assault, and brigandage. Although it was modeled on virtually identical military tribunals in the peninsula, the Council of the Indies recommended against approval on the grounds that its powers and jurisdiction were too vague. The king, however, disagreed and ordered the Council to approve Pezuela's tribunal because of the circumstances in Peru.[53] Lima also possessed a Santa Hermandad—the special police agency for the protection of public highways—but it had virtually ceased to exist because of the lack of finances. Its standard source of income was a tax on every Negro slave imported into Peru, and since there had been no traffic in slaves for some years the Santa Hermandad could not pay its patrolmen. In 1818 the Council of the Indies agreed to support it with new taxes on chicha, but this apparently paid for no more than six patrolmen. The provincial alcalde of the Santa Hermandad, Tomás Vallejo y Zumarán, warned Spain that if the bandits were not soon exterminated they would shortly be too powerful for the government to control. His prediction came true, for after San Martín landed in 1820 many of the bandit groups converted into partisan guerrillas in support of independence and were of immense help to the rebel side.[54]

The capstone of the royal regime's economic and political disintegration was the revolution that occurred in Spain in 1820. Viceroy Pezuela was secretly informed by foreigners on 28 May 1820 that the huge expeditionary force that had been gathered at Cádiz to launch a counterattack against Buenos Aires had revolted. The uprising, which began in January 1820, spread to other military garrisons in Spain, and in March the king was forced to reestablish the radical Constitution of 1812.[55] For the Peruvian government the reestablishment of the Constitution—disruptive though it was—was not as serious a setback as the cancelation of the expedition to reconquer Buenos Aires, for Pezuela had based all his policy for the past year on the assumption that he would throw his army against Upper Peru and the northwestern Argentine provinces in conjunction with the peninsular attack on Buenos Aires, making for a powerful royal offensive that promised to knock out Buenos Aires, thereby providing a death blow to Chile. He now had to abandon his plan of launching an offensive and his last hope of receiving peninsular reinforcements.[56]

Pezuela remained wary of the Consitution. He was not a reactionary like Abascal but was concerned about the potentially disruptive effect of the radical charter, for he was aware that San Martín's army was almost ready to embark for Peru. In July he received word from Panama that the Constitution had been reestablished and that America was again to swear its oath. Fearing that the information might be false, he determined to do nothing—not even announce the restoration of the Constitution—until specific royal orders arrived. After definite news came from Rio de Janeiro, he announced in the *Gazeta* of 13 July that the Constitution would be declared whenever he received an official order.[57] Within a few days public broadsides appeared throughout the capital demanding that the Constitution be proclaimed, to which Pezuela replied by announcing in the *Gazeta* that his government intended to do so shortly. He feared popular unrest at so critical a moment. Consequently, throughout August Lima was preoccupied by two great events— the departure of San Martín's expedition from Chile and the imminent promise of vast political reforms.

The two shattering events occurred virtually simultaneously. On 4 September the viceroy received the official order to proclaim the Constitution, and on 10 September San Martín's expedition of about four thousand men with nine frigates and two smaller ships landed on the Peruvian coast at Pisco. The next few days, to judge from Pezuela's diary entries, were little short of surrealistic. On 11 September he sent San Martín a cease-fire proposal on the grounds that the Constitution was about to establish the political reforms the dissidents sought. On 15 September he proclaimed the Constitution with suitable pomp. The viceroy noted in his diary, "Not a viva was heard nor the least demonstration of joy, until in the Plaza of Santa Ana the oidor Osma threw a handful of silver to the multitude of Negroes and Zambos who followed the official party, and this animated them to shout a few vivas to see if they could get more silver, but neither these people nor the most important people nor the other classes manifested either joy or repugnance for the event; it seemed, and I believe, that they were indifferent to it all." On 17 September, the day the oath was taken in the parishes, Pezuela again commented on the lack of interest. He wrote: "García Camba, Valleumbroso, and Bazo brought a multitude of Negroes and Zambos to the palace shouting 'Long live the Constitution' and 'Come out to the balcony viceroy!' but they retired, and nothing else happened."[58] He thought the popular apathy toward this major change of government was very strange indeed.

Pezuela's testimony disputes the contrary report later offered by Manuel Abreu—the peace commissioner sent out by the Cortes. Abreu testified in 1822 that the Constitution had been received in Lima in October 1820 with "such general enthusiasm that it cost the viceroy much to contain the people."[59] In fact, however, Abreu's testimony was merely the product of his own partisanship. He was not in Lima in October 1820; indeed, he did not arrive there until April 1821. Besides, Abreu was off by a month, for the Constitution was proclaimed in September, not October. On the other hand, in the same letter Abreu himself sets to rest the frequently used argument that Pezuela was a reactionary who opposed the Constitution.[60] He declared there was no delay in implementing the Constitution, that the audiencia observed it, and that "the viceroy required the same from the other authorities." The Constitution was received on 4 September and implemented on 15 September. There was no delay, only apathy.

During the last week of September the royal government and representatives of San Martín conferred about a possible settlement at the suburb of Miraflores outside Lima. Pezuela agreed to negotiations because he had been ordered to do so by the new government in Spain. San Martín agreed to talk because he had frequently proclaimed that his object was not to conquer Peru— an impossibility in any case, given his small army—but to provide an alternative to help Peruvians make up their own minds about their political future. But the talks came to nothing. On 30 September the negotiations broke off after Pezuela interviewed the rebel delegates at his country home, Magdalena.[61] On 4 October hostilities reopened, and on 1 November the rebel forces drew up outside Ancón, very near Lima.

In the intervening month of October Pezuela made his greatest mistake. Already very unpopular with the chief commanders of the army for his quarrels with General La Serna, his appointment of Osorio to lead the ill-fated expedition to Chile, his insistence on concentrating on Upper Peru, and his political policy, he now argued with them over the defense of Lima. On 1 October Pezuela received from La Serna and the other generals a plan for the defense of Lima that had been discussed and worked out without his knowledge. He was very angry because he thought everything had already been arranged, and he took it as an unfriendly act on La Serna's part. He informed his Junta of War—the committee composed of the commanders of the various sections of the army—that the necessary orders had already been given and that he would not agree to the generals' suggestions.[62]

It is not known what Pezuela objected to in the defense plans put forward by La Serna, but it is clear that the two men differed profoundly over the role Lima should play in the crisis now confronting them. Generals La Serna, José Canterac, and Jerónimo Valdés particularly were convinced that it was impossible to defend Lima owing to the difficulties in supplying the city, its vulnerability to Chilean naval blockade, and the apparent increase of political dissidence among its civilians. Recognizing that San Martín's objective was to encircle Lima, they decided that the best way to defend the entire royal regime would be to withdraw from Lima if it seemed to be in danger, guaranteeing that the army and navy would not be trapped there. Pezuela's thinking was diametrically opposite. In a meeting of the Junta de Arbitrios on 20 October he announced that in no circumstances would Lima be abandoned, for it was the key to the control of Peru and to the survival of the royal army. He said: "I assured the Junta that . . . the capital would be sustained as long as I existed, for it is taken as certain in the regular order of thinking that once Lima is lost, all the territory of Upper and Lower Peru will last only a short time, and that the capital is the only base that can conserve Peru for the king and the nation."[63] Antonio Vacaro, commandant of the naval forces at Callao, later testified that the royal army was bitterly divided over this question, with Pezuela convinced that Spain would still send aid, while La Serna, Canterac, Valdés, and most of the higher officers felt certain they could no longer afford to wait upon the possibility of reinforcements from a distraught Spain in the midst of its own revolution.[64] The basic disagreement related to whether Lima was essential to the defense of Peru—Pezuela insisted it was the key, La Serna insisted it was irrelevant. As it turned out, La Serna's was the correct assessment of the Peruvian reality, but it had to be proved by the events of the next few months.

Chapter 7

# 1821

THE NINE MONTHS from November 1820 to July 1821 were critical for the survival of the royal regime. During this period it suffered a serious—though not definitive—setback when it was forced to give up Lima and allow the rebels control of much of the coast as well as the symbolically important creation of an independent state. Most authors conclude their consideration of these events at July 1821—when San Martín took the capital. Yet Peru was not independent, properly speaking, until December 1824, when the battle of Ayacucho permanently expelled royal troops from the country. The rebels' acquisition of the capital was by no means the final step in the process of emancipation, for Lima became independent by default. The royal regime, too weak to hold the city, abandoned it in July 1821 as a tactical decision to save the army from the chaos and confusion that characterized the capital. The San Martín regime, however, was far too weak to complete the liberation of Peru, and it was itself destroyed by the very exigencies of supply and finance that the royalists had fled. The inhabitants of Lima themselves never made a clear-cut decision.

The process by which the royal regime was crippled revolved around Lima's supply problems and the lack of confidence in which Viceroy Pezuela was now held by his own commanders. The capital's great vulnerability—which La Serna and most of the other officers considered the greatest danger they faced—was dramatically pointed out in late October and early November

163

1820 when Cochrane established a firm blockade of the coast with his fleet of twenty-two Chilean ships.

The Chilean fleet was so powerful and so daring that on the night of 5 November 1820 it entered the straits of Callao and launched a successful surprise attack on the Spanish flagship *Esmeralda* at anchor there, cutting it out of the fleet and capturing it. The *Esmeralda*, a forty-four-gun frigate, was the best royal warship on the Pacific. As word of the daring attack and of the loss of the *Esmeralda* spread through Callao on the following morning, the inhabitants of the port expressed their fury against the foreigners who commanded the Chilean squadron and against the foreign neutrals who had become so active in the trade and commerce of Peru by attacking all the foreigners they could find on the streets of the town—including the crewmen of the British royal navy ships *Hyperion* and *Andromache* and the United States warship *Macedonian*. Pezuela estimated that fourteen to sixteen foreigners were killed, including two from the *Macedonian* and five from the British ships. Another source, however, said that only six or seven foreigners died. The American minister in Spain lodged a firm protest. An infuriated Pezuela wrote in his diary: "The people have not erred in their idea that the foreigners are our enemies; the examples of the bad faith of such men are many and, even ignoring the part they played in the surprise of the *Esmeralda*, they have done and are doing us all possible harm."[1]

The loss of the *Esmeralda* convinced the rest of the royal commanders that Lima was expendable. In the immediate wake of the attack Pezuela encountered his first unified resistance from them. On 14 November he noted that General La Serna had disobeyed a direct order and that the commanders had requested the establishment of a junta of generals to direct the war. He resisted their request—fearing that they intended the junta to be "a corporation superior to the viceroy"—but in the end he was forced to give in, realizing, he wrote, that if he alienated the officers he would be without any means of resisting the "general opinion in favor of independence."[2]

By the end of November the rebels had various interior locations under attack—including Jauja, Tarma, and Cerro de Pasco. Lima's communication with the interior was broken. On 3 December the Numancia regiment of the royal army went over to the rebels—a serious blow to the regime—after its officers were bribed with promises of rewards, payment of gambling debts, and even women.[3] Further disasters ensued. Guayaquil—the second most important port on the Pacific—rebelled in October. The status of Lima's jurisdiction over Guayaquil was unclear at that time. A royal cédula of 23 June 1819 had returned Guayaquil to the jurisdiction of the audiencia of Quito in all criminal, civil, and treasury matters, but Peru remained responsible for its military defense.[4] Many citizens of Guayaquil thought of themselves as a part of Quito, whose capital was only eighty leagues away, rather than Peru, whose capital was three hundred leagues away, and others aspired to an altogether separate existence. This would lead to later disputes between Peru and Ecuador. On 28 December the marqués de Torre Tagle rebelled and led Trujillo, Peru's northernmost coastal province, into independence.

San Martín pursued the initiative by sending private letters to selected opinion-makers in Lima, such as the city councilors, the archbishop, and the publicist Gaspar Rico. San Martín appealed to the archbishop in the name of religion to accept the inexorable desire of the American people to be independent. He swore, "I am nothing but the instrument of the destiny of my country" and assured the archbishop that "in a war in which opinion is worth more than force, arms and resistance can increase distress, but they cannot end the revolution." He promised the archbishop to consolidate a government of order that would guarantee the security of clerical and private property. In a long letter to Rico, San Martín argued persuasively for the inevitability of independence, concluding, "I say to you that cold reason indicates the party you should choose." In propaganda appeals to the soldiers and militiamen, he promised a new era. In his propaganda to the nobility he declared that "the revolution is not and has not been against your true privileges." Under the royal regime, he said, the nobles were "an inert class without function," but under an independent regime they could play a genuine role in government. To every class, from the highest to the lowest, San Martín promised something.[5]

Lima's tension grew daily. A series of personal letters from Sebastian de Ugarriza, a merchant in the city, provides a glimpse of the inhabitants' mood. Two months before San Martín's arrival on the coast the capital had already been brought to a standstill by the Chilean blockades. Ugarriza wrote a friend this laconic description of what was happening: "Not doing anything, spending money, commerce paralyzed." The same day he wrote to another friend to say that news of the restoration of the Constitution was spreading throughout the city, "and I hope to God it will help us all." After San Martín's arrival he informed another friend that the royal partisans were doing nothing; only a small cavalry group had left the city to keep watch on the rebels' movements. By October he was complaining that the failure of Cádiz to send the expected reinforcements had cost Peru the possible reconquest of Guayaquil and Quito, and that normal commerce and traffic in Lima were at a complete halt owing to the absence of friendly ships. On 25 October he said that Pisco, Chincha, Yca, and all the coast between those towns had been ruined by the depredations of the rebel army, causing 2 million pesos worth of damage, "yet to this point our side has taken no major action." By December the situation was much more serious. Ugarriza wrote on 6 December, "We are surrounded here by insurgents on sea and on land; at sea the ships are blockading from Chilca to Barranca, and on land all these places and even to Caravayllo. . . . In short, we find ourselves exhausted, and I pray that before eight days we may have some action." Finally, on 18 December he wrote: "Nothing enters by land or sea, because the insurgents have Callao blockaded with three, four, or more warships, and even when a foreign ship arrives they capture it."[6] The mood these letters reflected was a combination of growing desperation occasioned by the privation of the blockade and a clear annoyance with the viceregal government for taking no concerted military action against the rebels. Many citizens believed the rebel army could be defeated if decisive action were taken by the larger and better-trained royal forces. Viceroy Pezuela's chief commanders felt the same way, and they chafed at his refusal to strike.

By November and December 1820 Pezuela's leadership was a topic of public debate. The regime was coming apart at the seams. Pezuela proved himself totally inadequate to the crisis. Even the letters he sent to San Martín hinted at his fear. For example, on 30 October, the last day of the negotiations with San Martín's representatives at Miraflores, the viceroy sent a petulant letter to the rebel commander concerning the rebels' use of the term "Liberating Army" for what Pezuela insisted on calling the "Army of Chile." He told San Martín that while he was free in his propaganda to claim that the Peruvian people were oppressed and clamoring for a liberator, he must not say such things in his correspondence with the viceroy. The next day San Martín, from his ship off the coast, replied that the army he commanded was given the title "libertador" by those who sent it, and that that was the title it would use. Throughout December the correspondence between the two leaders dealt with topics such as the exchange of prisoners, but underlying their business was a continuing debate between them about whether Peru wished to be independent. On 24 December 1820 San Martín ended this debate when he told Pezuela that the recent elections for a constitutional city council offered positive proof of the drift of public opinion. He pointed out that the cabildo was clearly worried about the extent of public apathy toward the regime and the lack of unanimity among the populace, and he reminded Pezuela that he should discount the many public expressions of love for the Constitution and for Spain, "given the fact that they were spoken under the influence of your bayonets." He warned that "when an entire people ask for peace there is no salvation in war for those who contravene their desires."[7]

In a way, however, both men were already caught up in their own private dreamlands, where wishful thinking colored their perception of reality. If Pezuela refused to press the attack against the rebel armies in the belief that Lima must be defended at all costs and that to go out to the rebels would endanger the capital, San Martín also erred in his assumption that his mere presence in the vicinity of Lima would be sufficient to sway the population to independence. Both men overestimated the popular support for independence. Whereas Admiral Cochrane and others urged San Martín to attack Lima in the wake of the capture of the *Esmeralda* while royalist defenses were in confusion,[8] he stalwartly adhered to his self-assumed, nonempirical, and ultimately erroneous conception that he was merely the initiator of a genuinely Peruvian rebellion. In these very weeks he expressed to Captain Basil Hall, commander of a British naval vessel anchored off Callao, that his policy was "not to advance a step beyond the gradual march of public opinion." Declaring that he would use public opinion as the "engine" for the establishment of independence, he remarked, "Of what use would Lima be to me, if the inhabitants were hostile in public sentiment? How could the cause of Independence be advanced by my holding Lima, or even the whole country, in military possession?"[9]

Thus each of the leaders wasted precious opportunities to strike, while their subordinates chafed and both armies grew weaker. Driven by this realization, General La Serna and his supporters finally induced Pezuela to give his tentative approval to the initiation of an aggressive counterattack against the rebel army in the vicinity of Lima. On 12 December 7,200 men from the large royal army moved out to the encampment of Aznapuquio in preparation for field activities. On 14 December Pezuela discussed with his generals the creation of a Military Tribunal of Vigilance to oversee public tranquility in the capital; but since this was one of the assignments of the cabildo—whose prerogatives Pezuela did not wish to ignore—he instead called upon the cabildo to do whatever it could in view of "the circumstances of ferment in which this city finds itself."[10]

Simultaneous with these developments, the new constitutional city council of Lima was elected. On 7 November Viceroy Pezuela ordered the incumbent cabildo to proceed with drawing up voter lists and urged it to make haste "because I expect that within a very short time our circumstances will vary, since the enemy is at hand." On 7 December 1820 the new cabildo was chosen. It included a number of Lima's most noted liberals: as alcaldes, the conde de San Isidro and José María Galdiano; as regidors, Francisco de Zarate, Simón Rávago, Diego de Aliaga, the conde de la Vega del Ren, Francisco Vallés, the marqués de Corpa, Pedro de la Puente, José Manuel Malo y Molina, Francisco de Paula Mendoza, Mariano Vasquez, Manuel Pérez de Tudela, Manuel Sáenz de Tejada, Juan Bautista Gárate, Manuel María del Valle, Miguel Vertiz, and Manuel Alvarado; and as syndics, Tiburcio José de la Hermosa and Antonio Padilla.[11] It is no surprise, therefore, that from this point onward the cabildo rendered only grudging cooperation with the regime's efforts to resist San Martín. As one of its first acts, the cabildo sent Pezuela a petition it had received from seventy-two prominent citizens asking that the interrupted negotiations at Miraflores be reopened, so as to "free this loyal city from the furor and ravage of an enemy invasion." Pezuela declined the request. On 16 January 1821 the cabildo discussed, and finally rejected, a suggestion that it throw itself on the mercy of the commander of the British flagship *Andromache*, requesting him to place Lima under British naval protection.[12]

Other signs of royal disintegration were clear. The Consulado—once-proud bastion of Spanish commercial colonialism and valued lieutenant to the viceroys—was in total disarray. In a report to Spain it poured out its laments. The insurgent forces on the coast were intercepting all vessels bound for Peru. All commerce ceased and communications were broken. The mines were entirely inoperative. The Chilean army was going to attack Lima, and the Consulado apparently felt the invaders would be successful. Later it begged Spain to send three warships, saying that if aid did not soon arrive, the loss of Peru, of many fortunes, and of many loyal Europeans would be unavoidable, while all of America would succumb to "the fever of a premature independence."[13]

The merchant Félix D'Olabarriague y Blanco, who left for Spain at this critical point, gave a detailed description of the state of Lima in December 1820. He reported that since Pezuela took office the situation in Peru had been grave, and it was agreed that if the government of Chile had been in the hands of more competent men, Lima would have fallen long before. Taking it for granted that the loss of Lima would be the loss of Peru, he complained that San Martín met no obstacles whatsoever in his disembarkation at Pisco. Although he believed Lima would not necessarily succumb from hunger, he agreed that its situation was "truly critical." Livestock and bread were very expensive, and supplying the troops as well as the civilian population was becoming very difficult. San Martín and Cochrane had been so impolitic as to sack haciendas along the coast owned by Americans and Europeans, weakening their popular support, but also endangering Lima's food supply. He felt certain Lima could sustain these sacrifices "for at least a year and a half" if it received reinforcements. His most significant remark, however, concerned Pezuela: "The greatest danger is that all the inhabitants of Lima, without distinction as to classes or colors, as to Europeans or Americans, and even including the chiefs and troops of the army, have for a long time been discontented with the operations of the viceroy, and particularly, with his inaction since San Martín's arrival in Pisco."[14]

This refrain was repeated by many other eyewitness reports of the period. For example, an anonymous officer reported: "I arrived in Lima on December 12, [1820], and found it in the greatest disorder. Everyone in the cafes spoke at will about whatever they wanted, and with the greatest rashness. The government [was] without opinion; the gazettes carried San Martín's proclamations announcing liberty; . . . San Martín's troops [were] eight leagues from the capital." The diarist added that a few days later Pezuela was forced to surrender effective military command to La Serna, who was named commander-in-chief, with General Canterac as his second.[15] Similarly, the marqués de Valleumbroso and Antonio Seoane, the representatives of La Serna who later traveled to Spain to present his case, said that everyone in the country was convinced "that Peru would be lost not for lack of means of defense, not because of the superiority of the enemy, but because of the erroneous system and limited success of Joaquín de la Pezuela."[16] Another source, an anonymous officer in command of a regiment, wrote that the regime's "situation worsened every moment and what made it more terrible was having a government with neither military nor political credit. . . . Support for the enemy grew in proportion to the discredit of our government." The officers were convinced that San Martín's army was only half as large as the royal army and that if it were attacked in time it could be destroyed, but Pezuela refused to give the command. As a result of Pezuela's "lack of judgment for command, the absolute discredit into which he had fallen, the apathy that characterized him in everything dealing with the improvement of our army, the arbitrariness with which he resisted the other classes in the state, and the progressive increase in support for the enemy, . . . it was indispensable . . . to put at the head of the government a man who would merit public confidence and who would at least give life to this anguished country."[17]

Consequently, on 29 January 1821, nineteen of the chief army commanders, at their camp of Aznapuquio, signed a petition asking Pezuela to resign the viceroyalty in favor of General La Serna. The officers' formal statement to the viceroy was an eloquent summation of his "political and military errors." It accused him of taking insufficient steps to resist San Martín's army; of being unaware of the danger of treason within the Numancia regiment; of appointing unfit officers to certain commands; of decreeing unequal pay to different regiments; of error in appointing the highly suspect marqués de Torre Tagle intendant of Trujillo and Brigadier José Pascual de Vivero governor of Guayaquil; of failing to stop silver contraband and of tolerating free trade; of establishing unequal and punitive taxes and of malversation of funds; and of mistaken decisions in the campaign against the rebels in the interior. Declaring that in Pezuela's hands the country was lost, the officers asked him to turn power over to La Serna. To deliver their demands the commanders chose a young officer named Juan Loriga, secretary of the Junta of War, who had already asked for the hand of Pezuela's daughter Juana in marriage. He went to the palace on the morning of 29 January and, after a few moments of embarrassed confusion, presented the viceroy with the army's demand that he resign within two hours or face the risk of the army's coming from Aznapuquio to force him to. In the presence of the Junta of War, therefore, Pezuela agreed to abdicate. To avoid possible turmoil, the viceroy and his family were required to transfer that same day to their country house at Magdalena. An eyewitness testified that Pezuela was serene and cooperative, but his wife was highly incensed and emotionally accused her intended son-in-law Loriga of playing "with two packs of cards."[18]

General La Serna's account claimed that he was called to the Junta of War and informed that the officers wanted him to assume command. He said he was "surprised by such an unexpected event," but he acceded to the request, "taking on the weight of repairing the effects of our past misfortunes, of reanimating the public spirit, . . . of reestablishing the lost credit and public confidence, and of directing the common defense." He added that his assumption of power provoked new patriotism and will to resist among the Europeans, "but everything will be useless and will produce no other result but the ruin of the country and death—later yes, but inevitable—if His Majesty does not send to these seas considerable forces to protect our coasts." La Serna remained dedicated to the idea that Pezuela's government was about to lose Peru, and several years later he testified that Peru would have been lost if Pezuela had remained in command, "for his system was not the correct one for the critical circumstances in which these territories had been placed."[19] Valleumbroso and Seoane were immediately sent to Spain, via Rio de Janeiro, to testify that La Serna's assumption of office had improved everything and that "discretion, unity, and concurrence presided over all undertakings." To defend Lima, La Serna immediately conscripted 1,500 slaves—promising them emancipation after six years' service—and called up reinforcements of 3,000 men.[20] At the same time he sent various divisions to the mountains to attack San Martín's guerrilla partisans. Another source testified of La Serna's takeover: "Things are a thousand times better compared to the previous state." And yet another officer wrote: "This change . . . renewed the people's enthusiasm . . . and gave a new tone to all political subjects."[21]

Pezuela reacted to the coup with shock, followed by anger, then acquiescence. On 29 January he wrote in his diary: "This is as far as the diary goes, because of the unheard-of mutiny undertaken by the officers of the army." The day after the coup, many people came out to Magdalena to see him—including the archbishop, the oidors, officers, merchants, gentlemen, and all the generals except La Serna. But he received only the archbishop, delegating his wife to interview the others. Pezuela wrote that the archbishop was sad "to see command in the hands of such immoral, presumptuous, bold, and ambitious men." The former viceroy vented his emotions against the officers, accusing them of being "shameless, impudent, insolent, and disrespectful of the king, who is the only one who can appoint and remove viceroys," while he referred to himself as "a general full of military glory who had not lost a battle, who had rooted out . . . independence, . . . who had reconquered the rich provinces of Upper Peru." On 1 February Pezuela dictated to the auditor general, Bartolomé de Bedoya, a secret protest to be sent to the peninsula, in which he pointed out that La Serna and his accomplices must now be held responsible for the "ominous consequences" of their coup.[22] La Serna subsequently placed Pezuela's house under guard.

In April 1821 Pezuela wrote a book-length *Manifesto*, later published in Spain, in reply to all the charges the officers had leveled against him. He insisted that his government had done as much as was humanly possible to rescue the rapidly deteriorating royal authority in a country in which, he believed, the majority of the people favored independence. Furthermore, he testified that many "of those who appeared most loyal and judicious" in his administration had been secret rebel partisans. The ex-viceroy effectively countered the fundamental argument of the officers—that he had lacked energy and skill in prosecuting the war and defending the national honor—and attached fifty-seven documents to prove his government's effectiveness in military affairs and La Serna's errors as commander-in-chief of Upper Peru from 1816 to 1819. Pezuela defended himself in great detail, showing La Serna's frequent insubordination, arguing that Torre Tagle had shown no sign of disloyalty and that he had transferred him to Trujillo away from the intendancy of La Paz to which the king had appointed him because he understood Torre Tagle was not sufficiently experienced for the militarily sensitive Upper Peruvian intendancy, and arguing that the toleration of foreign commerce was based on "the law of necessity."[23]

The bitterness of Pezuela's defense, and the extent of the controversy among his supporters and opponents, makes it clear that the royal cause was seriously damaged by this internal power struggle. For months afterward, propaganda for and against Pezuela appeared in the form of pamphlets, reports to Spain, and editorials in the partisan press. On 19 February 1821, the former viceroy sent a secret letter to various royal officers, oidors, prelates, and bureaucrats requesting them to testify in his behalf—to say whether his political and military command had been inept and whether his overthrow reflected public sentiment. Colonel Juan Antonio Monet testified that Pezuela had been a skilled military commander; the marqués de San Juan Nepomuceno said every citizen understood that the viceroy had resigned merely to avoid civil war among the royalists; Pedro Antonio Fernández de Córdova, a clergyman, testified that the clergy and people had nothing to do with the coup; Tiburcio José de la Hermosa, a cabildo syndic, said neither the cabildo nor the population took part in it; and similar responses came from the rector of the university, members of the audiencia, members of the Provincial Deputation, and other prominent figures.[24] All agreed that Pezuela's overthrow was the work of only a few members of the General Staff. The ex-viceroy, after a desperate search for a ship that would carry him home, finally left Peru in July 1821, in the same week that Lima fell to San Martín.[25]

How then shall we assess the impact of Pezuela's removal from office? Clearly the army officers did not act out of hand. The General Staff turned against Pezuela to a man—including even young Loriga, the viceroy's intended son-in-law. They were all convinced that the military situation was hopeless under Pezuela's rule and that his insistence on holding Lima at all costs was threatening everything. Yet civilians and ecclesiastics responded with shocked dismay to the military takeover. The coup marked a major heightening of tension. Suddenly it became clear that Lima was in danger, and from that moment on it was every man for himself.

Now citizens began to go out to the rebels in significant numbers. The coastal haciendas were entirely disrupted by the confiscations of both armies and by the conscription of slaves. By mid-February Lima was running dangerously short of food. One source testified that three and a half ounces of bread cost one real, as did "three small sweet potatoes," and he bought two white potatoes the size of eggs, he said, for half a real. A loaf of bread at this rate might cost the incredible price of one peso, the equivalent of one United States dollar in 1821. Captain Basil Hall reported provisions so scarce in Lima that he had to sail to Huacho to find food and water for his ship. In addition, circulating specie had almost disappeared. Viceroy La Serna was able at the beginning of July to work out a special agreement with San Martín to permit the emergency provisioning of Lima with 3,000 fanegas of wheat and a thousand lots of rice, but La Serna calculated that the city needed 4,000 fanegas of wheat a week just to survive. Meanwhile, the viceroy admitted that since it was impossible to reopen supply lines to the interior, the city would have to go without meat, potatoes, vegetables, and other necessities. A North American ship sold its cargo of 1,100 casks of flour at 75 pesos a cask.[26] Simultaneously, both the rebel and the royalist armies were stricken by an epidemic of what appears to have been cholera. The royalists, however, were more seriously affected because of their shortage of supplies. In Lima the hospitals were filled to overflowing, and the convent of San Francisco de Paula had to be pressed into use as a hospital. In June, twenty soldiers a day were dying, and at least half the royal army was stricken.[27]

Meanwhile, the city council became increasingly bold in its resistance to La Serna's demands for supplies and money. In response to his demand for a public war contribution, the cabildo countered by proposing the issuance of paper or copper money. Although La Serna made the cabildo responsible for collecting 70,000 pesos as a forced contribution from the inhabitants, he also agreed to issue 500,000 pesos worth of bonds at 8 percent interest, guaranteed by the sale of property belonging to the Temporalidades and to the recently extinguished Inquisition. The bond issue was never implemented, and only 16,000 pesos of the forced contribution was collected. And all the while the cabildo continued to send frequent notes to La Serna warning him against the military confiscations of livestock and grain in outlying haciendas, pointing out that this threatened the capital's future food supply.[28]

In view of all these difficulties, Viceroy La Serna determined to abandon Lima. His plans were temporarily postponed, however, by the arrival in April of naval captain Manuel Abreu, the peace commissioner sent out from Spain by the new government of the Cortes with instructions to negotiate a settlement with the rebels. Abreu had already spent four days with San Martín at the rebel headquarters in Huaura. Now in Lima he was received by a reluctant La Serna, who had been ordered by Spain to facilitate the peace mission. Negotiations between representatives of the royal government and representatives of San Martín commenced at the hacienda of Punchauca, five leagues north of Lima. La Serna disliked Abreu intensely both because of the commissioner's noted friendliness toward San Martín and also because the army high command was suspicious of this naval captain who now had the authority to negotiate a settlement with the rebels.[29] On 23 May a twenty-day armistice was agreed to, and on 2 June Viceroy La Serna and General San Martín met personally at the hacienda. Later the negotiations moved from Punchauca to Miraflores, and later still they moved aboard the frigate *Cleopatra* in Callao harbor. However, except for agreements on the exchange of prisoners and the movement of livestock and food supplies, no concrete settlement was reached. On 6 June the Lima city council sent the viceroy an impassioned plea for peace. Written by Manuel Pérez de Tudela, it lamented because the armistice was about to run out and urged La Serna to be active in the search for an agreement. La Serna replied to the cabildo on 8 June in a remarkably candid letter, saying he too wanted peace, but it must be an honorable peace. War was like a game, he said, and while the royalists might be losing this particular encounter, the match itself was far from over.[30]

Nonetheless, Abreu continued to negotiate with San Martín —who apparently wanted some sort of settlement—long after the royalists abandoned Lima in July. The rebels' final proposal was for an armistice of eighteen months, during which time the viceroy would name two deputies, the government of Chile one, and San Martín a fourth to go to Spain to negotiate directly with the Cortes. Nothing further came of this proposal because it would have submitted Peru indefinitely to the prospect of supporting two contending armies and, most important, because La Serna hated Abreu and by November 1821 was accusing him of acting "more like an agent of the dissidents than a deputy of His Majesty." Each man accused the other of being uncooperative, abusive, and disrespectful.[31]

At any rate, once it became clear that the peace negotiations would lead nowhere, La Serna proceeded to complete his planned evacuation of Lima. In a letter to the conde de Casa Flores, the viceroy wrote that by June the critical situation that had brought him to command in January was even more difficult. There was a total blockade by sea and a siege by land that attracted more and more groups of montoneros (guerrillas) and royalist deserters every day; the negotiations forced on him by Abreu had badly weakened the royal government's prestige; public opinion was increasingly favorable to the rebels; and the army was desperately weakened by the deaths of 1,500 soldiers in the epidemic. In such circumstances, La Serna said, he was convinced that the army was going to be destroyed, for the capital was bound to fall, and he considered it safer to withdraw from Lima so as to save the army to fight another day.[32]

The public began to realize La Serna's momentous decision when on 25 June General Canterac left Lima with half the infantry and cavalry. In a general proclamation on 4 July La Serna announced that he was abandoning Lima because it did not provide a suitable military base from which to defend the rest of the country. "After vacillating for many days," he said, "[in deciding] whether to abandon a city which for so many reasons I will always appreciate, or to try to defend it at all costs, leaving myself buried forever in its ruins and cadavers, I decided at last to accede to my duties and obligations as a public figure." He promised that if the rebels occupied the capital they would not stay long.[33] When the viceroy himself foresaw nothing but "ruins and cadavers," it is easy to understand why panic swept the city. On 5 July La Serna placed military and civil command of the capital in the hands of the retired creole field marshal, the marqués de Montemira. He sent Montemira a letter to give to San Martín, in which he asked the rebel commander to exact no reprisals from the people of Lima. The audiencia protested the viceregal decision, accusing the viceroy of leaving the citizens at the mercy of the invaders and begging him not to withdraw until it was absolutely essential to save the army. La Serna's reply was to announce on the night of 5 July that he had placed two hundred rifles at Montemira's disposal—enough to assure the peace of the city, but not enough to allow hostile action against the rebels, thus avoiding bloodshed.[34]

The evacuation itself was conducted with considerable skill and was aimed at cutting all possible liabilities that might impede the royal army's progress. On 30 June La Serna transferred 900 ill soldiers to the fortress of the Real Felipe in Callao where, under command of subinspector general La Mar, he hoped they would recover their health and defend the fort. Of these men, however, 520 died from the plague between 2 July and 21 September. Meanwhile, La Serna ordered the rest of the army to take along whatever might be of use to the enemy. The treasury was emptied, the artillery was evacuated, arms were stored in the castles at Callao or destroyed. Because of the lack of mules to transport everything, La Serna was forced to deposit the papers of the viceregal secretariat in Callao.[35] Such exigencies help explain the relative scarcity of documents from the La Serna administration. All the silver on hand in the Casa de Moneda was carried away, and the machines were broken up so they could not be used by the rebels. La Serna also attempted to evacuate not only the silver from the cathedral but even the archbishop, both of which were refused him. On the eve of the evacuation La Serna insisted that the archbishop accompany him to the interior, but on 4 July Las Heras declined, saying he could not abandon his flock at such a critical time.[36]

The only criticisms that later appeared against the decision of La Serna and his officers to abandon Lima to its fate came from highly prejudiced sources. When the peace commissioners returned home to Spain in 1822 they submitted a report declaring that they were "ignorant of the motives Viceroy La Serna had for evacuating Lima" but could testify to its effect. They declared that it allowed the rebel army of San Martín, which at the time of its entry into Lima was undermanned and badly provisioned, to refresh itself at the capital's expense. At any rate the commissioners expressed their conviction that La Serna should have defended the capital. The commander of the naval forces at Callao—Antonio Vacaro, a decided partisan of Pezuela—also wrote a report after his return to Spain that was highly critical of La Serna's decision. He testified that the objective of the generals all along had been to hold the Sierra but to give up Lima and that Pezuela, having opposed it, was removed from power. But he insisted that in abandoning Lima the royalists had handed San Martín something for nothing. An even more partisan declaration of support for Pezuela came in the form of an anonymous pamphlet published in Rio de Janeiro in 1821. It insisted that La Serna was the tool of a cabal of ambitious officers who staged the "rebellion of Aznapuquio" for personal advancement.[37] The author was almost certainly a member of Pezuela's party, which landed in Rio de Janeiro in late 1821.

The truth is that La Serna's decision was entirely correct. By abandoning Lima he was able to extricate his army from the morass of supply, morale, and defense problems that characterized occupation of a large city that was vulnerable to both land and sea attack and impossible to provision. Now the rebel forces of San Martín would suffer the difficulties of occupying such a city. A few months later La Serna asserted in a letter to Spain: "What is certain is that the evacuation of Lima is what has paralyzed the progress of the enemy and saved Peru from the dissolution that would have overcome it if I had remained in Lima."[38]

On 6 July the marqués de Montemira wrote to San Martín that it was now possible to make the necessary agreements to guarantee the well-being of the population of Lima. He specifically asked San Martín to control the "Indians and guerrillas who surround the city and who, in this time of surprise, could cause many disorders if you do not act opportunely to prevent it." The next day San Martín replied to the city council, welcoming the citizens of Lima among the "free people of America" and promising he would take no reprisals. "I am disposed to throw a veil over past happenings and to ignore the political opinions manifested by each person before now." He promised his troops would protect the city.[39] With these letters the rebel commander and the marqués de Montemira began discussions for the takeover of the capital. At long last the moment of decision had arrived for the people of Lima.

And yet when independence was actually declared by act of an open town council meeting (cabildo abierto) on 15 July 1821, it did not in fact constitute a clear-cut decision on the part of the citizens. Quite simply, Lima had no choice but to declare independence. The Declaration itself consisted of but one brief sentence. The cabildo abierto declared: "All the gentlemen present, for themselves and satisfied of the opinion of the inhabitants of the capital, said: That the general will is decided in favor of the Independence of Peru from Spanish domination, and that of whatever other foreign power. . . ."[40] After the act was signed in the cabildo abierto it was put on display so that the public at large could further ratify it. The time for the collection of signatures was even extended, and in the end 3,504 persons signed.[41] This documentary evidence is normally assumed to be proof of a general consensus in favor of independence among the literate upper and middle classes of Lima.

The truth was quite different. This point has been argued at length elsewhere, and so here a brief review of the argument will suffice.[42] The Declaration did not reflect the genuine wish of Lima's inhabitants because it was impossible for them to refuse. Furthermore, there is considerable evidence that the Declaration was the work of a group of ambitious letrados—lawyers, priests, and professionals—who forced it upon a desperate and starving capital whose citizens were intimidated by armed force, threatened by imminent social chaos, and coerced by violence and fear. The fundamental premise of San Martín's campaign to liberate Peru was that the Peruvians themselves wanted independence. Consequently, it was necessary that Lima give extraordinary public manifestation of its desire for the new system.

According to Basil Hall, Lima was in a state of indecision and uncertainty after the royalists' evacuation. Hall attended a meeting called by Montemira among "the principal inhabitants as had not fled to Callao." The meeting was characterized by aimlessness and paralysis of purpose.[43] Since there was nothing to do except invite San Martín to occupy the city, the participants decided to do so. The next day the same notables met with Montemira to hear San Martín's reply. The rebel leader asked them to declare whether it was the general will of the people that he should enter. Having no alternative, the gentlemen said yes, and on 12 July San Martín entered Lima without ceremony. But two affirmations were still not enough for the man who had promised "not to advance a step beyond the gradual march of public opinion," and so on 14 July San Martín asked the city council to call a cabildo abierto the next day to discuss the future status of Peru. It was this meeting that declared independence.

A simple narration of these events, however, fails to capture the spirit that reigned in Lima and the motivation of many of the signers of the Declaration. The spirit was one of confusion, fear, and terror, and for many of the signers the motivation was the desire to escape the expected fury of the conquerors. Antonio Vacaro told Spain that it must interpret San Martín's success in light of the "horror with which the public viewed the conduct of our chiefs" when the viceroy's plan to abandon Lima became known.[44] Even more to the point, Pedro Angel de Tado, a dedicated royalist priest who lived in Peru for thirty-two years, described these events in a long letter to a former Lima oidor. Tado insisted that Lima was terrified of the rebel army because of the many months of pillage of rural haciendas, conscription of slaves, and arming of brigands that had preceded the army's arrival outside Lima. Tado insisted that the landowners, slaves, and peasants of Chincha, Pisco, Yca, Chancay, and Huaura all fled from the rebel army and that rural Peru unanimously rejected independence. It was only when the rebels directed their subversion toward the capital that their fortunes improved. As they neared Lima they began to attract the support of a wave of creditless petty lawyers, clerics without appointments, friars with no sense, and civil servants "who judged themselves aggrieved in not having the highest offices in Peru." Tado's version is that independence was the result of the desire for reward and appointment among this segment of the population, which he insisted was not representative of Peru as a whole or of Lima in particular.[45]

It will readily be recognized that Tado is a highly prejudiced source. Nonetheless, his letter constitutes a serious indictment of the rebels' claim that independence was the "general will" of Lima. In particular, Tado charged that the cabildo abierto was a scene of confusion in which there was no serious discussion of available options; that people signed out of fear of reprisals from San Martín, or that death, exile, and confiscation faced those who refused; that not enough of the "persons capable of expressing an opinion" signed the Declaration—in other words, that the signers were some nonrepresentative faction of the population; and that many signers later lamented their signatures but were restrained by fear from openly repudiating the Declaration. All of these allegations can be substantiated.

The cabildo abierto itself was a scene of considerable enthusiasm in which no calm deliberation was possible. The only major speech of the meeting was given by José de Arriz, a professor of law and a founder of the *Mercurio Peruano* who was later appointed to the High Court of Justice that superseded the audiencia. Arriz urged the people present not even to consider the question of independence on its merits. "We should not now occupy ourselves," he said, "in the justice, necessity, convenience or legitimacy of this resolution. . . . What the moment requires is to determine and to decide courageously."[46] From the balconies of the building and in the streets outside there were shouts of enthusiasm. Arriz and Manuel Pérez de Tudela wrote the one-sentence Declaration of Independence, while in the streets royalist sympathizers were urged to follow La Serna in his retreat.

In the next few days there is substantial evidence of outright coercion to sign the Declaration. Even before San Martín's minister, Bernardo Monteagudo, launched his persecution of Spanish nationals, there were, according to letters of royalists fleeing Lima, many types of pressure brought to bear on Europeans. The general situation of the city—surrounded by guerrilla troops made up of escaped slaves from the haciendas or of Indian brigands, in dire need of food and other necessities and abandoned by the royal army—was enough pressure for most. What other choice did Lima have? Even so, direct threats and coercion were exercised. Manuel Pardo, former regent of Cuzco, related that some Europeans and even creoles who refused to swear to independence went into hiding to protect themselves from the excitement of the day. "In this critical situation," he said, "the existence of every European, of their families and of their goods, was dependent upon the caprice of the populace, and on the ferocious despotism of a sanguinary chief." Particular pressure was exerted on the clergy to give their support to the new order. Manuel Méndez, a priest, fled to Spain and reported that the persecution of the Spaniards was meant simply to force them to swear to support independence. Nicolás Tadeo Gómez, sacristán mayor of the Lima cathedral, reported that he was confined at Chancay for refusing independence and that his goods were confiscated. Pedro Gutiérrez Cos, bishop of Huamanga, who had fled to Lima from his diocese as the rebels landed at Pisco, reported that after independence was declared San Martín tried to force him to give his oath of support and to send a pastoral letter to his diocese urging his people to do the same. When he refused, he was expelled from Peru.[47] The best-substantiated case of pressure on an individual to sign the Declaration of Independence was that of José Antonio Prada, a wealthy creole hacendado whose hacienda, which he valued at 700,000 pesos, was confiscated by the patriot army. Many sources—including former viceroy Pezuela, the former contador mayor, several former oidors, and others—testified that Prada was subjected to considerable persecution when he refused to sign. The conde de Montemar said that Prada refused to sign "in spite of the danger of being sacrificed." Manuel Pardo said he knew "the dangers that creole men of honor who thought like Prada" ran, for "D. José and a very few others of his class [that is, creoles] were the object of the persecution of the caudillo [San Martín]." Former oidor Manuel Genaro Villota testified that Prada went into hiding and ran a great risk. And Manuel de Arredondo testified that Prada "was one of the few and first Americans . . . to expose himself to the persecutions of that government."[48] There were many other reports of effrontery and insults, as well as outright threats, being directed against members of the elite. Nor were women exempt. For example, though the royalists had permitted the marquesa de Torre Tagle to leave Lima to join her husband after he had rebelled in Trujillo, the wives of several prominent royal officers were not so gently treated after the rebel takeover. The wife of General Juan Ramírez, who replaced La Serna as commander of Upper Peru from 1819 to 1820, was reported to have been insulted by a patriot officer at a ball, and many noble houses were forced to quarter rebel officers.[49] Basil Hall summarized the dilemma faced by members of the Lima elite at this critical moment:

> The Spaniards, who formed the wealthy class, were sadly perplexed: if they declined entering into San Martín's views, their property and their persons were liable to confiscation; if they acceded to his terms, they became committed to their own government, which, it was possible, might return to visit them with equal vengeance. The natives, on the other hand, . . . were even more alarmed at the consequence of their present act. Many doubted San Martín's sincerity; many his power to fulfill his engagements.[50]

For almost all the elite, therefore, the only choice was to sign the Declaration of Independence or to flee. In the days just before and just after the Declaration, many peninsulars and loyal creoles fled, abandoning their wives and families, homes and businesses. A year later the independent government conducted an investigation among all the city's escribanos to see which peninsulars had fled Lima and what their property dispositions had been. Every escribano reported many bills of sale, transfers of property, and powers of attorney drawn up in June and July 1821 by fleeing Europeans. In addition, within two weeks after the Declaration of Independence forty-three of the sixty-four members of the Consulado fled. Only seventeen members of the Consulado signed the Declaration. So many merchants closed down, indeed, that San Martín ordered all businesses owned by Spaniards to reopen or face confiscation.[51] Although it is impossible to arrive at a precise estimate of the numbers of the elite who fled, it seems clear that they included at least half the nobles, two-thirds of the Consulado members, one-fifth of the ecclesiastical cabildo, and half the audiencia. Nor were these invariably peninsulars; some were creoles.

Those Europeans who did not flee were soon subjected to outright persecution by the government of San Martín's ministers, notably Monteagudo. Spaniards were subjected to a six o'clock curfew, forced to make large punitive contributions to the government, harassed by a public campaign of vilification in which San Martín himself participated, exiled in large numbers, and finally destroyed. In early 1822 all unmarried Spaniards who had not acquired letters of Peruvian citizenship were ordered to leave the country, giving up half their goods to the state. In September 1821, when General Canterac's forces drew up outside Lima, more than 2,000 Spanish civilians were forcibly confined in the Merced Convent. For the next year, every ship leaving the coast of Peru carried Spanish emigrants. Three hundred Spaniards were repatriated on board the *Laura*, *Mercurio*, *Pacífico*, and *Sara*. When four hundred others were sent to Chile on board the *Monteagudo*, several hundred more waited in Lima to be expelled. A refugee officer newly arrived at Cádiz reported that between 8 and 29 November 1821, the English ships *Galen*, *Saint Patrick*, and *Lord Lyndock*, the Spanish *Cleopatra*, and the French *Estafeta* left Callao carrying Spanish families, while the American *Carabana* was receiving more passengers ready to sail. The consul in Rio reported that refugees paid up to 500 pesos for their passports from San Martín and 2,500 pesos for passports from Lord Cochrane.[52] Paz Soldán said that when the rebels landed at Pisco there were more than 10,000 Spaniards in Lima, but that in July 1822 no more than 600 remained. Gaspar Rico, who accompanied La Serna's army in the Andes, estimated in 1824 that 12,000 Spaniards had been killed or exiled in Peru in the past three years. Basil Hall testified that by July 1822 "the ruin of the old Spaniards was complete."[53]

Countless examples of the tragic plight of the old Spaniards could be cited, since most of those who fled to Spain later told their stories when they applied to the crown for new positions in the peninsula or for the special pension of 12,000 reales a year that was granted to each official who emigrated from America. A few cases, however, will illustrate the extent of their personal losses. For example, the conde de Vallehermoso, an oidor, was ordered expelled from Peru for refusing to accept independence. Like most others, however, he had a very difficult time finding passage. He successively boarded five ships—British, North American, and French—but was refused passage on each by intervention of San Martín. Then he was processed for conspiracy and lost his wife's extensive property by having it sequestered or by forfeiting it as bond. Once he got to Rio de Janeiro he remained there—as did many other emigrants—waiting to see if events in Peru might allow his return. Finally, convinced that Peru was lost, he traveled on to Spain. His wife and children remained behind in Cuzco. Other royalists fled to Callao, but when it fell to San Martín in September 1821 they had to leave Peru. Francisco de Puga, an official of the mails in Lima, had such an experience. After the castles at Callao capitulated to the republican government, he returned to his home in Lima, where he was arrested four months later. He was finally released after three months' incarceration and ordered to leave Peru within fifteen days. The conde de Montemar lent him the money for his trip, but he left his family behind in Peru. Antonio Caspe y Rodríguez, an oidor, was another royalist who fled to the castles at Callao. When they capitulated he became an indigent refugee. He fled Peru leaving his wife and nine children behind. In Rio de Janeiro he was forced to borrow from a Spaniard in order to survive.[54] Another type of story occurred to the conde de Montemar y de Monteblanco. At first unprepared to flee Peru—as were many other members of the elite—he swore an oath of allegiance to the new regime, even though San Martín's expedition had been responsible for the destruction of his haciendas to the north of Lima in 1820. On 18 August 1821 the *Gaceta* published a letter in which he abjured his loyalty to Spain and thoroughly embraced the cause of independence. The independent government, "in view of the spontaneous and frank retraction that [Montemar] made of his former opinions," returned to him his confiscated goods. In 1822 he even sponsored a series of public bullfights to raise money for the patriot government. Later that year, however, he availed himself of his opportunity and, despite his oath of loyalty to independence, fled to Spain.[55] Other nobles who took an active part in the independent government would attempt to emulate this example.

Although many prominent persons signed the Declaration of Independence and subsequently fled the country, there were a few who neither signed nor fled. These included persons who were so notable that the rebels preferred their silence even to their signatures. For example, out of all the audiencia members, only one, the peninsular Manuel María del Valle, signed the Declaration. But six others—the peninsulars Tomás Ignacio Palomeque, Gaspar Osma, and José de la Iglesia and the creoles José Santiago Aldunate, José de Irigoyen, and Francisco Moreno—asked San Martín to permit them to remain in Lima after independence but did not sign the Declaration.[56] They chose to remain in Lima not because they positively accepted the idea of independence, but because their incomes and properties were in Peru. Of the heads of departments and directors of the bureaucracy, only a handful signed. The highest-ranking were Antonio Chacón, contador mayor of the Tribunal of Accounts, and Félix de la Roza, former administrator of the mails, whose conduct in office had long been under investigation. Pedro Trujillo, director of the tobacco monopoly, was reported to have offered his services, but San Martín expelled him.[57]

Of course there were many prominent persons who willingly signed the Declaration of Independence, and these people are often cited as proof that independence was popular. In some cases, however, people signed simply because they were creoles who were unable to face the thought of expatriation or peninsulars whose families, properties, and sources of income were in Peru. For example, there were forty-nine holders of noble titles (títulos de Castilla) in Lima in 1821.[58] Of this number, eight were women, who could not sign the Declaration. But forty-one were men (most of whom were definitely in Lima at the time), and of that number only nineteen signed (see table 10). On close inspection, however, it appears that most of those nineteen were either young men who had only recently inherited their titles, such as Vega del Ren, Vistaflorida, San Juan de Lurigancho, or San Juan Nepomuceno, or holders of very "new" titles granted since the beginning of the century, such as Casa Boza, Casa Saavedra, Casa Dávila, and Torre Antigua del Orué. These men were usually born and reared in Lima and held titles that were granted specifically to reward creole families. They identified with Peru and would have been strangers in the very Castile from which their titles came. Hall remarked, at any rate, when referring to nobles like Torre Tagle, that independence offered "to persons so situated a great increase of fortune and consequence."[59] When older nobles, holders of older titles, or men who had a source of income or a family in Europe signed, like the conde de Montemar, they tended to flee the country shortly afterward because they had the option of flight.

It is true, too, that the upper clergy in Lima signed the Declaration of Independence. Archbishop Las Heras, Dean Francisco Javier de Echagüe, and most of the cathedral chapter signed. The explanation, again, is the extent of their identification with Peru. The archbishop, though a peninsular, had lived most of his life in America. He was eighty years old, and he had stalwartly refused to abandon his flock when called upon by the viceroy to do so. He knew how deeply Lima cared for him, and he loved Lima in return. In the last decade before independence the city council and the cathedral chapter had proposed his appointment as a cardinal in honor of the "triumph of Lima's fidelity."[60] The motivation for the remainder of the cathedral chapter is even clearer, for, contrary to the prevailing myth—as exacerbated by too literal a belief in creole propaganda such as Riva Agüero's "28 Causes"—the majority of the Lima chapter was American. Twenty of the twenty-six members, from Echagüe on down, were Americans; sixteen of them were Peruvians; and ten of those were Limeños.[61] The cathedral chapters at Trujillo and Arequipa were also predominately creole.[62]

Two other truly elite groups who signed the Declaration of Independence were the medical doctors and the leading import-export merchants. The motivation for the medical doctors is clear. They were exclusively creole, some even were nonwhite, and they had been advocates of political reform for many years.[63] More unusual were those great merchants who signed— including José Arizmendi, Pedro Abadia, Manuel and Fernando Exhelme, the conde de San Isidro, and the conde de Villar de Fuente. Their motives, however, are also clear, for most of these men were among the merchants who had long advocated foreign trade and had themselves been leaders in it. The first four mentioned, at any rate, had been opponents of the Consulado and its commercial exclusivism. All of the rich merchants were later disappointed by the disruption in trade and the incessant demands for contributions to the new independent government. Nearly all of them were bankrupted by 1823 and either fled to join the royalists—as did both the nobles mentioned—or went into exile. This last group included Arizmendi, Lima's richest merchant, whose company earned 120 million reales a year and whose assets were valued after he fled Peru at 2,172,000 pesos. After a brief imprisonment by San Martín, Arizmendi fled to Mexico, then to the Philippines, and finally to Spain. His partner, Abadia, who Proctor said was famous even in Europe, was completely ruined and lived the rest of his life a poor man.[64]

TABLE 10

LIMA TÍTULOS DE CASTILLA IN 1821

| Title | Comment |
|---|---|
| SIGNERS OF THE DECLARATION | |
| Marqués de Casa Boza | Inherited title in 1820–21 |
| Marqués de Casa Dávila | |
| Marqués de Casa Muñoz | Title created in 1817 |
| Conde de Casa Saavedra | Title created in 1820 |
| Marqués de Corpa | |
| Conde de Lagunas | |
| Marqués de Montealegre | |
| Conde de Montemar y de Monteblanco | Fled later |
| Conde de San Carlos | |
| Conde de San Isidro | Inherited title after 1812, died in Callao |
| Conde de San Juan de Lurigancho | Inherited title in 1817, died in Callao |
| Marqués de San Juan Nepomuceno | Inherited title in 1821, fled and properties confiscated |
| Conde de Torre Antigua de Orué | Title created in 1810s |
| Conde de Torreblanca | |
| Marqués de Torrehermosa | Inherited title in 1820–21 |
| Conde de la Vega del Ren | Inherited title in early 1800s as a youth |
| Marqués de Villafuerte | Inherited title in 1810s |
| Conde de Villar de Fuente | Later turned royalist, died in Callao |
| Conde de Vistaflorida | Inherited title in 1818 |
| Total = 19 | |
| NONSIGNERS | |
| Conde de Cártago | |
| Marqués de Casa Calderón | |
| Conde de Castañeda | |
| Marqués de Castel Bravo del Rivero | Oidor, fled |
| Marqués de Castellón | Neapolitan title, inherited after 1807 |
| Marqués de Feria | Stayed in Lima |
| Marqués de Fuentehermosa | |
| Marqués de Lara | Perhaps the premier noble family (Manrique de Lara), related to Montemira, Montemar, Feria, and San Carlos |
| Marqués de Montemira | Interim governor of Lima |
| Marqués de Monterrico | |
| Conde de Montesclaros | |
| Conde de Polentinos | |
| Marqués de la Real Confianza | |
| Conde de San Xavier | |
| Marqués de Salinas | |

(TABLE 10 con't.)
LIMA TITULOS DE CASTILLA IN 1821

| Title | Comment |
|---|---|
| Conde de Sierrabella | |
| Marqués de Tabaloso | |
| Marqués de Torre Tagle | Not living in Lima in 1821, intendant of Trujillo |
| Conde de Torre Velarde | Stayed in Lima |
| Conde de los Torres | |
| Marqués de Villablanca | |
| Conde de Valleumbroso | Royalist commander |
| Total = 22 | |
| | |
| Marquesa de Casa Concha | |
| Marquesa de Negreyros | |
| Condesa de Pozos Dulces | |
| Condesa de Premio Real | Mother of intendant of Arequipa, Juan Bautista Lavalle |
| Marquesa de Rocafuerte | |
| Marquesa de San Felipe | |
| Marquesa de Santa María | |
| Marquesa de San Miguel | |
| Total = 8 | |

SOURCE: "Lista de los individuos que poseen fincas en esta ciudad," 17 May 1820, ANP, Superior Govierno, L. 37, C. 1335.

It seems, then, that Tado's allegation that the Declaration of Independence was the work of the letrados and office-seekers is largely correct, at least when interpreted in light of what must have been Tado's very traditional and narrow sense of who constituted "persons capable of expressing an opinion." The simple fact is that refusal to sign the Declaration was for many men the equivalent of signing their own warrant for arrest, confiscation, and exile. As Tado said, "who would not sign it under those circumstances?" The vast majority of those signers I have been able to identify were men who had not yet reached the peak of their professions, who felt that their advancement was blocked by real or imagined impediments, or who, quite simply, never aspired to reach the top. They ascribed their failure of advancement to the inflexibility of Spain's imperial institutions rather than to their own failings, and each one kept a wary eye on the main chance.

From the historical point of view, of course, it is not surprising that the aspirants to office were the chief supporters of independence. One would naturally expect that. The point, however, is that these aspirants would have to be satisfied by the new government. They were not, for San Martín was no more able to turn Lima into a cornucopia to reward his followers than was La Serna or Pezuela. Furthermore, of those who signed the Declaration of Independence, many later reverted to the royalist side, or at least gave no indication of subsequent positive support for the rebel government. This alone impugns the assumption that all signers of the Declaration were active supporters of independence. Within six months San Martín's regime collapsed amid general apathy and even opposition, and the rebellion ground to an ignominious halt. To be sure, San Martín won Lima, but his victory turned out to be empty.

San Martín's object in acquiring so many signatures on the Declaration of Independence was to bind the undecided to his cause. He organized two other ceremonial occasions to pursue this objective. He called for, and received, oaths of loyalty from every government office, corporation, school, and institution in Lima. Hall noted that the signatures on these oaths "deeply committed many men who would have been well pleased to have concealed their acquiescence in the matter." In addition, on 28 July San Martín held a splendid public ceremony to proclaim independence. Amid great pomp, he made the historic announcement: "From this moment Peru is free and independent, by the general wish of the people." The ever-perceptive Hall, who stood near San Martín that day, declared: "It was a business of show and effect, and quite repugnant to his taste. I sometimes thought there might be detected in his face a momentary expression of impatience or contempt of himself for engaging in such mummery."[65]

Lima declared independence in July 1821 because it was the only alternative to the vacuum left by the viceroy's evacuation and the only method available to free the capital from the threat of attack or the depredations of marauding bands of guerrillas. At most, Lima merely acquiesced in a political development it was powerless to resist. And San Martín would soon learn how valueless that acquiescence was. The royal cause, of course, had been badly weakened by the abandonment of Lima, but it had managed to escape total ruin by cutting loose the albatross. Royal armies remained in the field, under aggressive and intelligent leadership, prepared if possible to reoccupy the capital. Both sides now settled in for what would prove a long stalemate, and the future of Peru remained undecided.

Chapter 8

# The Stalemate

NEITHER VICEROY LA SERNA in the Sierra nor General San Martín on the coast expected the military and political stalemate that gripped Peru from late 1821 to late 1824. La Serna anticipated that he would retake Lima fairly soon, or at least that he would be able to reinforce Callao (which at first remained in royalist hands), thereby preventing ships from unloading supplies at the harbor. He also planned to obstruct the supply of Lima from the interior and thus to starve the rebels out of the capital. San Martín's program, on the other hand, consisted of creating a functioning government in Lima and then expanding his crusade throughout the interior, using Lima as his supply base and chief support. Both plans were well grounded and sufficiently reasonable, and yet neither worked. The stalemate lasted three and a half years and constitutes the definitive proof, if any is needed, that Peruvians had not yet chosen to be independent.

San Martín and the independent government he now created controlled the politically active part of Peru. But he failed to establish his own credit or that of the entire enterprise of independence. La Serna, on the other hand, controlled the politically inert interior and highlands of Peru. Popular credit was not essential to his survival because his "government" consisted chiefly of an army that made its headquarters first in Huancayo and then after December 1821, in Cuzco. He possessed an enclave, but one that was too isolated, both politically and physically, to exert domination over the rest of Peru. Furthermore, La Serna was cut off from communication with Spain for periods as long as an entire year.[1] Thus Peruvians continued to be prohibited by circumstances from making a clear-cut decision on independence.

It was chiefly the failure of San Martín, who now bore the title protector of Peru, that permitted the survival of La Serna's royalist enclave in the highlands. It has never been fashionable in Peruvian historiography to use the word "failure" in reference to San Martín. The protector's voluntary withdrawal from Peru in September 1822 has always been treated as an act of self-abnegating heroism—the final glory of an honest man's distinguished career.[2] In fact, San Martín withdrew from Peru in 1822 because he had failed and he knew it. His failure is intimately bound up with the general question of whether Peru wished to be independent, for if his crusade had been supported by a true Peruvian consensus he would have succeeded. This essential fact can no longer be ignored. Having based his enterprise on the premise that Peruvians wanted independence and would rush to his side, San Martín paid the price for having misjudged the people he sought to liberate.

Three factors explain San Martín's failure. First, he stepped into a trap—the same trap La Serna had just avoided. He considered Lima the key to Peru, and from the capital he anticipated spreading independence to the hinterland. In truth, no army based in Lima could build the economic resources needed to carry its struggle forward. The added responsibility of creating and administering a civilian government divided the rebel leaders' attention and ultimately paralyzed their ability to function. In 1824, when Bolívar succeeded in destroying the royal army, he did so from the base of Trujillo and the northern countryside, not from Lima, and he concentrated his full talents on the military struggle, deputizing others to govern for him. Second, San Martín, quite simply, failed as a leader. Wracked by tuberculosis and addicted to opium, he could not provide day-to-day command or exercise the cunning brilliance that had brought him to Peru in the first place. His officers began to turn against him even as the citizens of Lima were doing so. Third, and most critical, Peru in general and Lima in particular—at least the politically active class—was not convinced that independence was desirable. In a

194

THE FALL OF THE ROYAL GOVERNMENT IN PERU

variety of ways, the San Martín government was clumsy, inept, and often wrong. It was not the swirling chaos of Lima's political factionalism that destroyed San Martín; rather, it was San Martín's failure that created the anarchy of 1823 and 1824.

That San Martín was in poor health throughout his entire period in Peru was public knowledge. In essence, it caused the loss of his leadership. Shortly after the Declaration of Independence, he went into virtual exile in the country house built by Viceroy Pezuela at Magdalena, half a league from Lima, leaving the actual government in the hands of three ministers, of whom Bernardo Monteagudo—minister of war and marine—was the most powerful and soon the most hated. Several informants reported to Spain that San Martín was inactive, that he suffered terribly, and even that he was expected to die. Pedro Gutiérrez Cos, bishop of Huamanga, reported that when he fled Lima in November 1821 San Martín was "gravely sick from bleeding from the mouth. It was doubted very much that he would recover his health." In November 1821 San Martín himself wrote Bernardo O'Higgins, supreme director of Chile, that he was convinced of the gravity of his illness and that if he continued working it would kill him. Luis Cruz, Chilean delegate to Lima, later informed O'Higgins that "General San Martín was passing through one of those crises that more than once have placed his health in danger."[3]

The full extent of San Martín's illness has only recently been detailed. According to Adolfo J. Galatoire, who traced his clinical history, San Martín suffered from the various direct and indirect symptoms of tuberculosis. Contracted when he was a child, the disease manifested itself only when he was an adult, and it was at its most virulent from 1814 to the early 1820s, the period of his active involvement in American independence. For relief from the agonies of his illness San Martín's physician prescribed the only reliable painkiller available to early nineteenth-century medicine—opium. San Martín became an opium addict. His personal advisers and friends, including Tomás Guido and Argentine Supreme Director Juan Martín de Pueyrredón, knew of his addiction, sympathized with him, and urged him to resist the habit. As Galatoire sketched it, the opium, in addition to being habit-forming, required increasing quantities as San Martín's tolerance to it grew. In San Martín's case the large doses caused not only the normal initial euphoria, but a sustained euphoria with functional behavioral changes, combined with respiratory depression and constipation. When the effect of the drug passed off, San Martín would be exhausted and depressed and would suffer from gastric pains and from extreme nausea and vomiting, requiring further doses to mitigate these effects.[4] His judgment may or may not have been impaired. Nonetheless, contemporaries and historians alike singled out certain crucial decisions for particular criticism—including his refusal to attack Canterac's army in September 1821 as it drew near Lima to relieve the royal garrison in Callao; his continued support for his widely hated and feared minister, Bernardo Monteagudo; his open courtship of the idea of establishing a European prince in Peru as monarch; and his endorsement of the counterproductive campaign of persecution against the Spaniards in Lima. His government's popular support plummeted, his troops deserted, and his armies stood about useless. It is the mark of San Martín's ability that he accomplished so much before his body and spirit wearied beyond hope.

The principal duties facing the government of the fledgling independent state included mounting an army large enough to defend and extend what had already been won by default, creating a functioning civilian regime, and winning the hearts and minds of Peruvians. These goals depended, above all, on stabilizing the economy. The object was not only to continue the war, but to prove to Peruvians that independence could provide "good government"—that it could find jobs for the letrados, satisfy the badly shaken elite, and control the lower classes. The patriot government failed to meet these goals because the destruction of the old elite—the Spaniards—paralyzed the economy. Every vacancy thus created in the bureaucracy had several aspirants waiting in line to fill it, but San Martín's most loyal followers, most of whom were outsiders, expected and received preference. Within a few weeks it was clear that San Martín's promises to every class in society could not be kept, and disappointment with the new regime swept Lima. When Basil Hall spoke of Lima as characterized by "an engrossing selfishness," he was referring to this.[5]

The San Martín regime embarked on an economic policy that, although it may not have been a conscious design, had the effect of despoliation. The destruction of the Spaniards was an economic catastrophe that threw into disarray the most economically active portion of the population, wiping out the accumulated value of properties, businesses, and haciendas. This in turn badly weakened the government's income base. In the first flush of victory the independent regime continued its forced confiscations and punitive legislation that ultimately came to look like a policy of outright persecution.

Some haciendas—those belonging to royalists—were directly confiscated. One group of valuable properties, with a value of more than 500,000 pesos, was confiscated and distributed in December 1821 as rewards to leading rebel officers. Distribution by lots was undertaken by the Lima cabildo, although many of the officers renounced their gifts. The cabildo ultimately turned against the policy of granting such rewards to officers, declaring in July 1822 that "nothing is more detrimental to the progress" of liberty. Apparently the largest confiscations were the properties taken from José Antonio Prada and from the intendant of Arequipa, Juan Bautista Lavalle.[6] Some properties were not directly confiscated—for example, the two haciendas of the religious order of Buenamuerte, whose father provincial was ordered to turn over all their produce to the state. Still other haciendas were simply ordered to surrender part of their land for the use of the government. In December 1821 the *Gaceta* published a list of seven large haciendas whose owners had been ordered to take 8,500 head of state-owned cattle to graze.[7]

Many of the haciendas suffered such extensive disruption that they ceased to be productive. The most serious problem was loss of slaves due to runaways or conscription into the army, followed by the confiscation of draft animals. In 1814 the royal government had estimated that there were 12,263 slaves in the immediate environs of Lima (partido del cercado) and 30,000 (one-fifth the total population) in the province of Lima as a whole.[8] In 1821 the royalists had conscripted 1,500 of these slaves. San Martín continued and expanded the policy, even though Stevenson attests that the protector was deeply disappointed by the lack of enthusiasm for service among the slaves. By January 1822 the rebel army included perhaps a majority of slaves (one contemporary estimated 4,000 to 5,000).[9] It is true that on 28 September 1821 San Martín decreed that the children of slaves born from that day forward were free, and in November he decreed the end of the import of new slaves into Peru. [10] But these decrees did not affect existing slaves, who were too valuable a source of manpower for immediate emancipation. In September 1821, as General Canterac's army drew near Lima for the first time, most slaves were armed. After the crisis had passed, San Martín decreed that as reward for their services twenty-five of the many hundreds of slaves who had taken up arms were to be chosen by lot and freed, but those who had not returned to the service of their owners were excluded from this token compensation. At any rate, slaves belonging to persons who had fled and those slaves who had been conscripted into the royal army but deserted were ordered incorporated into service and given their freedom after six years. In April 1822 the government called up a fifth of all the capital's slaves and a tenth of all those in the environs, promising to reimburse their owners within two years. Only a month later Torre Tagle, apparently ignoring the previous decree, simply ordered all male slaves enrolled. [11] Most of the slaves conscripted by San Martín were destined to make up the civil militia; later a Batallón de Cívicos Pardos was created.

The effect of this use of the slaves was easy to foresee. In March 1822 a group of hacendados in the valley of Cañete complained to the government that the patriots' seizure of some of their slaves had caused the rest to flee, leaving the land unworked. After the slaves were gone, the government continued confiscating draft animals and livestock from the haciendas. The patriot soldiers were extremely wasteful of confiscated livestock. Miller testified: "It was not an uncommon thing, at the commencement of the revolution, to kill half a dozen oxen merely for the sake of their tongues." In a matter of months the haciendas, upon which Lima depended for its domestic food supplies, were thoroughly ravaged. On 6 April 1822 the English visitor Gilbert F. Mathison traveled outside Lima to visit the haciendas in the valley of the Rímac. He reported that neither man nor beast could be seen for miles—all was empty and deserted. "I could have imagined myself in the Atacama desert that separates Chile and Peru rather than in the celebrated valley of the Rímac." The arming of the slaves and others not normally permitted to carry arms also led to widespread crime and robberies, as San Martín admitted in a decree of 7 September 1821. [12]

Because of this disruption of the haciendas Lima's food prices remained very high. The chief thing that saved the city from real starvation was the fall of royalist-held Callao to the rebels in September 1821. When Viceroy La Serna departed from Lima in July 1821, he left behind a large contingent of troops—2,022 men, many of whom were sick from the epidemic then raging among the army—to hold the royal fortresses at Callao. One of the most famous military episodes of the entire war occurred in September 1821, when royalist General José Canterac arrived at Callao with nearly 3,300 men from the royal army in an attempt to resupply the dwindling food in the castles and to remove those soldiers who had recovered from their illness. Finding it impossible to supply the forts, Canterac departed on 16 September taking 489 of the Callao defenders with him. San Martín's refusal to attack Canterac as he drew up outside Callao, and his refusal to attack the royal force as it retreated from Callao a few days later, was the single greatest blow to his prestige as a military commander.[13] For the next month the remaining royal soldiers in the forts were under siege, suffering horrible privations. Twelve to fifteen royal soldiers died every day, until the final surrender of the forts to San Martín on 19 September. La Serna's response was to claim that Canterac's unhindered withdrawal from Callao proved once again that the rebels' only victories were those the royalists handed them. Nonetheless, consular reports from Rio de Janeiro—which had now become Spain's chief listening post on Peru—said that the royalist emigrants living in Rio felt that if Canterac had attacked San Martín's main forces at Lima he would have won a quick victory.[14]

Despite the cost in prestige to San Martín, the acquisition of Callao was essential to Lima's well-being. It allowed Cochrane's blockade to be lifted and reopened Lima to wheat trade from Chile and coastal Peru. The Lima cabildo set the price of bread at ten ounces a real and continued publishing the price in the *Gaceta*, although it complained that wheat merchants were not reporting accurate figures in order to avoid entry duties. As late as May 1822 the need for food was still so great that the government ordered all foreign and domestic ships bringing in wheat, meal, rice, meat, or feeds to pay only the duties normally imposed on the coastal traders. It was not, however, until October 1822 that the *Gaceta* could officially boast, in reply to royalist propaganda saying that Lima was starving, that "provisions abound at present in

Lima." But it certainly overstated the case when it said that "never have more consumer goods been seen in Lima, nor at more comfortable prices."[15] What consumer goods there were came from the British merchants who now flocked in to set up shop under the direct protection of the British naval fleet in the Pacific. By October 1822 at least fourteen British merchant houses were already established in Lima.[16]

The independent government's sources of income were dangerously restricted. Throughout the San Martín period, and even after, the government published monthly reports in the *Gaceta* of the income and expenses of the public treasury. The figures show how weak the new state was. The first published figures, representing September 1821, showed total income to be only 130,659 pesos. Only about 30,000 pesos of this sum came from regular state sources of revenue—in this case from leftover sums in the customs at Lima and Cerro de Pasco and from the administration of tobacco. The rest came from private donations, confiscations, subscriptions, sales, and other irregular sources. Expenses, however, went for essential and regularly expected items—mainly military upkeep, which consumed four-fifths of all state funds. A year later, in September 1822 (San Martín's last month as protector), revenue had increased to 203,949 pesos, but at least half of it still came from irregular sources.[17] This gap between regular and irregular income was made explicit when, after San Martín's resignation and the accession of Congress, the minister of finance, Hipólito Unánue, informed Congress in December 1822 that actual income from what he called ordinary sources for the last six months of 1822 was 735,000 pesos, while actual expenditure was 1,526,000 pesos. Of this expenditure, more than 1,200,000 pesos, or nearly 80 percent of the total, was for military costs.[18]

The new government immediately turned its attention toward resurrecting the two fundamental sources of state revenue in Peru: customs and mining. In both fields the success was minimal. Although Lima's trade, long closed by Cochrane's blockade of Callao, was reopened after the royal surrender of the port in September 1821, it proved impossible to renew a very active foreign trade, because although Peru needed to buy almost everything, it had little to sell. San Martín immediately declared Callao open to all traffic and established new customs duties that favored Peruvian goods and goods from other South American republics. At first there was a rush of ships entering the port. From 28 September to 15 October 1821 twenty ships anchored, and in the next month twelve more arrived; but thereafter the trade became sparse. [19] More than anything else, this reflected the relative absence of Peruvian export commodities, for when these same ships left Callao they usually carried only ballast and, of course, the silver with which Limeños had purchased the badly needed supplies. The irregularity of trade made for highly irregular customs revenues. In most months it averaged about 40,000 pesos.

In the mining sector there was nothing the government could do. Almost all the mines had ceased producing, and many that were still worked lay in the territory controlled by La Serna. The abandonment of the mines, the disappearance of the chief investors (one Spaniard who fled Peru, for example, owned 420 mines), the dispersal of workers, the loss of animals, the shortage of mercury, and the devastation of major producing provinces like Pasco all added to the impossibility of reopening Peru's greatest source of wealth. Nonetheless, in October 1821 San Martín, referring to the mines as "the patrimony of Peru," created a General Directorate of Mines in Lima to replace the old Mining Tribunal. He also called for the creation of exchange banks for the state purchase of bullion at Pasco and Huancavelica. In November, Dionisio Vizcarra, first director general of mines, published a plan for the reform of the industry and for the creation of the exchange banks. [20] Nothing could be done, though, for Peru lacked the massive investment capital required to rebuild the industry.

Throughout San Martín's period in Peru, therefore, the government depended on voluntary and forced donations for half its income. This was a politically dangerous recourse, for the cabildo told San Martín that the common people believed independence would mean the abolition of nearly all taxes and duties, while the capitalists obviously were vulnerable to frequent exactions that could turn them against the regime. Genuinely voluntary donations accounted for very small sums, and even these were extracted through considerable social and political pressure. In January 1822, for example, the government announced that persons who intervened in behalf of the interests of Spanish nationals, or who bound themselves through personal ties to such enemies of the state, would have their names published in the *Gaceta* "so that the public might know those who prefer personal affections to the high interests of justice and of politics."[21] In other words, anyone not actively for independence would be deemed against it. Naturally the names of those people who did contribute were also listed in the *Gaceta*.

Forced contributions, however, remained essential. The largest sums were exacted from the Spaniards and from the Peruvian merchants. In August 1821 San Martín ordered the Consulado to collect 150,000 pesos for the government within six days; when it could not comply, the government simply confiscated 105,000 pesos outright. The problem was that many of the established merchants had fled, including nearly two-thirds of the Consulado. The cabildo, after being assigned a quota of 30,000 pesos, complained that it could not collect such a sum from leading citizens except by "extortion." In April 1822 the Spaniards still living in the city were forced to contribute 110,000 pesos.[22] And just after Congress took power a huge contribution of 400,000 pesos was levied against the merchants. In response to this last order, the entire community of British merchants living in Lima asked for their passports and received support from the commander of the British fleet in the Pacific, Captain H. Prescott. Ultimately, a compromise was arrived at whereby the British merchants would pay 73,400 pesos instead of the 100,000 pesos assigned them, but the government insisted that their nationality did not exempt them from future contributions.[23]

From the first moment of their presence in Lima, the rebels' foremost economic problem was the almost total absence of circulating specie—metal coins. The problem was partly caused by the flight of Spaniards from the city, as well as by the virtual collapse of the Casa de Moneda and the mining industry in general. The crisis was capped by the seizure of the government's entire bullion reserve by Lord Cochrane at Ancón in September 1821. Earlier that month, when Canterac made his first approach toward Lima, the government's bullion reserve had been moved to Ancón for safekeeping. At this very moment a tragic argument between San Martín and Cochrane reached its culmination. The Chilean navy, which Cochrane commanded and which had made the initial success in Peru possible, turned against San Martín because it was not paid. According to an agreement made with Chile, the navy was to be paid 150,000 pesos, plus a 50,000 peso bonus for the capture of the *Esmeralda*, once Lima was taken. When in August 1821 Cochrane demanded payment, San Martín said he thought Chile should pay. The government then tried to induce Cochrane's men to come over and form a separate Peruvian navy, but in October Cochrane and his fleet deserted San Martín, taking the bullion reserve with them. The treasure was worth 460,480 pesos.[24] The royalist propagandists seized with glee on this indication of dissension within the patriot ranks, and the government in Lima was so shocked that it even published in the *Gaceta* an itemized list of what Cochrane had taken. Months later the Ministry of Finance still blamed Cochrane for the inability of the Casa de Moneda to produce enough coins.[25]

The loss of the fleet was a less serious blow than the loss of the bullion. San Martín moved immediately to create a separate Peruvian navy; indeed, Stevenson alleged he set out to subvert the Chilean navy and bring its officers into Peruvian service.[26] Besides, there was no effective Spanish naval threat off Peru at the moment, the two remaining Spanish frigates, the *Prueba* and the *Venganza*, having sailed farther north. It was the loss of bullion that was crippling, for the government now had no reserves whatsoever.

By October 1821, only three months after the Declaration of Independence, San Martín's government was on the verge of collapse. The shortage of specie made it nearly impossible to purchase everyday goods, much less pay contributions and taxes. The situation was so strained that Chilean coins were declared legal tender at face value in Lima. The navy had already deserted for lack of pay. In addition, the army itself suffered heavy desertions and was extremely discontented because it was not paid. Deserters were replaced by conscripts, and some observers thought the entire army of about 4,800 men was composed of slaves. No more than 500 of the original contingent of Chilean troops remained. Ramón del Valle, a royalist, reported that the troops "are badly paid and most are barefoot." Former oidor Juan Bazo y Berri reported that the troops were "soldados de pintura"—soldiers in name only.[27] Salaries for the common soldier were extremely low, when they were paid at all. A soldier enrolled in the Batallón de Cívicos Pardos, for example, was paid only two reales a day—just enough to buy twenty ounces of bread at official prices.[28] San Martín and his most loyal commanders were deeply troubled by the existence of various plots among leading army officers to depose the protector. Aware of the dissension among his own commanders, San Martín chose not to reprimand them. Months later, as he was preparing to retire from Peru, he explained his tolerance to his friend Tomás Guido: "I'm going to tell you something. In order to sustain the discipline of the army it would be necessary to shoot some of the commanders, and I lack the courage to do that to companions who accompanied me in good days and bad."[29] By December 1821 there were pasquinades in Lima proclaiming "long live the king."[30]

In the midst of this grave crisis, Hipólito Unánue, the minister of finance, announced the creation of a paper money bank—the Banco Auxiliar del Papel-Moneda—to issue paper money as a means of rescuing the government from economic collapse. It was in many ways the boldest of the San Martín government's reforms, and only the second attempt in South American history to create a paper currency, but it failed utterly. The government gambled on the hope that paper money would permit the population to carry on daily market transactions while the state reserved metal currency to pay the troops, buy essential supplies from foreign ships, and keep the regime afloat. The paper issue, however, had no backing other than the word of the government, which by then was worth little. The money began to be issued in February 1822 and received no public support. Antonio Jaranco, a royalist exile, testified in February that it was "without circulation or credit." The royalist propaganda sheet *El Depositario*, published with La Serna's army, played on the public's suspicion of the whole undertaking by declaring that San Martín himself was the agent of "some usurious businessmen with whom he has been associated for four years in the enterprise of ruining our people in order to increase their private fortunes." By October 1822 even the government's own *Gaceta* allowed itself to say that the paper money "has given us some small discomfort."[31] In the same month in which the paper began to be issued, the government also began issuing a "provisional" copper coin, valued at two reales, to take the place of the silver cuartillos that had completely disappeared from circulation.[32] These new coins were preferred in the marketplace—since copper at least had some intrinsic value—and they immediately drove the paper money out of circulation. Both the paper and the copper currencies failed completely. A Spanish emigrant reported it was all a plot on the part of the leaders to line their own pockets with gold and silver, leaving the Peruvians only paper and copper in their place. Proctor said of the paper money: "Nothing, I am convinced, more disgusted the Peruvians with the independence cause."[33] In August 1822 the government ordered the withdrawal of the paper money, but the program to amortize it by collecting it in return for liens on future customs duties also failed. The government's credit was so low and the number of ships anchoring at Callao so few that holders of paper money refused to surrender even a worthless currency for a percentage of customs revenue. The royalist refugee José María Ruybál wrote that the failure of the amortization scheme clearly proved that the San Martín government was totally without probity.[34]

By the time San Martín surrendered the government of Peru to the Constituent Congress on 20 September 1822, it was clear that the first attempt to amortize the paper currency had failed. Congress then issued new paper stock in December 1822. A second attempt to amortize the paper, however, was undertaken in May 1823 during the presidency of José de la Riva Agüero. It too failed. A third attempt to collect both the paper currency and the copper coins was launched under the administration of the marqués de Torre Tagle in late 1823, and this time it succeeded. But in succeeding the amortization revealed the depth to which the independent government's finances had sunk. Torre Tagle was able to collect the paper money only by having it exchanged for copper. Then he liquidated the copper by ordering it exchanged at the rate of 75 pesos to each 100 with government notes drawn on the first of the great loans from London just then being made final. Deflated copper was employed to amortize worthless paper and then was itself redeemed by exchange at a 25 percent discount against borrowed money.

The attempts of the San Martín government to keep financing the crusade had failed. By early 1822 all was in disorder. The navy had deserted. The army was composed of slaves and conscripts whose meager salaries still cost 80 percent of the young state's total revenues. Even so, the soldiers were so rarely paid that they were selling or pawning their uniforms. Public order was disintegrating as a result of the widespread robberies and petty crimes of the armed but undisciplined soldiery. By mid-1822 the cabildo of Lima had stopped payment on its basic obligations. By September 1822 the troops were being paid only two-thirds of their salaries, and the civil employees had been paid only half of theirs since the year before. Meanwhile, the government had even recognized 6,500,000 pesos of debt inherited from the viceregal government.[35] The capital continued to suffer food shortages, lack of circulating specie, and discontent.

Furthermore, the San Martín government also lost its political credit because of its continued persecution of Spanish nationals. The Spanish civilians had been confined in the Merced Convent on 3 September 1821 when General Canterac drew near Lima. San Martín ordered their release on 18 September, and in a proclamation told the Spaniards that their confinement had been for their own safety and to prevent any of them from aiding the enemy. In the last months of 1821, however, the government, under the direction of Monteagudo, adopted a policy of more outright persecution of the Spaniards. In January 1822 several decrees ordered unmarried Spanish men to leave Peru. On 30 January the *Gaceta* editorialized that "the ingratitude of the Spaniards cannot be changed except by the use of force."[36] By February, Spanish consular officials in Rio de Janeiro reported to Madrid that "despite what [the rebels] say in their public papers the European Spaniards are persecuted in the most cruel and ignominious way," and that as a result, "the principal persons in Lima are very disgusted with San Martín and only the people of color and the lower classes are happy."[37] On 20 April 1822 San Martín's supreme delegate, Torre Tagle, instituted draconian restrictions on the freedom of movement of the Spaniards in a decree prohibiting all gatherings of two or more Spaniards, renewing the curfew against them after six o'clock in the evening (this had been in effect since 27 September 1821), denying them the use of all arms, and creating a Commission of Vigilance to supervise their activities. The penalty for any Spaniard breaking the curfew was death. A report of Francisco Xavier de Izcue to Monteagudo in April specified the quota each Spaniard was to pay in the forced contribution levied against them.[38]

The most famous Spanish victim of persecution—and one of the earliest—was the eighty-year-old archbishop Bartolomé de

Las Heras. Having refused to accompany the viceroy in his evacuation, Las Heras now fell to the arbitrary vindictiveness of Monteagudo. In a dispute over the government's expressed desire to close the religious retreat houses—which Monteagudo feared might become centers of pro-Spanish activity—the archbishop told the government that it had to accept his view that the houses were inviolate or else permit him to renounce his office. The impolitic reply of the government in early September 1821 was to accept the archbishop's resignation and order him to retire to Chancay within forty-eight hours, there to await transportation back to Spain. Las Heras bid goodby to his "esteemed friend" San Martín, thanking him for "having relieved me of a burden superior to my abilities." He arrived in Rio de Janeiro on 28 December 1821 and was joyfully received by the other Spanish emigrants. From there he went to Spain, where he died in 1823. His personal investments in the Lima Consulado were seized by the government, as were the payments owed him by various members of the clergy.[39] Dean Echagüe and the cathedral chapter assumed administration of the archdiocese for the next several years.

Several emigrants testified that the persecution of the Spaniards reached its peak in April 1822, after the defeat of the rebel forces at Yca on 7 April. The Spanish victory at Yca over the patriot army commanded by Domingo Tristan gave new hope to the royalists and deeply distressed the patriots. It was the first important field maneuver the rebels had attempted against the royalists. Miller wrote: "The moral effect was to dispel the idea, which until then had been entertained, of the superiority of the patriots; and to throw a damp over the mass of the population. . . . Union was restored in the royalist council, whilst the patriots were distracted by dissensions, and weakened by insubordination."[40] The peninsulars still living in Peru, however, paid the price for the success of royal arms. Gilbert Mathison reported that Lima was in great panic after the defeat at Yca, and that even the recluse San Martín "was now frequently seen on horseback in the streets."[41]

Among the victims of Monteagudo's persecution in the immediate wake of Yca was the popular former oidor of Lima, Pedro Mariano de Goyeneche (a creole), brother of the royalist general Manuel (conde de Guaqui) and of the bishop of Arequipa, Sebastian (future archbishop of Lima). In April 1822 he was ordered to give a special contribution of 40,000 pesos to the government to expiate the sins of his family. When he declared he did not have such money, Monteagudo ordered his house sacked, took 80,000 pesos, and sent him to jail in irons.[42] He later fled.

The long persecution of the peninsulars culminated on 2 May 1822 in an act of unparalleled violence and unprecedented abuse of human rights. The event was best described by the Englishman Gilbert Mathison. At three o'clock on the morning of 2 May government troops surrounded the houses of the remaining peninsulars and carried off at least six hundred of the men, not giving them time even to collect their personal belongings. The old and sick were carried on horseback, the rest were forced to walk. They were transferred to Callao and compelled to embark on the old merchant ship *Monteagudo* for deportation to Chile. Mathison wrote: "It was my misfortune to be a witness to this horrifying embarkation. Many showed their violent affliction at being unexpectedly forced in this way to leave their homes and families; some really had to be shoved into the boats by the soldiers' bayonets." He pointed out that many of the peninsulars had lived since childhood in Lima and considered it their home. On 3 May Mathison rode to Callao again, where he heard that two Spaniards had already died aboard the *Monteagudo*, "and that the misery that prevailed there exceeded belief." Many of the exiles were about to die of thirst, since no water had been provided for them in over a day. "To add to the horror of the scene, boats full of women and children surrounded the ship on all sides and filled the air with lamentations, vainly imploring permission to embrace their husbands, friends and family members one more time." Returning to Lima on 4 May, he found the road between the port and the city filled with carriages, horsemen, and pedestrians, as the city's inhabitants—apparently overcome either by their hatred of the peninsulars or by remorse—flocked to Callao to bid goodbye to the exiles. The government issued a decree announcing that the forced deportations were "a solemn act of expiation and a memorable example of vengeance" against the resident Spaniards for their irreconcilable refusal to adhere to independence. On 10 May the *Monteagudo* sailed for Valparaíso with its unhappy passengers, after two hundred of the deportees had been allowed to charter different ships for Rio de Janeiro.[43]

Stevenson, an avid supporter of Cochrane and therefore an out-spoken critic of San Martín, verifies every detail of Mathison's narrative, adding that those men not sent to Chile were the ones who could afford to buy the passports San Martín offered them at prices of 1,000 to 10,000 pesos each.[44] San Martín had repeatedly guaranteed the Spaniards' safety; yet he now condemned them to exile and financial ruin.

The people of Lima blamed Monteagudo for the persecution of the Spaniards and for the other unpopular actions of the ad-ministration. And it is true that Monteagudo was the most out-spoken opponent of the Spaniards in the government, having declared openly that his object was their total destruction. De-spite Paz Soldán's rather extreme claim that "Monteagudo with his politics acquired more triumphs against the Spaniards than did Cochrane with his ships," he soon became hated among all levels of Lima society.[45] He was particularly suspect because of his open advocacy of a monarchy, because of his social Jacobinism, and because he was an Argentinian, an outsider. No one was safe from his despotism. The Englishman Gilbert Mathi-son wrote: "Under the name of liberty and patriotism the existing government exercised the most despotic power and was obeyed more from fear than from love or true respect. A complete es-pionage system was maintained, and in place of talking freely about politics . . . the greatest caution and reserve was observed everywhere." Visiting Monteagudo, Mathison remarked that he spoke good English and was a good negotiator, but that he had a passion for power.[46] In July 1822, while San Martín was attending his famous interview with Bolívar at Guayaquil, a popular peti-tion signed by many of the foremost citizens of Lima was pre-sented to the cabildo asking for Monteagudo's removal from office. On the night of 25 July, and again the next day, the people surrounded the palace and city hall shouting for his fall. The cabildo approved the petition and urged the army not to fire on the demonstrators, pointing out that this was not sedition. It sent Francisco J. Mariátegui and two regidors to confer with San Martín's supreme delegate, Torre Tagle, about the people's de-mand. On 26 July Torre Tagle removed Monteagudo from the ministry and placed him under house arrest. To protect him from mounting public anger, he was quietly sent away from Lima on 30 July. Two and a half years later Monteagudo returned to Lima, where he was murdered on 28 January 1825 by a Negro water-carrier. Ricardo Palma and others have charged that it was a political assassination ordered, or at least permitted, by Bolívar or his minister Sánchez Carrión. There is no proof of the assertion.[47]

Some of the popular anger toward Monteagudo was directed against San Martín as well, and there is no question that Monteagudo cannot be made to bear all the blame for the government's arbitrary treatment of the Spaniards. Vargas Ugarte says that San Martín himself had previously proposed that the Spaniards should be made to pay for the war and that he was predisposed to acts of hostility against them. Basil Hall declared that, although the persecution of the Spaniards was largely Monteagudo's doing, San Martín still had to bear the blame; "It will not avail San Martín's friends to say they were the acts of another, for he was notoriously the main-spring of the whole government."[48]

The net effect of the San Martín government's failures in both economics and politics was a flood of resentment and opposition from among the Peruvians themselves. Basil Hall noted one critical fact about Lima's response to independence: "The Limenians, long pampered by luxury and security, and now for the first time fairly awakened to the real miseries and dangers of life, could not all at once acquire the faculty of balancing motives."[49] Here was the fundamental weakness of San Martín's fledgling state. Independence based entirely on self-interest would have to satisfy these aspirations. Ramón del Valle reported that by the end of 1821 the nobility and the middle class were already completely disillusioned by their failure to obtain positions, "and I do not believe those two classes are very attached to the government." Consular reports from Rio de Janeiro assured Madrid that "all the nobility . . . aspire to nothing else but to see the Spanish flag wave, in order . . . to incite rebellion against the celebrated liberator whom they hate in the extreme." Cristóval Domingo, a refugee, reported that the public indifference at San Martín's proclamation of his Provisional Statute on 8 October 1821 meant that he had lost much of his public support. José María Ruybál, another refugee, reported that "the most informed Peruvians, who had adhered to San Martín, disillusioned and convinced that he is not a new Washington, . . . generally abhor him." Gilbert Mathison's impressions in April and May 1822 were identical:

"Almost all the inhabitants [of Lima] have been more or less affected in their fortunes; and it is not a surprising fact that the government that occasioned their misfortunes and that was incapable of alleviating them . . . should be unpopular." He said that the number of those who had been financially ruined was very great and included not only Spaniards but all those creoles who had been clients or dependents of the Spaniards. He thought the fundamental fault was the government's sheer arbitrariness, which endangered the security and property even of the English merchants. John Miller summarized all these feelings when he wrote, "The people of Lima . . . grew tired of their liberators."[50]

San Martín could not possibly have failed to understand that his crusade was over and his personal leadership repudiated. No wonder he chose to give way to Bolívar. In January 1822 he announced his intention of meeting with Bolívar at Guayaquil and turned the government over to his supreme delegate, Torre Tagle, a weak and inept leader. San Martín left for Guayaquil in February but returned to Lima when he heard that Bolívar had decided to continue the campaign of Quito. Arriving in Lima on 3 March, he signed a decree keeping Torre Tagle at the head of the administration. In essence, therefore, San Martín separated himself from active political leadership six months before the actual meeting at Guayaquil, which took place in July 1822. The facts of life led this pragmatist to realize that aid from outside Peru was necessary to complete the independence struggle. The Bolívar movement, supported as it was by the grudging but nonetheless impressive aid of Gran Colombia, remained the best hope. The short public statement San Martín issued on 24 August 1822, after his return from meeting the Liberator at Guayaquil, reflected this unavoidable reality. It stated simply that Bolívar was going to send aid—troops and arms.[51] In the context of the moment, that was enough. It was a far more important question than whether San Martín himself would continue in the leadership.

On 20 September 1822, the Congress that San Martín had earlier called finally met. It consisted of fifty-one deputies representing the eleven districts into which Peru had been divided. Five of the eleven districts were still entirely in royalist hands (Cuzco, Arequipa, Huamanga, Puno, and Huancavelica) and had to be represented by delegates native to those regions but living in Lima. San Martín formally turned all his powers over to Congress. He declared to his friends: "Today is a day of true happiness for me. I have been relieved of a burden that I could not carry." When Tomás Guido went that night to see him, San Martín told him he was leaving for Chile. Guido urged him to stay, but he replied that he had to leave, adding; "Bolívar and I do not fit together in Peru."[52] At ten o'clock that night he embraced Guido, rode to Callao, and boarded the brigantine *Belgrano*, leaving Peru forever.

As the rebels in Lima sank into chaos and inactivity, La Serna's armies in the interior were also paralyzed by the total absence of communications from the mother country and by the sheer effort of trying to keep an army together in the vast interior. But La Serna remained confident of the possibility of ultimate royal victory. In March 1822 he reported to Spain the receipt of the first news from the peninsula in a year. In September 1822 he wrote from Cuzco urging the peninsula not to recognize the independence of America, as he had heard it was contemplating. He said he could still hold Peru, especially since he had given up the albatross of Lima, although he insisted that Peru could be reconquered only with naval support on the coast. Again in March 1822 he wrote from Cuzco to explain that in the disrupted state of Peru he had found it impossible to put all the provisions of the Spanish Constitution into effect and that it must not be expected of him. All three of these letters were intercepted by the rebels.[53]

Most royalists who actually accompanied La Serna in his retreat to the interior upheld his claim that only the abandonment of Lima had saved the royal cause from total destruction. A lively propaganda war was conducted over this question, with the public proclamations of La Serna often pointing out that the rebels had taken Lima only because he allowed them to; that possession of the capital would profit them little; and that he could retake it any time he wished. In reply to the viceroy's claim that Lima had been reduced to a "sad and horrible state" under the rebels, San Martín declared that the enemies were liars and that La Serna and Canterac would soon fall.[54] The publicist Gaspar Rico fled Lima with the viceregal armies and, making use of a small printing press carried by the troops, began publication of a royalist propaganda sheet called *El Depositario*. From 1821 until March 1824, one hundred and seven issues of this periodical appeared, churning out unsophisticated propaganda, exulting over the open dissent within the ranks of the rebel leadership, citing the apathetic public spirit that gripped Lima, and insulting San Martín and other leaders.[55] With Rico's help the royalists also published at Huancayo and Cuzco a *Gaceta del Gobierno legítimo del Perú*. In a letter to Spain in December 1821, La Serna explained that the low quality of the royalist propaganda was due to the loss of two printers, the supply of ink, and much of the type at Jauja. In 1824 La Serna testified in Rico's behalf that he was "the only state employee who accompanied me in my departure from Lima."[56]

The end of the San Martín era found Viceroy La Serna reporting to Spain that his army corps were filled but he was short of weapons. He asked for several thousand rifles and bayonets, and of course—in conjunction with every other royalist—for a large naval contingent. La Serna added, "and quick, quick."[57] When two French ships filled with Peruvian emigrants reached Spain in May 1822, one royalist reported that everyone agreed that if one ship of the line and two frigates could be sent to Lima "the destruction of San Martín's army would not encounter the slightest difficulty." In the same month the emigrant oidor, Juan Bazo y Berri, reported that Lima could be retaken at any time because San Martín had an army of only 6,000 men and "they are all Negroes taken by force from the haciendas, without the least discipline, and very discontented."[58]

Indeed, Bazo y Berri and the other eyewitnesses were correct in their prediction that the royalists could retake Lima anytime they wished. That was proved when the royal armies reoccupied the capital briefly in June 1823 and again for a much longer stay in February 1824. The rebels were simply too weak to resist. But three things were necessary for the royalists to effect a complete reconquest of Peru. They needed not only to continue controlling the highlands, but also to retake the capital, while at the same time reestablishing royal naval dominance on Peru's coasts. The first two they could do, the third they could not. Peninsular Spain, wracked by the domestic struggle between liberals and conservatives and the subsequent invasion in 1823 of a French army to restore Ferdinand VII to full power, was unable to send naval aid. The rebels, of course, also had to gain complete superiority in all three areas. They did control the sea, and they normally controlled Lima and its region, but they lacked the offensive capacity to drive the royalists out of the highlands. The English naval officer Alexander Caldcleugh, who visited Peru in 1819 to 1821, wrote of this period: "On examining the map it can be seen that this is a war entirely without recourse, and therefore, barring unforeseen circumstances, it will have to be long and full of ups and downs."[59] If the stalemate proved anything at all, it was that only a military solution remained. The Peruvians were not merely reactionary or shortsighted in their refusal to give wholehearted support to the cause of independence. The shattering failures of the independent regime—most of all its inability to make room for Peruvian participation—gradually convinced many that they really did have more in common with the Spaniards than with the pillaging Chileans, Argentinians, slaves, and mulattos who now seemed in control of their country. The stalemate continued and deepened.

Chapter 9

# Chaos and the Military Solution

IN THE TWO YEARS after San Martín's withdrawal, the independent part of Peru lapsed into chaos so intense that even the incomparable Bolívar at first despaired. When the government passed into the hands of Peruvian leaders, the state was crippled by internal factionalism, bankruptcy, and treason. By late 1823 Peruvian independence presented to the world a truly pathetic picture. Separate armies existed of Peruvians, Chileans, Colombians, and Argentinians. The political state was leaderless, with two different men claiming to be president of the republic. Congress collapsed under the pressure. The arrival of Bolívar in September 1823—a full year after San Martín's departure—added a new element to the mixture, one that many Peruvian leaders feared and tried to subvert. As Bolívar himself testified: "Peruvian affairs have reached a peak of anarchy. Only the enemy army is well organized, united, strong, energetic, and capable."[1] Bolívar's assessment was correct, for the royalist army under La Serna and his commanders had kept itself intact in the highlands and, making use of the considerable support for the royal cause that existed among the Indians, the mestizos, and the few whites of the interior and south, offered an ever-present threat to the cause of independence. Indeed, for several months in 1824— during the period when Lima was again in royal hands and while Bolívar lay sick at Pativilca—the royalists actually regained control of all except one province of Peru. They came very close to winning the war and smashing the independent regime. Only the leadership of Bolívar—unflinching and sometimes brutal—eventually stopped the rot and organized an effective patriot fighting force. Even so, independence came only as the result of a military contest, and the long siege of the royalist forces and their supporters at Callao throughout 1825 and into January 1826 proved once again that many Peruvians—including some of the most important leaders of the independent government—had still not committed themselves to independence. Peruvians never did decide. The independent regime had been founded at Lima in 1821 by default, it came close to being utterly eliminated in 1824, and by 1825 it had won a military campaign and had defeated the royal army; but true commitment had never been present.

Every author writing on Peruvian independence has commented, in one form or another, upon the essential phenomenon of Peru's inability to support independence. Masur ascribed it to the treason of the creole upper class: "When circumstances seemed to favor the cause of freedom they followed it; when the barometer of the new cause dropped, they quickly turned and, elusive as mercury, followed the Spaniards." Lynch pointed to the same factor: "The creoles were committed to neither cause; seeking only to preserve their own position, they awaited the victory of the strongest." Basadre ascribed it to the conflict between the continentalism of Bolívar and the nationalism of Peruvians, making a strong case to show that many Peruvian leaders viewed Bolívar as a new Napoleon, combined with the "anguish and the disillusion of the aristocracy facing a war that seemed a continuous carnage accompanied by endless exactions and permanent anarchy." Paz Soldán, with the outspoken fervor of a man who was witnessing the subsequent turmoils of the Peruvian state, blamed it on the treason and ignorance of the nobles. Vargas Ugarte attributed it, fundamentally, to the inability of Peru to support two contending armies and to the material devastation caused by the war from 1821 to 1824.[2]

From September 1822, when San Martín retired from Peru, to September 1823, when Bolívar arrived, the government of the independent regime was in the hands of the Peruvian aristocrats who had so long desired to hold power. They established three separate administrations, all three of which failed to hold the government together or to strengthen independence. Congress, to which San Martín surrendered power, created an executive, the Governing Junta, which consisted of three undistinguished men—José de La Mar, a former royalist officer; Felipe Antonio Alvarado, noted only as the brother of General Rudesindo Alvarado, general-in-chief of the patriot army of the south; and Manuel Salazar y Baquíjano, the conde de Vista Florida. The junta could do nothing, for its powers were too limited and the times needed energetic and active leadership. General conditions remained very bad. The government had no money, troops and civil employees were not paid, criminals infested Lima and its outskirts, the army of the center remained inactive, desertion was endemic, the navy was insubordinate and mutinous. Forced loans could be collected only with threats of confiscation and exile.[3] Writing in November 1822, the English Protestant minister James Thomson, who came to Lima to set up a Lancastrian school system and to distribute copies of the Bible, reported: "At the moment there exists a great anxiety in the government for lack of money. . . . This seems to be the principal obstacle impeding the general independence of Peru."[4] Finally, on 21 January 1823, the Congress's major military offensive collapsed with the defeat at Moquegua of the first Intermedios expedition. A royalist army encamped at Jauja, within easy reach of the capital. Parliamentary rule could not stand the pressure. The patriot army urged Congress to appoint a stronger executive and enforced its demands with threatening troop movements. On 27 February 1823, therefore, Congress did away with the Governing Junta and appointed José de la Riva Agüero as first president of the republic.[5]

Riva Agüero's administration lasted less than four months. Yet in that short period its accomplishments were more than those of either its predecessor or its successor. Riva Agüero, a long-time supporter of independence and a dedicated nationalist, concentrated on restoring the fast-disappearing military order of the republic. He immediately invited Bolívar to send a Colombian army to aid in the cause of independence, despite his intense fears of the impact of Bolívar's involvement in Peruvian affairs. An army of 4,000 Colombian troops arrived under command of Bolívar's chief lieutenant, Antonio José de Sucre, but Bolívar himself as yet forbore to enter the maelstrom of Peruvian affairs. Within Peru itself Riva Agüero created and dispatched the second

Intermedios expedition, composed of 5,000 troops. He reorganized the decadent navy, placing it under command of Jorge Guise. He created new battalions in several parts of the country and founded the Academia Militar. To help rescue the government from total bankruptcy, Riva Agüero presided over the first of the loans from London, negotiated by Juan García del Río and Diego Paroissien, who had originally been sent to Europe by San Martín. The first loan was for 1.2 million pounds. Riva Agüero also sent agents to Chile and to Buenos Aires in search of loans, but with little result.[6] The president even offered Viceroy La Serna a two-month armistice and treaty of peace, but the viceroy, certain of the imminent disintegration of the republic, rebuffed the suggestion.

Well might the viceroy bide his time, for the collapse of the republic was well advanced. Riva Agüero, who had been imposed by military pressure, did not even have the support of all the Congress. When the second Intermedios expedition departed from Lima, the capital itself was left with few defenses. Sucre, already on hand to send eyewitness reports to Bolívar, told his leader:

The army has no chiefs; the country is as divided as the troops of the different states; Congress and the Executive are in discord and this will not have a happy result; there are no supplies for the troops and the little that can be acquired is poorly used. . . . In short, a thousand evils show themselves to presage that all will be destroyed and in the disintegration the Colombian division will be part of the ruins.[7]

Seeing his opportunity, royalist General Canterac immediately moved down upon Lima. Unwilling to risk the newly arrived Colombian division in a futile defense of the city, on 17 June 1823 Sucre withdrew his forces to Callao, where he joined Riva Agüero, Congress, and the other civil political authorities who had already taken refuge there. The next day Canterac reoccupied Lima.

The civilian population of Lima responded to the royal reoccupation with what the cabildo called a "general emigration." This is confirmed by other sources. James Thomson said 10,000 persons fled Lima, and the British business agent Robert Proctor said that the only residents who stayed in Lima were those who were in no way identified with the patriot cause. Well might the civilians flee, for the royalists imposed a forced contribution of 300,000 pesos upon the city.[8] Nonetheless, not all the capital's residents resisted the Spaniards. A number of officials remained at their posts—for which they were later removed from office—and when the royalists departed a number of Limeños went with them.

Canterac, discovering once more that Lima was not defensible, abandoned it again in less than a month, on 16 July. When his army left the city it took what silver it could find from the churches, together with the machinery in the Casa de Moneda and many of the books and documents in the National Library—a total booty valued, according to Thomson, at more than 2 million pesos. When the royalists withdrew toward Cuzco, a number of Limeños threw themselves on royal protection and fled with them.[9] This was the second time Canterac proved he could come and go from Lima as he liked, and the second time the royalists voluntarily abandoned the capital on the grounds that it was a military liability.

While the patriots were taking refuge in Callao, Congress formally deposed Riva Agüero as president. Sucre was made supreme commander of the combined armies, and on 17 July Congress made the marqués de Torre Tagle chief executive. On 16 August he was formally created president of the republic by the part of Congress that continued to meet in Lima, but after Bolívar's arrival in Peru the next month Torre Tagle functioned merely as a figurehead in charge of the civilian government. Riva Agüero, meanwhile, transferred to Trujillo together with his supporters in the Congress, where he steadfastly refused to give up the presidential office or to recognize Torre Tagle. Torre Tagle replied by declaring Riva Agüero an outlaw and then by offering a reward to anyone who captured the tyrant dead or alive.[10] Peru now had two presidents, each of whom refused to recognize the legitimacy of the other. Torre Tagle proceeded to order the suspension or removal from office of all government employees who had remained in Lima during the month of Canterac's occupation, including the president of the High Court of Justice and several judges and departmental directors. This only guaranteed the further deterioration of civil government in Lima, already greatly disrupted. The interim president of the department of

Lima, the regidor José Freyre, had fled to join his benefactor Riva Agüero; he was replaced as president of the department by the alcalde Juan de Echeverría y Ulloa.[11]

In the outlying vicinity of Lima the situation had reached a new low of confusion and disruption. The patriot government, while it was located in Callao, had ordered the killing of two oxen from every hacienda in the region of the capital to provide meat. The hacendados and the Lima city council begged for relief, charging that this policy would destroy not only the output of the farms but its occupants as well. There was no help for the hacendados, however. Before another six months had passed the majority of them had been totally ruined. In January 1824 a hacendado from Miraflores, near Lima, reported that the army's extortions had left him without slaves, cattle, mules, or seed. An outside witness estimated that the losses to this one hacienda in only one year amounted to 34,400 pesos. The hacendado asked to have a debt he owed the government excused. The fiscal of the Ministry of Finance replied that the problem of the supplicant was no different from that of a hundred other hacendados; his request should not be allowed or else the others would clamor for the same relief.[12] Vergara Arias cites many other cases of haciendas that were destroyed by patriot montoneros who preyed on outlying farms to the point that it was often impossible to distinguish patriot guerrilla forces from bands of looters and common criminals. Proctor testified that the Spaniards took so many mules from Lima after their brief occupation in 1823 "that it cost more to carry merchandise from Callao to Lima than to bring it from England."[13]

Torre Tagle proceeded to organize a government, and he appointed as ministers Francisco Valdivieso for Foreign Affairs, Juan de Berindoaga for War and Navy, and Dionisio Vizcarra for Finance.[14] But as the time for Bolívar's arrival drew near it was clear that the independent state was absolutely bankrupt. All the fundamental sources of wealth had been exhausted. Special contributions continued to be decreed, of course, but they were simply not collected. Bolívar himself, shortly after his arrival, noted: "Lima is a large pleasant city which once was rich."[15] Robbery and civil unrest were uncontrolled. Major charitable agencies verged on collapse. The Lima public orphanage announced that it was unable to buy milk for the children and was about to close its doors. In November 1823 the dean of the arch-diocese reported that the cathedral had no money left for salaries, music, or sacred rites. Even the Colombian auxiliary troops suffered from lack of arms, clothes, and equipment. As a result, they joined the other undisciplined forces in robbery and assault.[16]

All pretense to government credit or orderly borrowing by a sovereign power was abandoned. A forced loan for 150,000 pesos decreed against the merchants in August had to be reduced to 80,000 pesos later in the month, and even that sum caused considerable vexation for the people. In November, Torre Tagle negotiated another loan from a number of merchants that proved the government's desperation. The contract with the group of private merchants called for them to grant the government 50,000 pesos in cash and 150,000 pesos in goods, in return for a 300,000 peso lien against future customs. This effectively absorbed all future customs revenue, and the man who held the contract, José Ignacio Palacios, was even given the right to appoint his own customs officers. In September, Torre Tagle asked Chile for a new loan of 2 million pesos against the London loan. Chile refused, having already lent Peru 1.5 million pesos. The government had already drawn more than 1.5 million pesos against the London loan, while in the Riva Agüero period alone it had issued new contracts for supplies and arms to a value of 2.5 million pesos.[17]

Peru now entered a sort of nether world. Words are inadequate to describe the gravity of the situation or the extent of the anarchy.[18] From July 1823 until December 1824, the patriot cause seemed close to defeat. After the second Intermedios expedition was defeated and destroyed, the rump government of Riva Agüero in Trujillo made this clear by opening negotiations for a settlement with Viceroy La Serna. Riva Agüero at first proposed the celebration of an armistice of eighteen months, during which time the definite peace with Spain would be arranged and joint Spanish-Peruvian forces would break up the rebel forces of the Lima government. Viceroy La Serna, encouraged by the collapse of the rebels and not able to decide which of the two presidents was the legitimate one with whom to negotiate, decided not to accept Riva Agüero's offer but appointed a representative to go to Trujillo to talk with him. In November 1823 Riva Agüero proposed a complete sellout, offering to establish a kingdom in Peru under a Spanish prince chosen by Ferdinand VII, with a provisional regency under La Serna, and based on the Spanish constitution. It would have been a type of independence—there is no question of that—but La Serna had no chance to reply to the proposal.

In the midst of the confusion one thing had become undeniable: the presence of Simón Bolívar himself was now required to prevent the total collapse of independence. Responding to the frequent appeals from the Peruvians, Bolívar sailed for Lima, arriving on 1 September 1823, more than a year after San Martín had made way for him. Despite the intense suspicion many Peruvians felt toward him—many of them viewed the Colombian president as a Napoleonic usurper—all the civil and ecclesiastical authorities turned out to greet him.[19] Bolívar allowed Congress to make him military dictator and commander of all the various armies in Peru. He immediately encountered the frustration of trying to deal with Peruvian suspicion of his motives, and he wrote: "I shall always be the foreigner to most people and I shall always arouse jealousy and distrust in these gentlemen. . . . I have already regretted that I came here."[20] Indeed, when Bolívar tried to initiate talks with Riva Agüero in Trujillo his approach was rejected by the rebellious ex-president, who viewed Bolívar as a tyrant and usurper. Torre Tagle was no less suspicious but depended too much on the Colombian forces to act freely.

Shortly after Bolívar's arrival the Peruvian army of the south disintegrated. Determined to secure the north if possible, the Liberator traveled toward Trujillo to try to effect a reconciliation with Riva Agüero. Before he could arrive there, however, Riva Agüero was overthrown, on 25 November 1823, by one of his own military aides, Antonio Gutiérrez de la Fuente. Convinced that Riva Agüero's negotiations with the royalists constituted open treason, de la Fuente marched to Trujillo and deposed him. The former president was imprisoned in Guayaquil, where he was eventually freed by Vice-Admiral Guise, commander of the Peruvian navy. He then went into exile in Europe.

After the disappearance of Riva Agüero, Bolívar returned to Lima. Finding it impossible to improve the military and supply situation there, he determined in late 1823 to move to the north, where he could regroup an army free of the pestilential anarchy of Lima. He wrote: "Providence only . . . can create order out of this chaos."[21] Traveling north by sea, Bolívar fell gravely ill. On 1

January 1824 he was carried from his ship to the little harbor of Pativilca, thirty miles north of Lima. There he lay for two months, fighting for his life against the first attack of the tuberculosis that eventually killed him. From his sickbed on 12 January he informed Torre Tagle that he would resign and return to Bogotá if fresh supplies and money were not sent to his Colombian army of the north within one month.[22]

And now, in the first months of 1824, the inevitable collapse of the patriot cause occurred. With the armies deserting, with the Liberator desperately trying to recover his health, the final straw came when Torre Tagle emulated his erstwhile opponent Riva Agüero in committing treason. Torre Tagle sent his minister of war, Berindoaga, to negotiate a settlement with the royalists. Bolívar was not opposed to a truce, which would allow time for the 8,000 Colombian reinforcements he had ordered to arrive. Torre Tagle, however, apparently contemplated more than a mere cease-fire. Berindoaga went to Jauja to talk with the royalists. The talks came to nothing, however, and Berindoaga returned to Lima, where Torre Tagle informed him that he and the vice-president, Diego de Aliaga, had opened negotiations of their own with the royalists, this time without Bolívar's knowledge or consent.[23] Torre Tagle's representative traveled to Yca to confer with the royalists who had recently taken the town, saying that the president desired to unite with the Spaniards in order to resist the Colombian usurper Bolívar. Whether an actual conspiracy for the royal seizure of Lima with Torre Tagle's connivance was formulated is not clear. At any rate, General Canterac, leading the royal forces that were advancing toward Lima, understood he would have Torre Tagle's support. Bolívar, still at Pativilca, understood the same, and he ordered Torre Tagle, Aliaga, and Berindoaga—the president, vice-president, and minister of war of the republic—to be arrested and sent to him. Torre Tagle interpreted this as an order for his execution, and he panicked. What was he to do now?

The answer came quickly. In the midst of these Machiavellian negotiations the patriot troops in Callao—now the only usable forces on hand in the capital—had been ignored by the civil authorities. Motivated by their lack of pay and unwilling to transfer to the north as ordered by Bolívar, the Argentinian and Chilean forces garrisoning Callao's forts mutinied on 5 February 1824, under the leadership of a sergeant named Dámaso Moyano. Unable to attract any attention to their privation, on 10 February the mutineers released all the royalist prisoners in the jails at Callao, and one of them, Colonel José de Casariego, assumed command of the place, raising the Spanish flag. Meantime, in preparation for the expected advance of royalist forces, Bolívar had ordered General Enrique Martínez to retire from the capital, leaving it undefended, and taking with him anything that might be useful to the enemy, including the horses and clothes of the civilians. Bolívar appointed General Mariano Necochea, an Argentinian, to command the capital. On 10 February Congress went into recess; on 17 February Torre Tagle turned his command over to Necochea; on 27 February—again motivated by the impossibility of defending the capital—Necochea abandoned Lima. Two days later the royalists, under General Juan Antonio Monet, occupied the city. This time the republic was in complete collapse. The civilians, with Callao denied them as a refuge, were unable to flee the Spaniards.

The disorder and chaos of that last week of February 1824 was on a scale Lima had never before experienced. Robert Proctor left a detailed account of the terror provoked by the mutiny at Callao. A few days before the mutiny, Proctor and his wife had traveled to Chorrillos—the "Brighton of Lima," as he described it—to take their oldest child to the pure air of that seaside resort. Hearing in the meantime that their newborn infant, left behind in Lima, had been taken critically ill, he and his wife rushed back to Lima on 27 February. It took them many hours to travel the few miles' distance, dodging royalist troops, mutinous patriots, bandits, and guerrillas. At the walls of Lima a band of patriot soldiers tried to force them to detour to royalist-held Callao. After bribing the soldiers, they entered the city and found to their horror that it was already in the hands of the mutinous Callao garrison, Necochea having retreated only that morning. Proctor's landladies, royalists like so many other propertied persons, were "overwhelmed by pleasure at the entry of their royalist friends," and only with effort could they be restrained from walking out into the streets to greet their liberators. The mutineers, however, were not rescuers but looters. As night fell, Lima embarked on a nightmare. Proctor stood on his balcony and watched the fighting swirl about him as rampaging soldiers from Callao sacked houses and shops at will. Mounted grenadiers smashed down the doors of neighboring houses and stripped them bare. "We saw much of what went on. . . . It was a horrible night for Lima." The next morning he ventured into the plaza, where he watched the officers of the mutineers shooting the looters without hearing or trial, and he noted that among those executed was the innocent servant of an English friend of his. "Everyone fervently prayed now for the entry of some respectable force, even though it be the enemy, for protection." That same night Proctor's house in Chorrillos was looted by Callao troops, and his child and the nursemaid were forced at gunpoint to reveal the hiding place of the valuables that had been transferred there for safekeeping. The robbers carried off the plate and valuables in bags made from the family's clothing. After smashing all the furniture in the house, the looters fled. The child and servant returned to Lima and reported that the highway was filled with bandit montoneros who insulted the servant girl and threw lighted matches at them through the carriage windows. Two days later the royal army of 3,500 well-disciplined men—Spaniards, creoles, Indians, and blacks—entered Lima, and the distracted and terrified population, forgetting all politics and politicians, silently watched their arrival.[24] The main body of royal forces marched on to Callao but left 200 soldiers behind to patrol the city.

The royalist General Monet offered amnesty to any inhabitant of Lima who would support the restored royalists. In the heat of the moment, and in a mad dash to save their own necks, almost the entire leadership of the republic went over. Since the royalists had refused Torre Tagle's request to regard him as a prisoner of war, he went over to their side instead. Following the lead of the president of the republic, others rushed to save themselves. They included the vice-president, Diego de Aliaga; Carlos Pedemonte, president of Congress and bishop of Trujillo, the patriots' choice for archbishop of Lima; Juan de Berindoaga, minister of war; the president of the department of Lima; various congressmen; many civil employees; and more than 240 military chiefs, together with many distinguished citizens.[25] The conde de Villar de Fuente— former head of the Consulado in royalist days—became governor of the city. There was no patriot army left; the royalists surrounded the city and were taking the provinces. Independence appeared lost.

Basadre makes a good case that the creole aristocrats who went over to the royalists were motivated chiefly by their exhaustion with the war and by the apparent impossibility of winning it. When Bolívar arrived and took leadership from them, they began to speak of the Liberator's regime in terms of "slavery," "tyranny," and "despotism." Viewing the War of Independence as nothing more than a civil war between Spaniards and Colombians, they determined that they were, after all, more closely aligned spiritually and culturally with the Spaniards. Their class prejudices led them to view the rough Colombian soldiers as their enemies, the cultivated royalists as their peers. Torre Tagle wrote Berindoaga: "I have resolved myself in my heart to be more a Spaniard than Don Fernando."[26] At Pativilca, Bolívar—faced with the defection of the entire leadership of the patriot cause—poured out his anger toward the Peruvians. "On all sides I hear the sounds of disaster. My era is that of catastrophe. Everything comes to life and perishes before my eyes as though struck by lightning."[27]

The extent of the turnabout in Lima was far greater than a mere temporary reoccupation by the royalists. The Spaniards held Lima from February until December 1824, with occasional retreats to Callao when patriot forces drew near. Callao was the bastion, and it remained in royalist hands without interruption until January 1826. General José Ramón Rodil held Callao and was governor and intendant. In Lima life returned to something resembling normality in the good old days of the viceroyalty. It is true that Viceroy La Serna remained in Cuzco, but in Lima life was much the same as before. The Consulado was reorganized under its former consuls Francisco Xavier Izcue and Manuel Exhelme and pledged its support to Rodil and the "legitimate cause." The cabildo met (though its acts have disappeared; probably they were later lost in Callao) and, most important, it consisted of many of the same members as in 1820. Such stalwart "republicans" as Juan de Echeverría (Torre Tagle's president of the department of Lima), Francisco Moreyra (the liberal of the 1812–14 period), the marqués de Montemira (son of the field marshal La Serna had left in command of Lima in 1821), and even the firebrand young radical of the 1810s the conde de la Vega del Ren sat placidly on the cabildo and collaborated with the royalists. The cabildo publicly thanked Rodil for creating a mobile column under Colonel Mateo Ramírez to defend the city from the rebel guerrilla bands that terrorized the vicinity. The royalist propaganda sheet *Triunfo del Callao* announced that perfect harmony reigned between the military authorities and the civil authorities of Lima and its environs.[28] Even the Protestant Thomson was allowed to keep open his Lancastrian school. It had 230 students and was housed in the former Dominican college.[29]

And in the most extraordinary act of all, on 6 March Torre Tagle issued a public manifesto, edited by Berindoaga, calling on the citizens to support the royalists:

> The tyrant Bolívar and his indecent satellites have wanted to enslave Peru and make this opulent territory a subject of Colombia.
>
> Peruvians: Bolívar is the greatest monster that has existed in this land. He is the enemy of all honorable men, of all those who oppose his ambitions. The national army offers you constant security, it has been joined by the leading authorities, the most distinguished men of the country.
>
> Men of all classes who live in Peru, unite and come to the salvation of the land that Bolívar wants to convert into a desert.[30]

In response to this plea, so many deserters came to join the royalists that they were able to create a volunteer Cuerpo de Cívicos of 600 men to keep order in the city.[31]

During the year of royal administration of Lima, several forced donations and loans were taken among the citizens, the 5 percent tax on urban real estate was reestablished, the customs was reopened, and various other sources of revenue were found. The royalists collected at Lima 511,644 pesos—all in silver—during the year. That was not, of course, on a par with revenues before 1820, but it was not bad in the circumstances. Lima spent almost all that sum on its own military expenses and pledged a further 238,000 pesos to the royalist army of the north. The naval headquarters at Callao spent 334,000 pesos more on the royal naval squadron that was now gathered. The squadron consisted of one ship of the line, one heavily armed corvette, three brigantines, and several transport and support ships, a total of ten vessels.[32] This force was sufficient to protect Callao but not to face open encounters with the combined naval forces of Peru, Chile, and Colombia that on the whole continued to command the coast. The Spanish fleet remained under the protection of Callao's forts until the Battle of Ayacucho, whereupon it abandoned American waters. The Peruvian squadron under Guise had established a blockade of Callao, but apparently it was not possible to hold it firm at all times. At any rate, the land forces thrown up by Bolívar under Colonel Luis Urdaneta to prevent communications between Lima and the royalists in the highlands were not successful. The royalists in Callao were able to come out of the forts to provision themselves, twice undertaking sallies into the Valley of Chancay, where the patriot militia and montoneros abandoned the field. Similarly, the outguards of the occupation forces in Lima ventured into the countryside in May and July without being stopped by the patriots.[33]

Even the Lima Casa de Moneda churned back into action under the royalists. Its new director was none other than the former vice-president Diego de Aliaga. He reported to Rodil in April that the mint was completely ruined but that he could make it serviceable again after some repairs. Incredible as it may seem—given that the mint was the first target of each of Lima's occupiers—Aliaga actually got it producing again. In May General Canterac in Huancayo sent Viceroy La Serna two pesos newly minted in Lima. Nonetheless, in June Viceroy La Serna decreed the creation of a new Casa de Moneda in Cuzco, because as long as Bolívar remained on Peruvian soil he did not wish to depend entirely on the reactivated mint in Lima. Furthermore, the mines at Cerro de Pasco, which supplied Lima, were not producing, whereas mines were active in the provinces of Cuzco and Puno, under royal control and closer to Cuzco. In recognition of what it apparently perceived as its increased status, in April the cabildo of Cuzco formally asked Spain to declare Cuzco the capital of Peru. The financial affairs of the royal forces were sufficiently stable that Rodil began granting permissions in Callao for the export of cash on foreign merchant ships, whereas in March Bolívar ordered a complete ban on the export of gold and silver from the territory under his control.[34]

By the end of March 1824 the powers of the patriots were at their lowest ebb. In that month Bolívar established his headquarters in Trujillo and watched more or less helplessly as royal forces took most of the rest of the country. Bolívar actually controlled only one province, though to be sure it was the one best situated for his purpose, which was to keep his army intact until the expected reinforcements could arrive from Colombia. For the time being he was forced to order his Peruvian troops to pitch their camps in the north of the province and the Colombians to camp in the south, thus preventing the Peruvians from going over to the enemy and the Colombians from deserting back home. His only immediate purpose was to wait, to survive, and to keep the army from disintegrating like the Chilean army in the south of Peru. He wrote: "I expect much of time. . . . What matters to us after all is to keep intact at any cost."[35]

La Serna, meanwhile, did not let down his guard. At no time was he prepared to predict success. But there was a certain air of cautious optimism about his letter to Spain in March 1824. Ferdinand VII had been restored to full absolutist powers in December 1823. La Serna now wrote to say that of all the dangerous elements he had faced in his command in Peru the most divisive had been the Constitution. Declaring that in the past he had not let his real feelings be known, he said that he had nonetheless abolished the constitutional system in every location that fell under his control during the campaign of 1823. He issued a formal decree on 11 March 1824 in Cuzco, abolishing all the acts of the constitutional government. Tadeo Gárate, royal intendant of Puno, reported that twelve provinces had now been reduced to royal control and that in abolishing the Constitution Peru had undergone a "happy transition from democracy or anarchy to a legitimate Government recognized by all the world."[36] In the first months of 1824, therefore, the royalist commanders had considerable grounds for self-congratulation; they appeared to be on the verge of complete success. Like Bolívar, they had consciously aimed at riding out the storm with their forces intact so as to be able to retake Peru as soon as the rebels had destroyed themselves through internal dissension.

Bolívar, however, did not give up. Dedicated to the proposition that, as he wrote Sucre, "We are the executors of South America," he turned his attention to rebuilding his forces in Trujillo. Perhaps at no other point in his career did his genius for organizing and commanding men and his commitment to the cause effect such a significant change in patriot fortunes. In only three months he drew together an army of almost 10,000 men, consisting of the Colombian forces and what survivors there were from earlier patriot forces. The army's training was entrusted to a polyglot group of officers—Colombian, Argentinian, Peruvian, and English. The civilian population of Trujillo was marshaled to sew uniforms, cloth was commandeered from the residents, tin and other metals collected. Windows were stripped of their iron grills, and even house keys were melted down. To keep his soldiers paid and loyal, Bolívar first reduced their pay to one-fourth, then confiscated the church silver in the province of Trujillo to pay them. He also ordered the temporary confiscation of all private property of anyone living in the territory controlled by the Spaniards, even if they were themselves patriot sympathizers.[37] To free himself and his commanders from civilian political turmoil—the downfall of each of the patriot leaders before him—he turned all government affairs over to one person, the Peruvian José Faustino Sánchez Carrión, a man of noted ability and patriotism. It was Sánchez Carrión, indeed, who was most responsible for provisioning the new army and for creating its revenue and supply networks. In March 1824 Bolívar created him "minister general of the affairs of the Peruvian republic." After the patriot victory, Sánchez Carrión continued as minister of government and foreign affairs until his death shortly after on 2 June 1825.[38]

In short, the great key to Bolívar's success was that he concentrated his attention exclusively on the creation and support of an army whose only job was to carry the war into the highlands that stretched from Jauja to Cuzco, where the royalists had their stronghold. With Colombia at his back to supply horses, mules, and manpower, Bolívar virtually ignored coastal Peru and most of all Lima. Indeed, retaking Lima was not even a serious objective. That would come in time, but it would be of value only if the main body of royal forces had been defeated in the mountains. Bolívar set his troops to work training in the mountains to help acclimate them to the altitude. He acquired 10,000 cattle as a reserve meat supply. The cavalrymen were given mules to carry their arms and supplies so that their service horses could be kept fresh. To bivouac the troops in their journey to the highlands, Bolívar ordered shelters stocked with food and water. If the royalists were to be defeated it could only be by military strength, and that was his objective. On 15 June Bolívar ordered his troops to begin their march to the highlands. He wrote, "I am possessed by the demon of war and am about to end this fight one way or another."[39]

Early in 1824 the patriots received an unexpected but critical assist through the defection of the royal commander of the army in Upper Peru since 1820, General Pedro Antonio Olañeta. General Olañeta despised Viceroy La Serna, General Canterac, and General Jerónimo Valdés, the three chief royal officers who had themselves once been his superiors in Upper Peru. In January 1824, having been informed via Buenos Aires of the fall of the liberal regime in Spain before La Serna himself knew of it, Olañeta openly mutinied against the viceroy, overthrowing the constitutionalist government in Upper Peru and replacing it with an absolutist regime of his own. Faced with virtual civil war within his own ranks, Viceroy La Serna sent General Valdés, commander of the royal army of the south, to deal with the revolt. On 11 February 1824 Olañeta entered Chuquisaca, where he proclaimed absolute monarchy and the abolition of the constitutional system. He appointed his followers to the audiencia and declared himself commander of the "Provinces of the Río de la Plata." Valdés realized he was unable to depose the entrenched Olañeta, who was surrounded by his own followers and family and widely supported by the conservative Upper Peruvian elite. On 9 March 1824 the two commanders signed an agreement by which Olañeta was permitted to remain commander in Upper Peru in return for recognizing La Serna's authority, furnishing troops to the royalists in Lower Peru, and submitting to Valdés's commands. When Valdés withdrew, however, Olañeta broke his agreement and assumed direct political command of Upper Peru.[40] It should be noted that Olañeta's treason occurred only a month before La Serna himself abolished the Constitution, which shows that it was more an attempt to seize power than a crusade to restore a particular political system.

The most damaging impact of the Olañeta rebellion was that it deprived La Serna of the security of a friendly Upper Peru, while it absorbed the attention of Valdés's army of the south at the very moment (March 1824) that Bolívar in the north was at his weakest and most vulnerable to a combined assault. In June 1824 Olañeta rejected an ultimatum from Viceroy La Serna ordering him to submit to his command. After the royalist defeat at Junín, General Valdés left Upper Peru to join the main viceregal army, leaving Olañeta in command of what would shortly become Bolivia. Bolívar, of course, rejoiced at this turn of events. He declared: "The Spanish now also suffer the influence of the evil star of Peru. The Pizarros and Almagros fought each other. La Serna fought Pezuela . . . now Olañeta is fighting with La Serna."[41] Recognizing that nothing more advantageous could possibly happen to him, Bolívar wrote Olañeta assuring him of his friendship, and the Upper Peruvian rebel replied in kind. A few months later the victorious army of Sucre defeated Olañeta in battle and mortally wounded him, thereby winning the independence of Bolivia.

The Spanish royalists in Peru were stunned by Olañeta's treason. In a long and bitter memorial, La Serna's representatives in Spain wrote to the peninsular government to survey the multitude of glories La Serna and his officers had achieved since they took power in January 1821. Reviewing the great royal campaign of 1822 and 1823, they concluded that the insurgents had lost nearly 18,000 men, mostly from desertion, in the same period that the viceroy had kept his armies intact and in fighting form. All of this campaign was now being risked by the treason of Olañeta. La Serna had saved Peru, he had saved the army, he was on the verge of victory, when suddenly the insubordination of one man wrecked his chance to recover all of Peru. They urged that Olañeta be called to court to answer for his conduct. The king, however, proved that he was unworthy of the loyalty of La Serna and his men by subsequently appointing Olañeta viceroy of Buenos Aires, on Olañeta's claim that he could reconquer the La Plata region. In an incredible Council of Indies consultation, the councilors voted to overrule the strong objections of La Serna, Canterac, and Valdés and allow Olañeta's appointment to stand, for Olañeta was the king's kind of man.[42]

Bolívar's army, which had set out from Trujillo on 15 June ascended into the Andes in a month. By 15 July the army crossed the Andes and reached Pasco. On 6 August, outside Canterac's headquarters of Jauja, the patriot army confronted the royalists in the battle of Junín. The royalists were defeated, breaking formation and fleeing from the field. La Serna's northern supply lines were cut, although Canterac managed to retreat to Cuzco with most of his army intact.

Four months passed quietly, as both La Serna and Bolívar collected their forces in preparation for what was now viewed as the decisive test. The Spanish highland bastion had been breached at last. Far away from Lima and the turbulent coastal desert the future of Peru would be decided, in the clear, cold air where Spain had first won Peru three centuries before. In the interim, Bolívar departed for the coast to organize his government throughout the districts that now fell into patriot hands. General Sucre was left in charge of the army in the mountains, with full authority to determine its future course of action. In September a blockade was established at Callao, and Lima began to undergo daily harassment from patriot guerrilla bands.

As Bolívar approached the capital, the royalist defense there fell apart. A series of skirmishes occurred, chiefly between unimportant guerrilla or montonero groups of both sides. The suffering of the Limeños during this period was great, not only from privation but from fear. Too many of them had deserted the patriot side to be content with the prospect of Bolívar bearing down upon them. Guerrilla forces from both sides entered and left the city at any hour, committing robberies and spreading terror. Thomson testified, "As a consequence of all this the anguish that existed in the city was very great, and it was aggravated by the increase in forced contributions. . . . This was, perhaps, in former times . . . the richest city in the world, but now, it can be said with all certainty, it is the poorest."[43] On 2 November the patriot vanguard was repulsed from outside Callao but took refuge in Lima. The patriots occupied Lima temporarily, and Colonel José María Equisquiza was named governor, but they had to abandon it quickly on 4 December owing to an attack from the defenders of the Real Felipe of Callao who entered the capital with two pieces of artillery. The royalists then retired to the castles, and the patriot forces again returned to take Lima.[44] On 7 December 1824, Bolívar entered the now patriot-held city and proceeded to organize its defense. Callao, however, remained securely in royalist hands, and thousands of civilian collaborators fled to the protection of the impregnable fortresses.

In November, Viceroy La Serna united all the highland royalist forces, some 9,300 men, and marched out of Cuzco in a concerted offensive in search of Sucre. For a month Sucre retreated while La Serna exhausted his men in a rapid march in search of the patriots. By 1 December the two armies were marching parallel to each other. La Serna mistakenly believed Sucre was becoming entrapped, but Sucre had received orders from Bolívar authorizing him to take the offensive whenever he chose. On 8 December Sucre stopped his retreat and faced La Serna across a series of deep ditches. Aware that defeat would mean certain destruction—the patriot army consisted of only 5,780 men and proroyalist Indians in the area had been armed to pick off any retreating patriots—Sucre counted on his army's fighting with extra valor. The royalist army, on the other hand, was exhausted, not only from the last month's forced march but, perhaps, from the last four years of resistance. The great battle of Ayacucho began on the morning of 9 December. After hours of fierce fighting the royalist lines collapsed under the enthusiastic charge of the Colombian infantry. Viceroy La Serna was taken prisoner, and the royalist army was defeated. Shortly thereafter, General Canterac appeared before Sucre with an offer of surrender. The capitulation was signed that same day. It consisted of eighteen articles, mainly allowing the royalist troops and officers to leave Peru in honor if they chose or to remain in their positions if they took an oath of allegiance to independence. The patriots renewed their pledge to recognize nonmilitary debts inherited from the viceroyalty. One clause called for royalist-held Callao to surrender within twenty days.

The battle of Ayacucho was a total patriot victory and the most decisive encounter in all the American wars of independence. Spanish power in Peru was broken. More than that, Spanish power was ended on the entire continent, for La Serna's army was the last major royal force still intact. For the first time the royalists had no backup, no territory into which they could retreat, no other army to call upon. Having thrown his combined forces into the battle, La Serna lost everything in a single blow. Sucre, now bearing the title marshal of Ayacucho, swept on to final victory over the rebel Olañeta in Upper Peru in April 1825, thus establishing the independence of Bolivia. The future of Abascal's great viceroyalty was decided on the battlefield.

Peru was now independent. On 21 December 1824 Bolívar called for the reinstallation of Congress. Still vested with the title of dictator, he turned his attention to organizing and governing a devastated country. Most of the leading Spanish officers left the country on various foreign merchantmen. La Serna and three of his generals sailed on a French ship.[45] On his arrival home, La Serna was given the noble title conde de los Andes, although in a way his higher honor might well have been the deference and respect paid to him and to Canterac and Valdés by Marshal Sucre in the days immediately after Ayacucho, for it was the respect the victor owed the vanquished for his long years of defending the king's patrimony. The story of the extinction of royal power in Peru should end there, but it does not. There is a final tragic footnote that shows the extent to which the decision of Ayacucho was a purely military solution.

The capitulation of Ayacucho called for the royal defenders of Callao to surrender as well. No one imagined that General José Ramón Rodil, Spanish governor of Callao, would refuse. Yet when Bolívar informed Rodil of the royal army's defeat, the commander refused even to receive a patriot representative. When Viceroy La Serna sent his own commissioner to order Rodil to give up the forts, he again refused to surrender. Rodil possessed two battalions and a brigade of artillery, a total of more than 2,500 soldiers, commanded by competent officers. The forts were well provided with livestock and other necessities, the towers and ramparts had been reinforced, and the commander expected help to arrive from Spain.[46] Furthermore, when Lima fell to the patriots in early December, at least 3,800 civilian refugees had sought protection with the royal forces in the forts. Among them were former president Torre Tagle and his family, former vice-president Aliaga and his family, former minister of war Berindoaga, nobles, merchants, members of Congress, and collaborators of the royalists. Though Rodil obviously felt no obligation toward the civilians, he was determined to restore the honor of the royal flag by holding on to the strongest fortification on the entire Pacific coast. Thus Callao came to play the role for which it was destined. Never conquered, never breached, it now became the last bastion of Spain in Peru. The year-long siege of Callao began. It was the final death watch not only of Spanish power but of the more self-serving members of the old Lima elite as well.

The patriots, distracted by the liberation of Bolivia and exhausted by their exertions, instituted an unenthusiastic siege. The naval blockade, which began in December 1824 with the Chilean fleet, ultimately came to include Peruvian and Colombian ships as well. To supply Lima, Bolívar had to declare Chorrillos the official port city. The land siege was established at Bellavista, a mile from the forts. In the midst of constant skirmishes, the patriots were able to deny the castles any further livestock or supplies. They did not, however, attempt a general assault.

In the castles, Rodil—who by most accounts was obsessed with the essentially pointless defense of the forts—imposed a regimen of espionage and terror. The occupants included not only Spanish and Peruvian veteran soldiers but patriot prisoners from the earlier rebellion of Moyanos, as well as civilian nobles, commoners, wives, and children. As many as 200 persons were executed by Rodil for conspiracy. A special espionage system was created, and the slightest sign of protest was cause for execution. When a priest named Marieluz refused to divulge to Rodil the secrets of the confessional, he was shot. Food supplies slowly ran out. Mariano Torrente says chickens sold among the refugees for 25 to 30 pesos each. As food supplies disappeared, Rodil determined that those civilians who had not brought six months' supplies with them were to be expelled. Little by little, 2,380 civilian refugees were forced out into the no-man's-land separating the forts from the patriot army. In the first weeks the patriots received the expelled civilians, but when they realized that the object of sending them out was to preserve supplies for the royalist soldiers, the patriots decided not to admit the civilians behind their lines. Many starved to death in the mile of land separating the two sides. In May, for example, twenty women were expelled from the castles but not allowed behind patriot lines. When they tried to gain readmittance to the forts Rodil ordered volleys fired over their heads. Ultimately the patriots relented and received them.[47] Rodil did release some patriot prisoners left over from Moyanos's mutiny the year before, not out of humanity, but to save precious stores and because he feared conspiracy. At one point, however, he executed thirty-six of these patriots after a riot.

After May 1825 Rodil ordered rations only for civil employees, soldiers, and collaborators. The refugees and soldiers ate horses, mules, cats, dogs, and even rats. When they were gone, the people began to die of starvation. An epidemic of scurvy and typhus swept the fort, adding considerably to the death toll. There is no consensus on the total number of deaths, and Rodil himself gave no figure for the civilians. Torrente says that 6,000 persons died of starvation and disease and 767 more died in actual military combat defending the forts. Mendiburu says that in the main fort, the Real Felipe, there were 7,000 persons, of whom only 2,300 survived. Vargas Ugarte says more than 5,000 died in the castles, not counting the 200 Rodil executed. When the forts finally surrendered in January 1826, only about 400 defenders remained alive among the soldiers, and of these only 94 chose to go to Spain, implying that the rest were Peruvians. When he returned to Spain, Rodil gave the death toll among the veteran soldiers as 2,095, with 444 survivors.[48]

Subtracting the military deaths from the total leaves anywhere from 2,700 to about 4,000 civilians who died. The lower figure is probably more accurate. These civilians included several of the foremost Peruvian leaders of the independent state. Former president Torre Tagle, who insisted till the end that he was actually a prisoner of the Spaniards, died after nine months of siege, as did his wife and son. Diego de Aliaga, the vice-president, also died, as did his brother Juan de Aliaga, conde de San Juan Lurigancho. Others included the conde de Villar de Fuente, former prior of the Consulado and governor of Lima during the Spanish occupation of 1824, and Isidro Cortazar, conde de San Isidro, the director of San Martín's paper money bank. Gaspar Rico, the royalists' most faithful propagandist, left Callao alive but died a few days later from the effects of the siege. Torre Tagle's minister of war, Berindoaga, attempted to escape on 2 October, disguised as a fisherman, but his boat was captured by a patriot patrol. He was sent to Lima for trial on charges of treason, found guilty, and executed in the main plaza on 15 April 1826. The fate of these representatives of the old-line creole elite puts the final capstone on their whole history of indecision and self-aggrandizement. Buried in unmarked graves, their names not even recorded, the last resisters of independence, like the viceroyalty of Peru itself, died a lingering, agonizing death.

On 11 January 1826 Rodil agreed to receive patriot negotiators, and an agreement for the surrender of the forts was signed on 22 January. Of the surviving defenders, most returned to Lima, while a few went to the dockside in Callao to try to get passage on the English frigate *Briton* then in port. Rodil and some other officers sailed on that ship. They arrived in Spain in August 1826, and before he could even disembark Rodil was granted the distinction of a commander's cross in the Order of Isabel La

Católica.[49] So high was Ferdinand's estimation of him that in the future Rodil became captain general of Cuba and of the Philippines, minister of war, and president of the Council of Ministers. He received the noble title marqués de Rodil, and upon Ferdinand's death he was made guardian of the king's two daughters.

To Spain it appeared that Rodil had upheld the honor of the flag in the face of universal defeat. Spain did not accept Peru's independence and continued for several years, partly inspired by last-ditch stands like Rodil's, to plan the reconquest of the "rebellious overseas provinces." Spaniards, of course, had a different perspective on Peruvian independence. What Spaniards saw was that the independence of Peru—which in itself constituted a mere separation, not a social or political revolution within the country—had been achieved in only two battles, in a decision of arms.

The image that lingers in the mind, at any rate, is the one provided by Torre Tagle, Aliaga, Berindoaga, and the other 3,800 or more civilian refugees in Callao. No matter how unedifying it may be, their conversion back to the royal side suggests that many politically active citizens had not yet chosen independence. Three thousand eight hundred persons was a considerable portion of the total population of Lima—three hundred more than the total number who had signed the Declaration of Independence in 1821. No matter how mixed their motives might have been, these people were still voting against independence with their feet. Even though the royal government had collapsed and its leaders had already fled the country, they preferred to cling to the belief that Spanish power might reassert itself. Submitting their destinies, and their lives, to the control of a fanatic megalomaniac was preferable to residing peacefully under the command of Bolívar and his Colombian army. Ayacucho—the glory of America—did not constitute a referendum for these Peruvians. Whether they were right or wrong, whether they misunderstood the motives of the victor and the purposes of the vanquished, across a century and a half they still bear stark witness that as late as 1825 the vigorous sentiment expressed in the 1821 Declaration of Independence—"That the general will is decided in favor of the Independence of Peru from Spanish domination"—was not unequivocally true.

Manuel Vidaurre—that troubled royal oidor of Cuzco who eventually supported independence and returned to Peru in 1824—wrote about this inability to give up the heritage of three centuries in his *Cartas Americanas* (1823). His words assume an immensely tragic significance when viewed in the light of the refugees in Callao, for their duality was his. He wrote:

> I love the Spanish nation like a grandmother, and the American like a mother. I weep to see these beloved persons destroyed. The one, old but inexperienced and with bad habits that impel it . . . to domination and conquest. The other, young, weak, without resources, going from desperation to faint-heartedness, from heroism to barbarity, with signs of virtue and with many vices.[50]

This was the Peruvians' dilemma. To give up the old empire, with all its ancient grievances of disrespect for American pretensions, monopoly, absolute monarchy, arbitrariness, and frustration meant throwing themselves blindly into a future that threatened many evils, social destruction, militarism, and possible foreign domination by their northern neighbors. No, Peru was not dragged kicking and screaming into independence. Neither did it embrace the new day of independence with joy and anticipation of good fortune. It staggered on, impelled by forces it could not control, afraid of the future but burdened by the past. None of the other Spanish American independence movements is so profoundly troubling. A considerable portion of the population of Lima resisted independence to the very end, and many paid with their lives. The event was accomplished, the deed was done, and Peruvians still had not decided.

# Notes

PREFACE

1. Timothy E. Anna, *The Fall of the Royal Government in Mexico City* (Lincoln: University of Nebraska Press,1978).

2. *Colección documental de la independencia del Perú* (hereafter cited as *CDIP*). Published by the Comisión Nacional del Sesquicentenario de la Independencia del Perú, dated Lima, 1971 (with the exception of a few volumes dated 1974) and edited by various specialists, this collection was originally planned to consist of 82 volumes in 30 tomes, most of which are not yet available. Most of its contents are available in earlier editions or in archives. Items from the *CDIP* will be cited here by the titles used in the collection rather than by their original titles.

3. Older English-language surveys tend to emphasize the foreign intervention, as Clements R. Markham, *A History of Peru*, and William Spence Robertson, *Rise of the Spanish American Republics as Told in the Lives of Their Liberators*. Obviously, so do Colombian, Chilean, and Argentinian studies of Peruvian independence. For example, the classic historian of San Martín, Bartolomé Mitre, *Historia de San Martín y de la emancipación Sud-Americana*, 3d ed., 6 vols. (Buenos Aires: La Nación, 1903–7), emphasizes the interventionist aspect of Peruvian liberation, though Mitre was a universalist dedicated to the idea that the struggle for independence transcended national boundaries. The Chilean Gonzalo Bulnes, *Historia de la expedición libertadora del Perú (1817–1822)*, 2 vols. in 1 (Santiago: R. Jover, 1887–88), and *Bolívar en el Perú: Ultimas campañas de la independencia del Perú* (Madrid: Ed. América, 1919), is said by Raúl Porras Barrenechea to be "anti-Peruvian." The major works on Bolívar would be in this group too, as, for example, Gerhard Masur, *Simón Bolívar*; Daniel Florence O'Leary, *Bolívar y la emancipación de Sud-America: Memorias del General O'Leary*, trans. Simón B. O'Leary, 2 vols. (Madrid: Sociedad Española de Librería, 1915); or Vicente Lecuna, *Crónica razonada de las guerras de Bolívar*, 3 vols. (New York: Colonial Press, 1950); also see Lecuna's defense of Bolívar, *Catálogo de errores y calumnias en las historia de Bolívar*, 3 vols. (New York: Colonial Press, 1956). Raúl Porras Bar-

renechea, in his *Fuentes históricas peruanas: Apuntes de un curso univer-sitario* (Lima: Instituto Raúl Barrenechea, 1963), p. 288, even takes to task Mariano Felipe Paz Soldán's *Historia del Perú independiente* on the grounds that it does not sufficiently appreciate the Peruvian contributions to independence, while also admitting that Paz Soldán is the "classic Peruvian historian of independence." For an excellent summation of the faults of the existing historiography and tentative solutions, see Heraclio Bonilla and Karen Spalding, "La independencia en el Perú: Las palabras y los hechos," in Bonilla et al., *La independencia en el Perú*, pp. 15–63.

4. Especially notable in this regard are the selections in *La causa de la emancipación del Perú*. Individual writings in that volume, however, contain a multitude of errors. Certainly the seminal work in this tradition is not by a Peruvian, but by a Chilean who lived in Peru for some time, Benjamin Vicuña Mackenna, *La independencia en el Perú*, first published in 1864. Closely following Vicuña Mackenna is Jorge Basadre's early work, *La iniciación de la republica*. In date of appearance one of the latest additions to this group—though written in the 1910s and 1920s it has only recently been published in its entirety—is Germán Leguía y Martínez, *Historia de la emancipación del Perú: El Protectorado*. Gustavo Vergara Arias has made a recent contribution in his *Montoneras y guerrillas en la etapa de la emancipación del Perú (1820–1825)*, a study of the rural and highland peasant guerrillas. Perhaps the most detailed of this nationalistic group is the document collection by José Manuel Valega, ed., *La gesta eman-cipadora del Perú*, 12 vols. (Lima, 1940–44). Other works supporting the nationalist view include Jorge Cornejo Bouroncle, *Pumacahua: La revolu-ción del Cuzco de 1814* (Cuzco: Editorial H. G. Rozas, 1956), and Javier Ortiz de Zevallos, ed., *Correspondencia de San Martín y Torre Tagle*. But the monumental work of Manuel de Mendiburu, *Diccionario histórico-biográfico del Perú*, remains the basic and original plea for recognition of the contributions of Peruvians. Vicuña Mackenna was heavily dependent on Mendiburu's work in collecting documents and personal testimony. Another early nationalist work is Francisco Javier Mariátegui's *Anotaciones a la Historia del Perú independiente de Don Mariano Felipe Paz Soldán* (Lima: Imprenta "El Nacional," 1869), which takes Paz Soldán to task for his alleged oversight of the secret conspirators in Lima's colegios and of the involvement of Peruvians in San Martín's regime. This list could be expanded indefinitely to include biographies of Peruvian participants and studies of Indian uprisings. The massive *Colección documen-tal de la independencia del Perú* obviously favors a nationalist interpretation whenever possible.

5. Felipe Barreda Laos, *Vida intelectual del virreinato del Perú*; Fernando Gamio Palacio, ed., *La municipalidad de Lima y la emancipación, 1821* (Lima: Sanmarti, 1944), and the second edition of the book, very much aug-

mented (Lima: Concejo Provincial de Lima, 1971); all citations here are from the 1971 book. Eduardo Mendoza Silva, *Historia de la masonería en el Perú: Masonería pre-republicana* (Lima, 1966); José Ignacio López-Soria, *Descomposición de la dominación hispánica en el Perú* (Lima: Editorial Arica, 1973).

6. Most such writers follow the thinking of Ricardo Palma or Hipólito Unánue. See Palma, *Tradiciones Peruanas*, 9th ed., 6 vols. (Madrid: Espasa-Calpe, 1958–63), and Unánue, *Observaciones sobre la clima de Lima*, intro. and comm. Carlos Enrique Paz Soldán (Lima: Imp. "Lux," 1940). A chief example is Jean Descola, *Daily Life in Colonial Peru, 1710–1820*, trans. Michael Heron (London: George Allen and Unwin, 1968); or Juan Manuel Ugarte Elespuru, *Lima y lo Limeño* (Lima: Editorial Universitaria, 1967). For critiques of Palma and Unánue see Ruben Vargas Ugarte, "Don Ricardo Palma y la historia"; John E. Woodham, "The Influence of Hipólito Unánue on Peruvian Medical Science, 1789–1820: A Reappraisal"; John E. Woodham, "Hipólito Unánue and the Enlightenment in Peru," Ph.D. diss., Duke University, 1965.

7. See E. Bradford Burns, "Ideology in Nineteenth-century Latin American Historiography," *Hispanic American Historical Review* (hereafter cited as *HAHR*), 58, no. 3 (August 1978): 409–31, for a discussion of the lasting effects of the great-man emphasis and other preoccupations of nineteenth-century historiography.

8. J. R. Fisher, "Royalism, Regionalism, and Rebellion in Colonial Peru, 1808–1815."

## CHAPTER 1

1. J. R. Fisher, *Government and Society in Colonial Peru: The Intendant System, 1784–1814*. See also Guillermo Céspedes del Castillo, *Lima y Buenos Aires: Repercusiones económicas y políticas de la creación del Virreinato del Plata*; Sergio Villalobos, *El comercio y la crisis colonial*; Oscar Febres Villaroel, "La crisis agricola en el Perú en el ultimo tercio del siglo XVIII"; Heraclio Bonilla, "La coyuntura comercial del siglo XIX en el Perú"; Carlos Camprubi Alcázar, *El Banco de la Emancipación*; Camprubi Alcázar, "El Banco de la Emancipación"; Timothy E. Anna, "Economic Causes of San Martín's Failure in Lima"; and Bonilla and Spalding, "La independencia en el Perú."

2. Both quoted in Descola, *Daily Life*, pp. 74–75.

3. "Plan demostrativo de la población comprehendida en el recinto de la Ciudad de Lima," Lima, 5 December 1790, published by the Sociedad Académica de Amantes del País, Archivo General de Indias, Seville (hereafter cited as AGI), Indiferente 1527; Abascal to Secretary of Ultramar, Lima, 21 July 1814, AGI, Lima 747; "Memoria sobre la población del reino de Nueva España, escrita por D. Fernando Navarro y

Noriega," Archivo General de la Nación, Mexico, Impresos oficiales, vol. 60, no. 48; Fisher, *Government and Society*, pp. 251–53; "Estado del población del vireynato de Lima, 1813," AGI, Indiferente 1524. Although the intendancy of Puno was added to the viceroyalty of Peru in 1795 and the provinces of Mainas and Guayaquil were annexed in 1802 and 1803, neither the 1795 census nor the 1813 census counted those three territories. Hipólito Unánue calculated that Puno, Mainas, and Guayaquil added 200,000 to the population; Fisher, *Government and Society*, p. 6.

4. Vasilii M. Golovnin, "Lima y Callao en 1818," in Estuardo Núñez, ed., *Relaciones de Viajeros*, CDIP, tome 27, 1:147–73.

5. William Bennet Stevenson, "Memorias sobre las campañas de San Martín y Cochrane en el Perú," in Núñez, ed., *Relaciones de Viajeros*, CDIP, tome 27, 3:119–46.

6. J. R. Fisher, *Silver Mines and Silver Miners in Colonial Peru, 1776–1824*; Fisher, *Government and Society*, p. 130.

7. Las Heras to Nicolas María de Sierra, Lima, 10 August 1811, AGI, Lima 1568.

8. Fisher, *Government and Society*, p. 205.

9. Ibid., p. 130.

10. Ibid., p. 136.

11. Ibid., p. 135.

12. Ibid., pp. 131, 134.

13. Anna, "Economic Causes," pp. 657–81.

14. Fisher, *Silver Mines*, pp. 120–22.

15. On the Nordenflicht expedition see Rose Marie Buechler, "Technical Aid to Upper Peru: The Nordenflicht Expedition"; and John Lynch, *Spanish Colonial Administration, 1782–1810: The Intendant System in the Viceroyalty of Río de la Plata*, p. 145. Both concern Nordenflicht's work in Upper Peru. For Lower Peru see Fisher, *Silver Mines*, pp. 54–73.

16. Fisher, *Silver Mines*, p. 120.

17. "Noticias curiosas en punto a derechos y otros particulares," n.d., AGI, Indiferente 1709; Biblioteca Municipal de Lima (hereafter cited as BML), Actas de Cabildo, book 44, 26 May 1815 and 18 December 1816; Fisher, *Government and Society*, p. 147; Robert Proctor, "El Perú entre 1823 y 1824," in Núñez, ed., *Relaciones de Viajeros*, CDIP, tome 27, 2:251.

18. Doris M. Ladd, *The Mexican Nobility at Independence, 1780–1826*, (Austin: Institute of Latin American Studies, 1976), pp. 25, 184–86; Expediente concerning José Arizmendi, Madrid, 1825, AGI, Lima 602.

19. Ladd, *The Mexican Nobility*, pp. 32–35; David A. Brading, *Miners and Merchants in Bourbon Mexico, 1780–1810* (Cambridge: At the University Press, 1971), pp. 169–207; D. A. Brading and Harry E. Cross, "Colonial Silver Mining: Mexico and Peru."

20. Basadre, *Iniciación de la república*, 1:2; Ladd, *The Mexican Nobility*, pp. 173–74.

21. Ladd, *The Mexican Nobility*, pp. 113–14.

22. "Testimonio del estado en que se halla la Tesorería general," Lima, 7 September 1812, AGI, Lima 1442.

23. Antonio Cano to Secretary of Hacienda, Cádiz, letters respectively 15 November, 21 July 1812, and 14 August 1813, AGI, Indiferente 1577.

24. Abascal to Real Hacienda, Lima, 11 January 1810, AGI, Lima 1442.

25. BML, Actas de Cabildo, book 41, 27 January 1809, 11 November 1808, and 20 June 1809.

26. Abascal to Secretary of Indies, Lima, 29 December 1815, AGI, Lima 752.

27. Report of Consulado of Lima, Lima, 26 June 1815, AGI, Indiferente 313.

28. Consulado to Regency, Lima, 7 September 1811, AGI, Lima 1539; "Razón de los individuos del Comercio de Lima que se han subscripto para mantener soldados en el Ejército del Desaguadero. . . ," Lima, 6 December 1811, AGI, Lima 1551.

29. "Estado de los productos naturales y artificiales del Perú en el vireynato de Lima, y computo de su valor comercial cada año," n.d., AGI, Indiferente 1525. This document appears with a group of estados from the general period 1807–9.

30. This is an average drawn from the agricultural export figures Fisher gives for the 1780s and 1790s, *Government and Society*, pp. 134–36.

31. Ibid., pp. 120–22; "Estado general de valores gastos y sobrantes . . ." for 1812, submitted to Secretary of Indies by Abascal, 20 March 1815, AGI, Lima 750, also in AGI, Lima 1136; Hacienda summary report, Cádiz, 28 September 1813, AGI, Indiferente 1708; "Expediente formado sobre el deficit," Lima, 1 February 1813, AGI, Lima 1443.

32. Ministry of Hacienda memorandum, Madrid, 1819, AGI, Lima 1471.

33. Fisher, *Government and Society*, pp. 251–53; Abascal to Secretary of Ultramar, Lima, 31 July 1814, enclosing census of 1813, AGI, Lima 747 (also AGI, Indiferente 1524).

34. Leon G. Campbell, "The Army of Peru and the Túpac Amaru Revolt, 1780–83."

35. "Plan demostrativo de la población comprehendida en el recinto de la ciudad de Lima," Lima, 5 December 1790, AGI, Indiferente 1527. The discussion to follow will show that I have taken account of the critique concerning my earlier enumeration of the Lima elite expressed by Mark A. Burkholder, "Titled Nobles, Elites, and Independence: Some Comments," *Latin American Research Review* 13, no. 2 (1978): 290–95. I believe, however, that the term "occupational elite" is valid as an index of status (especially in the absence of secondary data), and that enumeration of the "ruling elite" alone would be less illustrative of society in general, since the colonial structure effectively predetermined much of

the membership of the ruling elite. Since Lima was the capital of the viceroyalty and the center of international commerce, the occupational, "policy-making," and "ruling" elites were all disproportionately larger there than they would have been in a secondary center or in Peru in general. Unfortunately, for Peru we still lack the truly detailed data on education, position, income, and other indexes of status employed by Linda Arnold, who shared with me a manuscript entitled "Social, Economic, and Political Status in the Mexico City Central Bureaucracy: 1808–1822," to be published in *Memorias, V Reunión de Historiadores Mexicanos y Norteamericanos*, Pátzcuaro, 1977. Where the data exist, her work provides a model.

36. List of real estate owners, Lima, Archivo Nacional del Perú, Lima (hereafter cited as ANP), Superior Govierno, L. 27, C. 1335. For Mexico City, see María Dolores Morales, "Estructura urbana y distribución de la propiedad en la ciudad de México en 1813," *Historia Mexicana* 25 (January–March 1976): 363–402.

## CHAPTER 2

1. See Mendiburu, *Diccionario histórico-biográfico*, 1:33–35. Also see the introductory study to the political memoir of José Fernando de Abascal y Sousa, *Memoria de govierno*, ed. Vicente Rodríquez Casado and José Antonio Calderón Quijano; José Luis Pérez de Castro, "Rara y olvidada biografía del virrey Abascal," *Revista Histórica* (Montevideo) 31 (February 1961): 575–91, which reprints a *Biografía del Virrey Abascal* (Seville, 1851) assumed to be by Juan Manuel Pereira y Soto Sánchez Murillas y Jurado. Related material includes Fernando Díaz Venteo, *Las campañas militares del Virrey Abascal*; James Larry Odom, "Viceroy Abascal versus the Cortes of Cádiz"; and Timothy E. Anna, "The Last Viceroys of New Spain and Peru: an Appraisal."

2. Neuhaus, "Hacia una nueva clasificación," in *La causa de la emancipación del Perú*, pp. 12–19.

3. As two devotedly pro-independence scholars of an earlier age recognized. Vicuña Mackenna, in *La independencia en el Perú*, generally spoke highly of Abascal's rectitude, honesty, and wisdom. Leguía y Martínez got quite carried away in his praise (*Historia de la emancipación*, 1:402).

4. Leguía y Martínez, *Historia de la emancipación*, 1:403–18.

5. Abascal, *Memoria*, 1:129.

6. Abascal to Minister of Grace and Justice, Lima, 2 August 1814, AGI, Lima 748.

7. See Luis Durand Flores, *Independencia e integración en el plan político de Túpac Amaru* (Lima: P.L.V., 1973); J. J. del Pino, "Significado de la

revolución de Túpac Amaru frente al estudio de la causa de la independencia," in *La causa de la emancipación del Perú*, p. 28; Boleslao Lewin, *La rebelión de Túpac Amaru y los orígenes de la independencia de Hispano-América*, 3d ed. rev. (Buenos Aires: Editorial Paidos, 1967), pp. 131–89; and Carlos Daniel Valcárcel, *La rebelión de Túpac Amaru* (Mexico: Fondo de Cultura Económica, 1947).

8. Fisher, *Government and Society*, p. 23; see also Lillian Estelle Fisher, *The Last Inca Revolt, 1780–1783* (Norman: University of Oklahoma Press, 1966), which also treats the rebellion as a reformist movement.

9. Leon G. Campbell, "The Army of Peru and the Túpac Amaru Revolt."

10. Mark A. Burkholder and D. S. Chandler, *From Impotence to Authority: The Spanish Crown and the American Audiencias, 1687–1808* (Columbia: University of Missouri Press, 1977), appendix V, the standard authority on the makeup of the audiencias; Mark A. Burkholder, "From Creole to *Peninsular*: The Transformation of the Audiencia of Lima"; Leon G. Campbell, "A Colonial Establishment: Creole Domination of the Audiencia of Lima during the Late Eighteenth Century."

11. Fredrick B. Pike, *Modern History of Peru*, p. 35.

12. A recent, sound treatment of the college and its rector is Fernando Romero, *Rodríguez de Mendoza: Hombre de lucha* (Lima: Editorial Arica, n.d.). On the role of the university-trained professionals, see *La Universidad de San Marcos en el proceso de la emancipación peruana*, ed. and prol. Ella Dunbar Temple, *CDIP*, tome 19, vols 1–3.

13. Pike, *Modern History of Peru*, p. 42.

14. Baquíjano was appointed a councilor of state in 1812 and moved to Spain in 1813. After the restoration of absolutism in 1814 he was confined in Seville, where he died in 1817. BML, Actas de Cabildo, book 42, 30 June 1812; Miguel Maticorena Estrada, "Nuevas noticias y documentos de Don José Baquíjano y Carillo, Conde de Vistaflorida," in *La causa de la emancipación del Perú*, pp. 145–207; Mark A. Burkholder, "José Baquíjano and the Audiencia of Lima"; Baquíjano to Abascal, Lima, 30 December 1812, AGI, Lima 749.

15. Pezuela to Minister of Grace and Justice, enclosing reports on the college, Lima, 27 October 1817, AGI, Lima 757.

16. Abascal to Secretary of Indies, Lima, 27 March 1815, AGI, Lima 749.

17. Revata to Regency, Lima, 24 February 1813; Revata to George III, Lima, 23 February 1813, both in AGI, Lima 1016.

18. Revata to Infante Don Carlos María de Borbón, Lima, 29 July 1816, AGI, Lima 773; Revata to Regency, Lima, 7 September 1812, AGI, Lima 1014-A; Revata to King, Lima, 8 March 1817, AGI, Lima 774.

19. Revata to Infante D. Carlos, Lima, 29 July 1816, AGI, Lima 773;

Revata to Regency, Lima, 8 April 1810, AGI, Lima 1014-B; Las Heras to Regency, Lima, 10 August 1811, AGI, Lima 1014-B; Regency to Las Heras, Cádiz, 21 April 1812, AGI, Lima 1014-B.

20. Expediente about Revata, 1812, AGI, Indiferente 1833; "Defensa de D. Domingo Sánchez Revata sobre la calumnia que le fulminó D. José Sicilia y Fena," Lima, 30 April 1812, AGI, Lima 1016; Revata to Regency, Lima, 24 February 1813, AGI, Lima 1016; Baquíjano to Abascal, Lima, 14 April 1813, AGI, Lima 749. Revata was still active in 1821, when he reappears in the documents as a zealous comisario de barrio during the Monteagudo persecution of Spaniards. Vicente Freire to President of the Department Riva Agüero, Lima, 14 November 1821, ANP, L. 37, C. 1348.

21. Pérez to Minister of Grace and Justice, Lima, 22 October 1815; Pérez to Miguel de Lardizábal, Lima, 26 June 1815, both in AGI, Lima 773.

22. Pérez to Spanish government, Lima, 26 June 1815; Pérez to Minister of Indies, Lima, 14 April 1815; Pérez to Minister of Indies, Lima, December 1815, all in AGI, Lima 773.

23. Mariano Tramarria to King, Lima, 1 May 1816, AGI, Lima 773; Joaquín Jordán to Regency, Lima, 18 March 1814, AGI, Lima 773; Anonymous letter to Spain, Lima, 10 August 1810, AGI, Indiferente 1568. This last letter is one of a series of anonymous denunciations.

24. Masur, *Simón Bolívar*, p. 366; Basil Hall, *Extracts from a Journal Written on the Coasts of Chile, Peru, and Mexico, in the Years 1820, 1821, 1822*, 1:282.

25. BML, Actas de Cabildo, book 41, 12 August 1808.

26. Ibid., 5 August 1808.

27. Ibid., 4, 5, 10, 11, 13, and 15 October 1808.

28. On 18 March the formal oaths of allegiance to the Junta were taken. Ibid., 9, 17, 18 March 1809; Ecclesiastical cabildo of Lima to Junta Central, Lima, 16 April 1809, AGI, Lima 1568.

29. Vicuña Mackenna, *La independencia en el Perú*, p. 73.

30. Ibid., pp. 77–88.

31. For a review of the reaffirmation of Peru's loyalty in 1808–10, see Armando Nieto Vélez, "Contribución a la historia del fidelismo en el Perú (1808–1810)"; and María Consuelo Sparks, "The Role of the Clergy during the struggle for Independence in Peru."

32. José Manuel de Goyeneche to Conde de Florida Blanca, Lima, 22 April 1809, AGI, Lima 1442.

33. Vicuña Mackenna, *La independencia en el Perú*, p. 88.

34. Odom, "Viceroy Abascal versus the Cortes of Cádiz," p. 8; BML, Actas de Cabildo, book 42, 27 August, 7 September 1810, and 8 February 1812; Antonio Suazo to Miguel de Lardizábal, Madrid, 19 June 1814, AGI, Indiferente 1354.

35. Fisher, *Government and Society*, p. 204; for some background on the

social makeup of the Peruvian army see Leon G. Campbell, "The Changing Racial and Administrative Structure of the Peruvian Military under the Later Bourbons"; and Campbell, *The Military and Society in Colonial Peru, 1750–1810.*

36. Fisher, *Government and Society*, pp. 204–5; "Estado general . . . de Real Hacienda . . . año de 1812," Lima, 23 January 1815, AGI, Lima 1136, also in Lima 750; Abascal to Secretary of War, Lima, 31 January 1814, AGI, Lima 747; Fisher, "Royalism, Regionalism, and Rebellion."

37. Leguía y Martínez, *Historia de la emancipación*, 1:420, 1:226–27.

38. Odom, "Viceroy Abascal versus the Cortes of Cádiz," pp. 15, 18, 54; Barreda Laos, *Vida intelectual del virreinato*, p. 259; Alexandro Morales y Duarez to Regency, Lima, n.d., AGI, Lima 773.

39. John Preston Moore, *The Cabildo in Peru under the Bourbons*, pp. 208–9.

40. Salazar to Secretary of Indies, Madrid, 17 August 1814, AGI, Lima 1018-B.

41. About 25,000 mules left Salta each year for sale in Peru, of which 5,000 died on the trip. The mules were taxed six times in the course of their travels to Cuzco. Since they were valued at 20 to 25 pesos each, the customs produced about 30,000 pesos a year, but only 10,000 pesos of that reached Lima. The rest was lost in graft. Salazar asked that the mules be submitted to only one customs, as they entered Peru, and that the tax per head be reduced. The Cortes agreed to the first request and rejected the second, but it appears the decision was never implemented. Minutes of Cortes, Cádiz, 8 March 1813, AGI, Lima 1015; José de Limonta to Secretariat of Cortes, Cádiz, 8 March 1813, AGI, Lima 1444.

42. Salazar repeated all these requests in 1817; Report of Salazar, 15 September 1817, place not given, AGI, Lima 613.

43. BML, Actas de Cabildo, book 42, 23 November 1810.

44. Ibid., 19 January 1811; Fisher, *Government and Society*, pp. 153–54.

45. Quoted in Fisher, *Government and Society*, p. 154.


CHAPTER 3

1. Odom, "Abascal versus the Cortes of Cádiz," pp. 49, 50, 52.

2. The most appropriate studies of the Cortes include Odom's dissertation, which covers several issues; Luis Alayza y Paz Soldán, *La Constitución de Cádiz, 1812: El egregio limeño Morales y Duarez* (Lima: Editorial Lumen, 1946); Cesareo de Armellada, *La causa indígena americana en las Cortes de Cádiz* (Madrid: Ediciones Cultura Hispánica, 1959); and to gain some idea of the general scope of the Cortes's actions in America see Nettie Lee Benson, ed., *Mexico and the Spanish Cortes, 1810–1822: Eight Essays* (Austin: University of Texas Press, 1966).

3. Abascal to Secretary of Hacienda, Lima, 31 December 1814, AGI, Lima 746.

4. Juan José de Leuro to Secretary of Hacienda, Lima, 7 December 1811, AGI, Lima 1014-A.

5. BML, Actas de Cabildo, book 42, 29 October 1811, discussing the letter of Orue to Abascal, dated 26 October; and 12 November 1811.

6. Abascal to Secretary of Hacienda, Lima, 24 February 1813, AGI, Lima 744.

7. Abascal to Secretary of State, Lima, 23 May 1814, AGI, Estado 74; Abascal to Secretary of Hacienda, Lima, 25 February 1813, AGI, Lima 744; Consulta of Council of Indies, Cádiz, 23 March 1812, AGI, Lima 602; Eyzaguirre to Regency, Lima, 31 May 1813, AGI, Lima 1015.

8. Abascal to Council of Indies, Lima, 27 February 1813, AGI, Lima 604; Eyzaguirre to Cortes, Lima, 3 April 1813, AGI, Lima 799.

9. Eyzaguirre to Cortes, Lima, 8 August 1812, AGI, Lima 977.

10. Expediente about Eyzaguirre, 1812–16, AGI, Lima 977.

11. Eyzaguirre to Regency, Lima, 5 October 1812, AGI, Lima 1015; Isidro Vilca to Regency, Lima, 19 February 1813, AGI, Lima 1016; Abascal to Secretary of the Indies, Lima, 24 October 1815, AGI, Lima 749.

12. Royal order, Madrid, 30 September 1817; Eyzaguirre to King, Lima, 18 March 1816; Pezuela to Minister of Grace and Justice, Lima, 4 June 1818, all in AGI, Lima 977.

13. Extract of letters of Abascal, Lima, 25 February 1813, AGI, Lima 1443; "Expediente formada sobre el deficit," Lima, 1 February 1813, AGI, Lima 1443; Abascal to Secretary of Hacienda, Lima, 31 March 1814, AGI, Lima 747.

14. Baquíjano to Regency, Madrid, 10 January 1815, AGI, Lima 1017; Rivera to Pedro Cevallos, Lima, 7 March 1816, AGI, Lima 773.

15. Abascal to Secretary of Hacienda, Lima, 31 December 1814, AGI, Lima 746; Eyzaguirre to Cortes, Lima, 8 August 1812, AGI, Lima 977; Abascal to Secretary of Hacienda, Lima, 25 February 1813, AGI, Lima 744; Isidro Vilca to Regency, Lima, 4 February 1813, AGI, Lima 1443.

16. Abascal to Secretary of Ultramar, Lima, 25 February 1813, AGI, Lima 1443; Abascal to Secretary of Ultramar, Lima, 1 August 1814, AGI, Lima 746.

17. Baquíjano to Regency, Madrid, 10 January 1815, AGI, Lima 1017.

18. Vilca to Regency, Lima, 31 May 1813, AGI, Lima 1016; Vilca to Regency, Lima, 26 January 1813, AGI, Lima 1015; Torre y Vera to Regency, Quartel general de Tupiza, 25 January 1814, AGI, Lima 1568. For Indian legislation after independence see Thomas M. Davies, Jr., *Indian Integration in Peru: A Half Century of Experience, 1900–1948* (Lincoln: University of Nebraska Press, 1974), pp. 19–23.

19. Rivera to Pedro de Macanaz, Lima, 3 February 1815, AGI, Lima 773.

20. Manuel Alvarez Guerra to Secretary of Hacienda, Madrid, 1 April 1814, AGI, Lima 1443; Consulta of Council of State, Madrid, 27 July 1814, AGI, Lima 1016; Pezuela to Secretary of Hacienda, Lima, 17 June 1818, AGI, Lima 1444.

21. Fisher, *Government and Society*, p. 122.

22. Abascal's decree, Lima, 11 March 1815, ANP, Superior Govierno, L. 35, C. 1197.

23. BML, Actas de Cabildo, book 42, 19, 25, 26 April and 17 May 1811; Abascal to Regency, Lima, 31 July 1812, AGI, Lima 1016; Odom, "Abascal versus the Cortes of Cádiz," p. 60.

24. Abascal to Regency, Lima, 15 April 1812, AGI, Lima 1016.

25. Abascal to Secretary of Hacienda, Lima, 12 May 1812, AGI, Lima 743; Abascal to Regency, Lima, 31 July 1812, AGI, Lima 1016.

26. *El Peruano*, 5 June and 9 June 1812.

27. Abascal to Secretary of State, Lima, 26 June 1812, AGI, Estado 74; Consultas de Governación de Ultramar, 1813 and 1814, the Rico case, AGI, Lima 1016; Juan Acevedo y Salazar to Regency, Cádiz, 25 February 1813, AGI, Lima 1016.

28. *El Satélite del Peruano*, 1 March 1812.

29. *La Abeja Española*, 15 March 1813; Abascal to Regency and to Minister of Grace and Justice, Lima, 31 July 1813, AGI, Lima 1016; Antonio Cano Manuel to Abascal, Cádiz, 6 November 1812, AGI, Lima 1016.

30. Order of King, Madrid, 21 August 1818, including related documents, AGI, Lima 795.

31. Abascal to Secretary of Indies, Lima, 22 March 1815, AGI, Lima 749; Expediente about Angel de Luque, AGI, Lima 1017; Luque to Miguel de Lardizábal aboard Frigate *Resolución* in Bay of Cádiz, 10 August 1815, AGI, Lima 1017.

32. Abascal to Minister of Grace and Justice, Lima, 31 July 1813, AGI, Lima 1016.

33. *Verdadero Peruano*, 22 September and 1 October 1812.

34. Ibid., 25 February 1813.

35. Ibid., 8 October 1812.

36. Lyda Gordillo de Delucchi, "La conspiración de San Fernando, Estudio crítico de sus fuentes," in *La causa de la emancipación del Perú*, pp. 526–37.

37. *Verdadero Peruano*, 25 February 1813; the letter of resignation was dated 18 February.

38. *El Investigador*, 3 September, 7 September, and 23 October 1813.

39. Abascal to Cortes, Lima, 8 January 1814, and 2 August 1814, AGI, Lima 746, also in Lima 748

40. José M. Velez Picasso, "Propaganda subversiva," in *La causa de la emancipación del Perú*, pp. 485—90.

41. *El Investigador*, 9 and 10 July, 29 October 1813.

## CHAPTER 4

1. Carl J. Friedrich, *Tradition and Authority*, pp. 97–98.
2. Fisher, *Government and Society*, pp. 207–12.
3. Council of Indies Consulta, Madrid, 28 June 1815, AGI, Lima 602.
4. Joaquín de Molina to Regency, Quito, 30 September 1811; Torre Tagle to Regency, Lima, 12 November 1810; Abascal to Ministry of Grace and Justice, Lima, 11 October 1812, all in AGI, Lima 1014-B.
5. BML, Actas de Cabildo, book 43, 30 July 1813; Council of Indies Consulta, Madrid, 28 June 1815, AGI, Lima 602; Las Heras to Abascal, Lima, 22 September 1812, AGI, Lima 1014-B.
6. Secret order, Regency to Abascal, Cádiz, 21 January 1812; Abascal to Minister of Grace and Justice, Lima, 11 October 1812, both in AGI, Lima 1014-B.
7. Ramón de Posada to Ignacio de la Pezuela, Cádiz, 17 November 1811, AGI, Lima 1014-B; Solicitude of Arequipa Cabildo, Cádiz, 1812–14, AGI, Lima 1016.
8. Abascal to Secretary to Grace and Justice, Lima, 2 August 1814, AGI, Lima 748.
9. Council of Indies Consulta, Madrid, 28 June 1815, AGI, Lima 602.
10. Cámara de Indias minutes, Madrid, 22 January 1816, AGI, Lima 602.
11. "Estado de todas las audiencias de ultramar," Madrid, 5 June 1820, AGI, Indiferente 1565; Expediente concerning Anzotegui, 1821, AGI, Lima 795; Cámara de Indias Consulta, Madrid, 13 September 1817, AGI, Lima 602; Council of Indies Consulta, Madrid, 2 March 1818, AGI, Lima 604.
12. Abascal to Secretary of Grace and Justice, Lima, 13 October 1812, AGI, Lima 799; Junta Preparatoria de Elecciones, Lima, October 1812–January 1813, AGI, Lima 745.
13. Cortes minutes, Cádiz, 25 June 1813, AGI, Lima 1015.
14. Abascal to Secretary of Ultramar, Lima, 3 November 1814, AGI, Lima 746.
15. BML, Actas de Cabildo, book 42, 7 and 13 December 1812; and Cabildo to Regency, Lima, 5 January 1813, AGI, Lima 799. Both syndics had also been electors.
16. Abascal to Secretary of Grace and Justice, Lima, 13 October 1812, AGI, Lima 743; Abascal to Regency, Lima, 27 February 1813, AGI, Lima 604.
17. Abascal to Secretary of Cortes, Lima, 14 April 1813, AGI, Indiferente 1524; BML, Actas de Cabildo, book 43, 2 April 1813.

18. *Verdadero Peruano*, 17, 24, and 31 December 1812, 14 January, 4, 11, 18, and 25 February 1813.

19. BML, Actas de Cabildo, book 43, 23 March, 23 April 1813.

20. Abascal to Secretary of Ultramar, Lima, 31 May 1813; Regency to Abascal, Isla de Léon, 28 October 1813, both in AGI, Lima 1016.

21. BML, Actas de Cabildo, book 43, 19 December 1813, 1 January 1814.

22. Rivera to Regency, Huancavelica, 2 July 1811, AGI, Lima 1622; Fisher, *Government and Society*, p. 217.

23. Fisher, *Government and Society*, pp. 224–25; Abascal to Cortes, Lima, 30 November 1813, AGI, Lima 1016.

24. Miguel Tenorio, Antonio María Bazo and Andrés García Mancebo to Cortes, Lima, 24 May 1814, AGI, Lima 799.

25. Abascal to Secretary of Grace and Justice, Lima, 30 November 1813, AGI, Lima 744; Abascal to Secretary of Ultramar, Lima, 31 July 1814, AGI, Lima 747.

26. Cabildo to Regency, Lima, 28 September 1813, AGI, Lima 799.

27. Gálvez to Secretary of Indies, Lima, 29 March 1815, AGI, Lima 1116; Stevenson, "Memorias de las campañas," in Núñez, ed., *Relaciones de Viajeros*, CDIP, tome 27, 3: 149–52.

28. Las Heras to Minister of Ultramar, Lima, 20 December 1813, AGI, Lima 1568.

29. Gálvez to Cortes, Lima, 23 December 1813, AGI, Lima 1017 and Lima 1605; Audiencia to Regency, Lima, 3 August 1813, AGI, Lima 1017.

30. Abascal to Secretary of Indies, Lima, 22 May 1815, AGI, Lima 749.

31. Abascal to Secretary of Indies, Lima, 29 March 1815, AGI, Lima 749.

32. Expediente about José Ruiz Sobrino, 1818–19, AGI, Lima 1022.

33. Félix de la Roza to Alfonso Batanezo, Lima, 28 May 1813, AGI, Lima 1015; Roza to Juan Facundo Caballero, Lima, 14 May 1812, AGI, Lima 1014-A.

34. Abascal to Secretary of Indies, Lima, 27 March 1815, AGI, Lima 749.

35. Fisher, *Government and Society*, pp. 227–31; Fisher, "Royalism, Regionalism, and Rebellion."

36. Cámara de Indias Consulta, Madrid, 28 November 1818, AGI, Lima 603, and Lima 1563; Fray Marcos Duran Martel to King, Ceuta, 8 July 1814, AGI, Lima 1015; Abascal to Minister of State, Lima, 19 August 1811, AGI, Lima 1014-A.

37. Leon G. Campbell, "The Foreigners in Peruvian Society during the Eighteenth Century."

38. Abascal to Minister of Hacienda, Lima, 18 June 1810; Council of Indies Consulta, Cádiz, 7 January 1811, both in AGI, Lima 1016.

39. *Gaceta del Gobierno de Lima*, 22 July 1812; Eyzaguirre to Abascal, Lima, 17 July 1812, and to Regency, 4 August 1812, AGI, Lima 977; José Figueroa to Minister of Ultramar, Cádiz, 16 January 1813, AGI, Lima 1016; Commander, Port of Cádiz, to Secretary of Navy, Cádiz, 2 February 1813, AGI, Lima 1016; Pedro Antonio Madarriaga to Cortes, Lima, 10 October 1812, AGI, Lima 1014-A.

40. Abascal to Secretary of the Indies, Lima, 27 March 1815, AGI, Lima 749.

41. Ibid., testimony number 1.

42. Ibid., testimony number 2.

43. Report of Ramón Vendrell to Abascal, Lima, 19 November 1814, AGI, Lima 749.

44. BML, Actas de Cabildo, book 43, 2 and 13 December 1814; Testimony number 4 in Abascal to Secretary of the Indies, Lima, 27 March 1815, AGI, Lima 749; Council of Indies Consulta, Madrid, 16 June 1819, AGI, Lima 603; Salvador Alvarez y Moreno to King, Madrid, 17 December 1819, AGI, Lima 603.

45. For biographies of Vidaurre, see Mercedes Jos, "Manuel Lorenzo Vidaurre, Reformista Peruano"; José Guillermo Leguía, *Manuel Lorenzo Vidaurre, Contribución a un ensayo de interpretación sicológica* (Lima: Imp. "La Voce d'Italia," 1935); and Estuardo Núñez, *Manuel Lorenzo de Vidaurre, ciudadano de América* (Lima: Biblioteca de Cultura Peruana Contemporánea, 1945).

46. Jos, "Vidaurre," pp. 451–52; Council of Indies Consulta, Madrid, 28 September 1814, AGI, Lima 1619; Extract of Council of Indies, Madrid, 1820, AGI, Lima 1022.

47. Jos, "Vidaurre," pp. 463–69.

48. Extract of Council of Indies, Madrid, 1820, AGI, Lima 1022; Abascal to Secretary of Grace and Justice, Madrid, 12 January 1818, AGI, Lima 1022.

49. Vidaurre to Miguel de Lardizábal, Lima, 15 October 1815, AGI, Cuzco 8; Jos, "Vidaurre," p. 489.

50. Vidaurre to King, Lima, 2 April 1817, AGI, Indiferente 1568.

51. Ibid.

52. José Guillermo Leguía, as quoted in Jos, "Vidaurre," p. 446.

53. Ibid., p. 533.

54. BML, Actas de Cabildo, book 43, 7 October 1814; Abascal to Secretary of Ultramar, Lima, 25 October 1814, AGI, Lima 748.

55. BML, Actas de Cabildo, book 43, 4, 8, and 11, November, 2 December 1814.

56. Ibid., 18 December 1814; Cabildo to King, Lima, 4 January 1815, AGI, Lima 1017.

57. BML, Actas de Cabildo, book 44, 31 December 1814; Fisher, *Government and Society*, p. 234.

58. Abascal to King, Lima, 14 April 1815 and 3 November 1815, both in AGI, Lima 751; BML, Actas de Cabildo, book 44, 7 May 1816.

59. "Notas de los deputados de las Américas a quienes se les ha comunicado la circular de 17 de junio de 1814," AGI, Indiferente 1354.

60. Mariano de Rivero to Minister of Indies, Madrid, 28 July 1814, AGI, Lima 1020, also in AGI, Indiferente 1354; Tadeo Gárate to Minister of Indies, Madrid, 27 July 1814, AGI, Indiferente 1354; Pedro García Coronel to Minister of Indies, Madrid, 8 July 1814, AGI, Indiferente 1354; Martín José de Múxica to Minister of Indies, Madrid, 21 July 1814, AGI, Indiferente 1355; Council of Indies Consulta, Madrid, 17 January 1816, AGI, Lima 602, and extract, 6 February 1816, AGI, Lima 1515.

61. Rivera to Pedro de Macanaz, Lima, 3 February 1815, AGI, Lima 773; Council of Indies Consulta, Madrid, 7 March 1818, AGI, Lima 1019.

62. Memoria of Conde de Vistaflorida, Madrid, 31 August 1814, AGI, Estado 87. See Maticorena, "Nuevas noticias . . . de Don José Baquíjano," in *La causa de la emancipación del Perú*, pp. 145–207.

CHAPTER 5

1. Bonet to Secretary of Hacienda, Lima, 16 February 1815, AGI, Lima 751; "Libro manual de cargo y data de la Caja Matriz de Lima," 1814, Archivo Nacional del Perú, Archivo Histórico de Hacienda (hereafter cited as ANP, AHH), 1211; "Libro manual de cargo y data de la Caja Matriz de Lima," 1813, ANP, AHH, 1206: Joaquín de la Pezuela y Sánchez Muñoz de Velasco, *Memoria de Gobierno*, ed. and prol. Vicente Rodríguez Casado and Guillermo Lohmann Villena, p. 105.

2. Félix de la Roza to Alfonso Batanezo, Lima, 28 May 1813, AGI, Lima 1015.

3. Abascal to Consulado, Lima, 15 September 1814; 29 October 1814; 19 June 1815; 2 January 1816; and 30 March 1816, all in ANP, Superior Govierno, L. 35, C. 1162; Abascal to Secretary of Hacienda, Lima, 4 February 1815, AGI, Lima 1550.

4. Directors of the Company of the Philippines to José de Ybarra, Madrid, 20 January 1816, AGI, Lima 1467.

5. BML, Actas de Cabildo, book 42, 11 August 1812; Report of Fernando Zambrano to Directors of Public Hacienda, Lima, 30 July 1814, AGI, Lima 773.

6. "Memoria, Plan General de Arbitrios," Lima, 28 April 1815, AGI, Lima 751.

7. "Informe de la Comisión sobre un emprestito patriótico al govierno de 500,000 pesos fuertes," Lima, 28 April 1815, AGI, Lima 751.

8. General meeting of Junta de Arbitrios, Lima, 28 April 1815, AGI, Lima 751; Real Acuerdo of 28 April 1815, ANP, Superior Govierno, L. 35, C. 1191.

9. Council of Indies Consulta, Madrid, 3 June 1817, AGI, Lima 602.

10. "Libro de cargo y data de la Real Caja Matriz de Lima," 1817, ANP, AHH, 1223.

11. Pedro Alcantara Bruno to Ministry of Hacienda, Madrid, 17 July 1820, AGI, Lima 1470.

12. Camprubi Alcázar, *El Banco*, p. 29.

13. BML, Actas de Cabildo, book 44, 26 May, 24 November, and 1 December 1815, and 19 April 1816; Vecinos of Barrio de Santo Domingo to Viceroy, Lima, 21 August 1816, ANP, Superior Govierno, L. 35, C. 1214.

14. Audiencia of Lima to Secretary of Hacienda, Lima, 4 February 1815, and Chiefs of the Royal Hacienda of Peru to Secretary of Hacienda, Lima, 30 January 1815, AGI, Lima 749, audiencia's letter also in AGI, Lima 794; José Manuel de Aparici to Council of Indies, Madrid, 14 February 1817, AGI, Lima 1069; Royal order, Madrid, 10 August 1815, AGI, Lima 749.

15. Consulado to King, Lima, 16 June 1818, AGI, Lima 1551.

16. "Informe de la comisión nombrado por el Real Tribunal del Consulado de esta capital para la habilitación y armamento de la escuadrilla destinada a perseguir a los piratas de Buenos Aires," Lima, 1 March 1816, AGI, Lima 1551; Consulado to King, Lima, 16 June 1818, AGI, Lima 1551.

17. Consulado to King, Lima, 16 June 1818, AGI, Lima 1551.

18. "Informe de la comisión . . . ," 1 March 1816, according to a note added in Spain on 11 September 1816, AGI, Lima 1551.

19. Tribunal of Mining to Abascal, Lima, 1 March 1814; Abascal to Secretary of Ultramar, Lima, 21 March 1814; Abascal to Secretary of Indies, Lima, 17 April 1815, all in AGI, Lima 1358.

20. Abascal to Cortes, Lima, 14 April 1813; Tribunal of Mining to Regency, Lima, 4 October 1813, both in AGI, Lima 1358.

21. Pezuela to Ministry of Hacienda, Lima, 29 April 1817, AGI, Lima 1358 and Lima 756; Pezuela to Secretary of Hacienda, Lima, 8 March 1819, AGI, Lima 1358. See Fisher, *Silver Mines*, pp. 83–85, on mercury supplies in the last years of royal control.

22. Tribunal of Mining to Regency, Lima, 4 October 1813, AGI, Lima 1358. See Fisher, *Silver Mines*, pp. 96–97.

23. Ministry of Ultramar to Tribunal of Mining, Madrid, 24 March 1814, AGI, Lima 1358.

24. This document exists only as the extract of a letter from Abascal to some government ministry, extract dated Madrid, 4 February 1818, AGI, Lima 1358.

25. *Gaceta de Gobierno de Lima*, 8 February 1815; Pezuela to Minister of Grace and Justice, Lima, 24 October 1816, AGI, Lima 753. Fisher, *Silver Mines*, pp. 114–15. I follow Fisher's spelling of Uville; Spanish sources usually spell it Wille.

26. Agustín de Arpide to Regency, Lima, 16 October 1812; Council of Indies Consulta, Madrid, 16 October 1816, and King's Approval, 29 October 1816, all in AGI, Lima 1358.

27. Council of Indies Consultas, Madrid, 18 September 1817 and 11 August 1819, both in AGI, Lima 1358.

28. Martín José de Múxica to Cortes, Madrid, 4 October 1814, AGI, Lima 1358.

29. Regency to Ministry of Ultramar, Madrid, 24 March 1814; Tribunal of Mining to Regency, Lima, 4 October 1813; Mexican Mining Tribunal to Secretary of Ultramar, Mexico, 29 October 1814, all in AGI, Lima 1358.

30. Abascal to Ministry of Ultramar, Lima, 30 September 1813, AGI, Lima 1017.

31. BML, Actas de Cabildo, book 44, 11 October 1815; see also book 42, 9 and 17 July 1811. Abascal refused the annuity granted his daughter. In 1815 Ramona married Juan Manuel Pereyra, a royal army officer. Though she inherited her father's title, she was never wealthy.

32. Consulado to King, Lima, 21 October 1815, AGI, Lima 1539; "Consulta dirigida al Exmo. Sr. Marqués de la Concordia," Lima, 1816, AGI, Lima 795 and Lima 1551.

33. Vilca to Miguel de Lardizábal, Lima, 23 June 1815, AGI, Lima 772.

34. Gálvez to Directors of Public Hacienda, Lima, 20 July 1814; Gálvez to King, Lima, 13 February 1817, both in AGI, Lima 1116.

35. Council of Indies to Regent Anzotegui, Madrid, 8 November 1816, AGI, Lima 1017; Antonio Arroniz y Lainfiesta to King, Lima, 28 June 1815, AGI, Lima 1017.

36. Pedro Trujillo to Julian de la Vega, Lima, 8 July 1816, AGI, Lima 773.

37. BML, Actas de Cabildo, book 44, 15 and 22 March 1816, 28 January and 26 August 1817; Pezuela to Secretary of State, Lima, 12 July 1816, AGI, Estado 74; Council of Indies Consulta, Madrid, 1 August 1816, AGI, Lima 602; Tribunal of Accounts to King, Lima, 14 February 1817, AGI, Lima 1467.

CHAPTER 6

1. Pezuela, *Memoria*, pp. 74, 90.
2. Ibid., p. 97.
3. Ibid., pp. 108–17.
4. Ibid., pp. 120–21.
5. Ibid., p. 192.
6. Golovnin, "Lima y Callao en 1818," in Núñez, ed, *Relaciones de Viajeros, CDIP*, tome 27, 1:170; Bowles to John Wilson Croker, aboard *Amphion*, at sea, 4 January 1818, in Gerald S. Graham and R. A. Humphreys, eds, *The Navy and South America, 1807–1823, Correspondence of the*

256

*Commanders-in-Chief of the South American Station* (London: Navy Records Society, 1962), p. 218.

7. La Serna to Pezuela, Potosí, 1 November 1817, in Felix Denegri Luna, ed., *Memorias, Diarios y Crónicas, CDIP*, tome 26, 3:479–81.

8. Stevenson, "Memorias sobre las campañas," in Núñez, ed., *Relaciones de Viajeros, CDIP*, tome 27, 3:249–50.

9. Pezuela, *Memoria*, pp. 247, 258, 250.

10. Stevenson, "Memorias sobre las campañas," in Núñez, ed., *Relaciones de Viajeros, CDIP*, tome 27, 3:250; Pezuela, *Memorias*, p. 387.

11. Pezuela, *Memorias*, pp. 362, 380, 383, 385, 678.

12. BML, Actas de Cabildo, book 44, 28 February, 14 and 21 March, 15 July 1817.

13. Meeting of Junta de Arbitrios, Lima, 4 May 1818, ANP, Superior Govierno, L. 36, C. 1259.

14. Pezuela to Secretary of Hacienda, Lima, 16 June 1818, AGI, Lima 1550; Pezuela, *Memoria*, p. 279.

15. Pezuela, *Memoria*, pp. 295–96; Proposed plan for free trade with Rio de Janeiro and London, Manuel Pedro de Zelayeta, Lima, 2 June 1818, ANP, Superior Govierno, L. 36, C. 1264.

16. Extracts and notes added to letter of Pezuela to Secretary of Hacienda, Lima, 29 July 1819, AGI, Lima 1551; and the full letter and extracts of Junta de Arbitrios meeting, AGI, Lima 760.

17. Invoice of the *Syndey*, AGI, Lima 1550; Pezuela to Secretary of Hacienda, Lima, 26 April 1817, AGI, Lima 756; Pezuela to Secretary of Hacienda, Lima, 16 December 1817, AGI, Lima 758; Receipt signed by Félix de la Roza, Lima, 1 June 1818, AGI, Correos 115; Pezuela to Secretary of Hacienda, Lima, 3 November 1818, AGI, Lima 759.

18. Letter to Secretary of Hacienda, Lima, 31 December 1816, AGI, Lima 1468.

19. Translation of the English contract sent to Minister of Hacienda, Madrid, 10 May 1819, AGI, Lima 1550; Pezuela, *Memoria*, 396–99; Report of Rico, Lima, 30 January 1819, AGI, Lima 1551.

20. Extract of a private letter, author's name not given, Lima, 31 July 1818, AGI, Lima 1471; Consulado to King, Lima, 13 February 1819, AGI, Lima 1550.

21. Stevenson, "Memorias sobre las campañas," in Núñez, ed., *Relaciones de Viajeros, CDIP*, tome 27, 3: 255; Donald E. Worcester, *Sea Power and Chilean Independence*, pp. 39–40.

22. Pezuela, *Memoria*, pp. 413–17, 466.

23. Juez de Arribadas of Cádiz to Ministry of Ultramar, Cádiz, 8 August 1820, AGI, Arribadas 355. The Juez de Arribadas of Cádiz often sent Madrid its first news of events in America, received from arriving passengers who were still quarantined or otherwise unable to come ashore.

24. Lázaro de Rivera to Pedro de Macanaz, Lima, 3 February 1815, AGI, Lima 773; Vidaurre to King, Lima, 2 April 1817, AGI, Indiferente 1568. The 1818 census figure is contained in a report by the British consul to Lima, John McGregor, in 1847; Heraclio Bonilla, comp., *Gran Bretaña y el Perú: Informes de los cónsules británicos, 1826–1919*, 5 vols. (Lima: Instituto de Estudios Peruanos, 1975–77), 1:111–72.

25. Abascal to Secretary of Hacienda, Madrid, 29 June 1819, AGI, Lima 1505.

26. Cámara de Indias Consulta, Madrid, 8 February 1830, AGI, Lima 604.

27. Pezuela to King, extract, Madrid, 10 November 1818, AGI, Estado 74; Pezuela to Duke of San Carlos, Lima, 29 July 1818, AGI, Estado 74; Francisco María Pizarro y Zevallos to Ministry of Ultramar, Lima, 7 February 1821, AGI, Lima 1470.

28. Conde de Casa Flores to Marqués de Casa Irujo, Rio de Janeiro, 5 June 1819; *Gazeta de Buenos Aires*, 31 March 1819, both in AGI, Lima 1471.

29. Agustín Tavira y Acosta to Manuel Gonzalez Salmón, Madrid, 9 September 1819, AGI, Lima 1471; Golovnin, "Lima y Callao en 1818," in Núñez, ed., *Relaciones de Viajeros*, CDIP, tome 27, 1:151; Proctor, "El Perú entre 1823 y 1824," in ibid., 2:308–9.

30. Pezuela to Fernando de la Serna, Lima, 20 January 1818, AGI, Correos 115; Joaquín Bonet to Directors of the General Administration of Mails, Lima, 8 July 1819, and another to same, 10 February 1821, and the report of Bonet as visitador, AGI, Correos 115; Order of Pezuela, Lima, 4 May 1820, in Denegri Luna, *Memorias, Diarios y Crónicas*, CDIP, tome 26, 3:403–9.

31. Vicente Romero to Secretary of Hacienda, Madrid, 16 November 1820, AGI, Indiferente 2440.

32. Olarria to Government, Madrid, 29 July 1820; "Noticia de las deliberaciones que en nombre del virrey del Peru pide Francisco Xavier de Olarria," Madrid, 28 August 1820; Domingo Espinosa to Secretary of Ultramar, Madrid, 14 August 1820, all in AGI, Lima 1022.

33. Estados, ships entering Cádiz, year of 1820, Cádiz, 4 May 1821, AGI, Indiferente 2293; Resume of a letter of Consulado, Madrid, 3 May 1817, AGI, Indiferente 313, and report of the Contaduría General, Madrid, 23 April 1818, AGI, Lima 1538; Vicente Romero to Council of Indies, Madrid, 25 February 1819, AGI, Lima 1069; Company of the Philippines to Silvestre Collar, Madrid, 5 October 1818, AGI, Indiferente 2440; Opinion of Contador General José Texada, Madrid, 23 December 1818, AGI, Lima 610.

34. Royal order to Minister of State, Madrid, 6 March 1818, AGI, Lima 1551; P. Pascasio Fernández to Juan Palarea, London, 11 September 1820, AGI, Indiferente 2439; Blas de Mendizabal to Secretary of

Hacienda, London, 1 September 1821, AGI, Indiferente 2440; José Delavat to José Argüelles, Rio de Janeiro, 23 January 1821, AGI, Indiferente 2440. On the British intervention in the Peruvian market see Heraclio Bonilla, "La coyuntura comercial del siglo XIX en el Perú," pp. 159–87, and Bonilla and Spalding, "La independencia en el Perú."

35. Pezuela to Secretary of Hacienda, Lima, 28 January 1820, AGI, Indiferente 2440; Pezuela, *Memorias*, p. 646.

36. Francisco Ruiz de Tagle to King, Lima, 1 June 1818, AGI, Lima 773; Opinion of Manuel Aparici to Secretary of Hacienda, Madrid, 28 January 1817, AGI, Lima 1619; Royal order, Madrid, 22 May 1817, AGI, Lima 603; Publicity notices of Rico, Lima, 17 November, 1 December 1818, 20 January, 27 June, and 30 June 1819, AGI, Lima 1444; BML, Actas de Cabildo, book 44, 26 January 1819; Rico to Pezuela, Lima, 23 March 1820 and Rico to Secretary of Hacienda, Lima, 28 March 1820, both in AGI, Lima 1469.

37. Vicente Romero to Secretary of Hacienda, Madrid, 16 November 1820, AGI, Indiferente 2440; Pezuela, *Memoria*, p. 703.

38. BML, Actas de Cabildo, book 44, 11 and 26 January, 7 and 11 May, 1 October 1819; Royal order to cabildo of Lima, Madrid, 22 July 1819, AGI, Lima 1223; Pezuela, *Memoria*, p. 579; "Relación de los aportes contribuidos por los vecinos de la ciudad de Lima para cubrir el cupo forxozo impuesto por el gobierno," 1819–21, ANP, Superior Govierno, L. 37, C. 1308.

39. Pezuela to Secretary of State, Lima, 12 November 1818, AGI, Estado 74.

40. Ministry of Hacienda to Council of Indies, Madrid, 26 August 1819, AGI, Lima 603.

41. Pezuela to Secretary of Hacienda, Lima, 30 November 1818, AGI, Lima 76l.

42. Council of State Consulta, Madrid, 15 July 1820, AGI, Lima 603.

43. Riva Agüero to King, Lima, 23 July 1811, AGI, Lima 772; Royal order to Viceroy of Peru, Madrid, 27 May 1817, and accompanying documents, AGI, Lima 1467; Riva Agüero to Directors of Public Hacienda, Lima, 26 April 1814, AGI, Lima 1019; Council of Indies Consulta, Madrid, 24 November 1818, AGI, Lima 603.

44. Memo to Contador General de Indias, Madrid, 1 April 1815, quoting letter of Abascal, Lima, 2 June 1814, AGI, Lima 608.

45. Council of Indies Consulta, Madrid, 21 April 1818, AGI, Lima 1019; Council of Indies Consulta, Madrid, 24 November 1818, AGI, Lima 603; Royal order to Viceroy of Peru, Madrid, 28 August 1819, AGI, Lima 1471. The evidence presented here suggests we should abandon any thoughts that Riva Agüero supported independence as a means of resisting the liberal reforms of the Cortes in 1821, as suggested by Bonilla and Spalding, "La independencia en el Perú," p. 51.

46. Basadre, *Iniciación de la república*, 1:9; Vicuña Mackenna, *Independencia en el Perú*, p. 96.

47. So says Cesar García Rosell, "Riva Agüero y sus '28 Causas,' " in *La causa de la emancipación del Perú*, pp. 419–25.

48. Council of Indies Consulta, Madrid, 21 June 1816, AGI, Lima 602; Council of Indies Consulta, Madrid, 8 March 1817, AGI, Lima 603; Pezuela to Secretary of Hacienda, Lima, 28 March 1820, AGI, Lima 1121; Proctor, "El Perú entre 1823 y 1824," in Núñez, ed., *Relaciones de Viajeros, CDIP*, tome 27, 2:250.

49. Vicuña Mackenna, *Independencia en el Perú*, pp. 201–14.

50. Leguía y Martínez, *Historia de la emancipación*, 2:271–73.

51. Readers will find the most thorough accounting of dissident activity in ibid., 2:246–329.

52. Pezuela, *Memoria*, pp. 418–19, 465; Vicuña Mackenna, *Independencia en el Perú*, pp. 223, 225–26; Inquisitors of Lima to Superior Government, Lima, 26 May 1820, AGI, Lima 1022.

53. Pezuela to Minister of War, Lima, 10 October 1816, AGI, Lima 1019; Council of Indies to Minister of Grace and Justice, Madrid, 18 September 1818, AGI, Lima 603.

54. Council of Indies Consulta, Madrid, 15 July 1818, AGI, Lima 603; Report of Tomás Vallejo, outlined and discussed in Madrid, 19 May 1818, AGI, Lima 788; see Vergara Arias, *Montoneras y Guerrillas*.

55. Pezuela, *Memoria*, p. 716.

56. For another perspective on the expedition see Timothy E. Anna, "The Buenos Aires Expedition and Spain's Secret Plan to Conquer Portugal."

57. Pezuela, *Memoria*, pp. 728, 731.

58. Ibid., pp. 754–55, 763–64.

59. Fernando Farina and Manuel Abreu to Ministry of Ultramar, Madrid, 12 April 1822, AGI, Lima 800.

60. This inaccurate idea was first proposed by Paz Soldán, *Historia del Perú independiente*, part 2, 1:250, who thought that Pezuela was overthrown by La Serna and the other officers because they thought him too conservative.

61. Ruben Vargas Ugarte, *Historia general del Perú*, 6:79–83.

62. Pezuela, *Memoria*, p. 773.

63. Ibid., p. 782.

64. Jacinto de Romarate to Secretary of Ultramar, Aranjuez, 30 March 1822, AGI, Indiferente 1571.

CHAPTER 7

1. Pezuela, *Memoria*, p. 798; Juez de Arribadas to Ministry of Ultramar, Cádiz, 16 March 1821, AGI, Indiferente 2291; Juez de Arribadas

to Ministry of Ultramar, Cádiz, 23 March 1821, AGI, Indiferente 2293; Minister of Ultramar to Minister of State, Madrid, 31 January 1822, AGI, Indiferente 313.

2. Pezuela, *Memoria*, pp. 799–800.

3. Paz Soldán, *Historia del Perú independiente*, part 1, 1:101–10.

4. Minister of Grace and Justice to Secretary of Hacienda, Madrid, 29 May 1819, AGI, Lima 1471; Royal Cédula to Viceroy of Peru, Madrid, 23 June 1819, AGI, Lima 610.

5. San Martín to Las Heras, Huaura, 20 December 1820; San Martín to Rico, Huaura, 21 December 1820, both in AGI, Lima 800; San Martín's manifestos to American soldiers, Spanish soldiers, women, Europeans, and nobles, AGI, Indiferente 313.

6. Ugarriza to Matías de la Fuente, Lima, 2 July 1820; to Juan Bautista Odaondo, 2 July 1820; to Antonio de Finajas, 18 September 1820; to Matías de la Fuente, 25 October 1820; to Manuel Martín de Romaña, 6 December 1820; and to Antonio de Finajas, 18 December 1820, all in ANP, Superior Govierno, L. 37, C. 1325.

7. Pezuela to San Martín, Lima, 30 October 1820; San Martín to Pezuela, aboard the *San Martín*, 31 October 1820; Pezuela to San Martín, Lima, 3 November 1820; and San Martín to Pezuela, Huaura, 24 December 1820, all in AGI, Lima 800.

8. Worcester, *Sea Power*, pp. 58–60.

9. Hall, *Extracts*, 1:215–16.

10. Pezuela, *Memoria*, pp. 811–12.

11. BML, Actas de Cabildo, book 45, 9 November and 7 December 1820.

12. Ibid., 18 December 1820, 15 and 16 January 1821.

13. "Fragmento del expediente promovida por el Real Tribunal del Consulado . . . manifestando la situación en que se encuentran las costas del Perú . . . , año de 1820," ANP Govierno Superior, L. 37, C. 1324; Antonio Real de Asua, Apoderado of the Lima Consulado, to King, Madrid, 31 August 1821, AGI, Indiferente 313.

14. "Situación política de Lima," a report by Félix D'Olhaberriague y Blanco, Madrid, 19 June 1821, AGI, Lima 1023.

15. Anonymous letter, "Es de Lima de sugeto fide digno," AGI, Indiferente 1570.

16. Marqués de Valleumbroso and Antonio Seoane to Conde de Casa Flores, Rio de Janeiro, 29 June 1821, AGI, Indiferente 313.

17. Anonymous letter, Lima, 30 April 1821, AGI, Indiferente 1570.

18. Manifesto of officers to Pezuela, Aznapuquio, 29 January 1821, in Denegri Luna, ed., *Memorias, Diarios y Crónicas, CDIP*, tome 26, 3: 353–58; Account of Juan Martín de Larrañaga given in editors' introduction to Pezuela's *Memoria*.

19. La Serna to Secretary of War, Lima, 9 February 1821, AGI, Indifer-

ente 313; La Serna to Minister of Grace and Justice, Cuzco, 15 March 1824, AGI, Lima 762.

20. Conde de Casa Flores to Minister of Ultramar, Rio de Janeiro, 7 July 1821, AGI, Indiferente 313.

21. Anonymous letter, "Es de Lima de sugeto fide digno," AGI, Indiferente 1570; Anonymous letter, Lima, 30 April 1821, AGI, Indiferente 1570.

22. Pezuela, *Memoria*, p. 841; Pezuela to Secretary of War, Magdalena, 1 February 1821, in Denegri Luna, ed., *Memorias, Diarios y Crónicas, CDIP*, tome 26, 3:486–99.

23. "Manifiesto en que el virrey del Perú D. Joaquín de la Pezuela refiere el hecho y circunstancias de su separación del mando . . . ," Magdalena, 8 April 1821, in Denegri Luna, ed., *Memorias, Diarios y Crónicas, CDIP*, tome 26, 3:267–505.

24. Ibid., pp. 433-57, various letters, and "Tres folletos a favor del virrey Pezuela," pp. 510–46.

25. The story of Pezuela's escape is narrated in an appendix to his *Memoria*, pp. 847–63.

26. Anonymous letter, "Es de Lima de sugeto fide digno," AGI, Indiferente 1570; Hall, *Extracts*, 1:263; La Serna to peace negotiators, Lima, 12 June 1821, AGI, Lima 800.

27. Vargas Ugarte, *Historia general del Perú*, 6:164; Paz Soldán, *Historia del Perú independiente*, part 1, 1:162.

28. BML, Actas de Cabildo, book 45, 10 and 20 February, 11 and 25 April, 22 May, and 8 June 1821.

29. Vargas Ugarte, *Historia general del Perú*, 6:152; Paz Soldán, *Historia del Perú independiente*, part 1, 1:163.

30. Vargas Ugarte, *Historia general del Perú*, 6:166.

31. Ibid., 6:158–60; La Serna to Abreu, Huancayo, 2 November 1821; Abreu to La Serna, Lima, 12 November 1821, both in AGI, Lima 800.

32. La Serna to Conde de Casa Flores, Andahuaylas, 11 December 1821, AGI, Indiferente 313.

33. "El virey a los habitantes del Perú," Lima, 4 July 1821, AGI, Indiferente 1571.

34. La Serna to Montemira, Lima, 5 July 1821, AGI, Indiferente 1571; Audiencia to La Serna, Lima, 5 July 1821, AGI, Lima 800 and Indiferente 1571; "El virey a los habitantes del Perú," Lurín, 8 July 1821, AGI, Indiferente 313.

35. La Serna to Secretary of Hacienda, Cuzco, 19 October 1822, AGI, Lima 762; Vargas Ugarte, *Historia general del Perú*, 6:169.

36. Ibid., 6:167–68.

37. Pedro Fernando Farina and Manuel Abreu to Secretary of Ultramar, Madrid, 12 April 1822, AGI, Lima 800; Antonio Vacaro's report, submitted in letter of Jacinto de Romarate to Secretary of Ultramar,

Aranjuez, 30 March 1822, AGI, Indiferente 1571; "Analisis de las circunstancias del General La Serna. Virey intruso del Perú," by "El Observador," Rio de Janeiro, 1821, AGI, Indiferente 1569, also published in Denegri Luna, ed., *Memorias, Diarios y Crónicas CDIP*, tome 26, 3:539–46.

38. La Serna to Secretary of War, Cuzco, 22 February 1822, AGI, Indiferente 313.

39. BML, Actas de Cabildo, book 45, 6 and 7 July 1821.

40. Ibid., 15 July 1821. Copies of the declaration and of the cabildo meetings immediately before and after have been printed, in edited form, in Gamio Palacio, *La municipalidad* (1971). A facsimile of the declaration and the signatures was published in 1971 by the Concejo Provincial de Lima under the title *Acta de la declaración de la independencia nacional*.

41. This sum was arrived at by counting the signatures on the facsimile copy. The *Gaceta del Gobierno de Lima Independiente* published a special edition on 10 August 1821, containing an incomplete list of 3,136 signatures.

42. See Timothy E. Anna, "The Peruvian Declaration of Independence: Freedom by Coercion."

43. Hall, *Extracts*, 1:219–32.

44. Report of Vacaro in letter of Jacinto de Romarate to Ministry of Ultramar, Aranjuez, 30 March 1822, AGI, Indiferente 1571.

45. Pedro Angel de Tado to Marqués de Castell-Bravo de Rivero, Madrid, 14 November 1823, AGI, Lima 1024. This letter was sent to Castell-Bravo, an emigrant Lima oidor; he turned it over to the fiscal of the Council of Indies, who suggested it be published as propaganda. The Council read the letter in a session on 17 January 1826, but there is no indication it was ever published. Tado had a long career as a parish priest among the Peruvian Indians. After he returned to Spain he requested a benefice in some church in Spain. His relación de méritos and letters of recommendation in his behalf from Archbishop Las Heras and Castell-Bravo are in AGI, Lima 1563. In February 1826 the Cámara de Indias agreed to find him a position; Cámara de Indias Consulta, Madrid, 27 February 1826, AGI, Lima 604.

46. Gamio Palacio, *La muncipalidad*, p. 42.

47. Manuel Pardo to Minister of Grace and Justice, Rio de Janeiro, 12 February 1822, AGI, Lima 1619; Manuel Méndez to King, Madrid, 16 September 1823, AGI, Lima 1024; Council of Indies Consulta, Madrid, 26 January 1824, AGI, Lima 604; Bishop of Huamanga to Minister of Grace and Justice, Mexico City, 8 March 1822, AGI, Indiferente 1571.

48. Expediente concerning José Antonio Prada, Madrid, 1824, AGI, Lima 1024. This is not the former regent of Lima, Manuel de Arredondo y Pelegrín, who died in 1821, but his nephew and heir Brigadier Manuel de Arredondo y Mioño.

49. Unsigned diario, Rio de Janeiro, 26 December 1821, AGI, Lima 1023.

50. Hall, *Extracts*, 1:254–55.

51. "Relación elevada al Sr. Presidente del Departamento por los escribanos de Lima" ANP, Superior Govierno, L. 38, C. 1365; Conde de Villar de Fuente to San Martín, Lima, 2 August 1821, ANP, AHH, PL 1-10: the names of Consulado members are taken from a letter of the Consulado to Pezuela, Lima, 27 July 1818, AGI, Lima 155; Decree of San Martín, Quartel General de la Legua, 19 July 1821, AGI, Lima 800.

52. *Suplemento a la Gaceta del Gobierno*, 22 May 1822; *Gaceta del Gobierno*, 2 and 26 January 1822; Martín de Aramburu to Minister of Ultramar, Rio de Janeiro, 2 September 1822, AGI, Lima 798; Cristóval Domingo and others to Juez de Arribadas, Cádiz, 19 March 1822, AGI, Lima 1619; "Relación de los sugetos que han salido de la ciudad de Lima . . . abordo de la *Especulación*," Cádiz, 15 March 1822, AGI, Indiferente 1571; Letters of Juez de Arribadas de Cádiz to Ministry of Ultramar, Cádiz, 15 and 19 March 1822, AGI, Indiferente 2294 and Indiferente 1571; Unsigned diario, Rio de Janeiro, 26 December 1821, AGI, Lima 1023.

53. Paz Soldán, *Historia del Perú independiente*, part 1, 1:314; Rico's figure reported in letter of La Serna to Minister of Hacienda, Cuzco, 2 April 1824, AGI, Lima 762; Hall, *Extracts*, 2:87. Paz Soldán's and Rico's figures for numbers of Spaniards were estimates.

54. Conde de Vallehermoso to King, Madrid, 25 August 1825, and Hacienda to Contador General, Madrid, 12 October 1825, both in AGI, Lima 1472; Francisco de Puga to King, Madrid, October 1823, AGI, Lima 1470; Antonio Caspe y Rodríguez to King, Madrid, 28 April 1822, AGI, Lima 1470.

55. *Gaceta del Gobierno de Lima Independiente*, 18 August 1821; Order of Torre Tagle, Lima, 16 February 1822, ANP, AHH, OL 29-21; Conde de Montemar to King, Madrid, 27 September 1823, AGI, Lima 1023.

56. Expediente concerning Francisco Tomás Anzotegui, Regent of Lima, 1821, AGI, Lima 795.

57. Unsigned diario, Rio de Janeiro, 26 December 1821, AGI, Lima 1023.

58. This figure is drawn from the list of real estate owners in 1820, ANP, Superior Govierno, L. 37, C. 1335.

59. Hall, *Extracts*, 1:114.

60. Council of Indies Consulta, Madrid, 16 June 1817, AGI, Lima 1018-B. The king actually agreed to send a formal request to the Holy See for Lima to be raised to the cardinalate, although no one expected it to happen, since there were as yet no American cardinals. Other documents on the question are in AGI, Lima 1568. When asked his opinion, former Viceroy Abascal endorsed Las Heras in the highest terms.

61. "Estado de la Iglesia metropolitana de Lima," 1820, AGI, Lima

264
NOTES

1566. There was only one European, four whose birthplaces were not given, and one appointee who had not yet arrived.

62. In 1820 Trujillo had a Spanish bishop and a chapter of four creoles and three Europeans; Arequipa had a creole bishop and a chapter of four creoles and three Europeans. This has not been emphasized in several studies of the clergy in independence, including Ruben Vargas Ugarte, *El episcopado en los tiempos de la emancipación*, or Sparks, "The Role of the Clergy during the Struggle for Independence in Peru." See Antonine Tibesar, "The Peruvian Church at the Time of Independence in the Light of Vatican II"; and idem, "The Lima Pastors, 1750–1820: Their Origins and Studies Taken from Their Autobiographies."

63. Jorge Arias-Schreiber Pezet, *Los médicos en la independencia del Perú*, p. 108.

64. Expediente concerning José Arizmendi, Madrid, 1825, AGI, Lima 604; Proctor, "El Perú entre 1823 y 1824," in Núñez, ed., *Relaciones de Viajeros*, CDIP, tome 27, 2: 309.

65. Hall, *Extracts*, 1:260–61; Gamio Palacio, *La municipalidad*, pp. 68–77.

CHAPTER 8

1. In March 1822 La Serna reported to Spain the arrival of the first news from the peninsula in a year. La Serna to Minister of Ultramar, Cuzco, 12 March 1822, AGI, Lima 1023.

2. The most worshipful treatment of the protector's withdrawal and of all other aspects of his career is Ricardo Rojas, *San Martín: Knight of the Andes*.

3. Report of a group of officers from the *Especulación*, Cádiz, 19 March 1822, AGI, Indiferente 2294; Cos to Minister of Grace and Justice, Mexico City, 8 March 1822, AGI, Indiferente 1571; San Martín to O'Higgins, quoted in Adolfo J. Galatoire, *Cuáles fueron las enfermedades de San Martín*, p. 26; Cruz, quoted in ibid., p. 77.

4. Ibid., pp. 107–13, 139.

5. Hall, *Extracts*, 1:282–83; Anna, "Economic Causes of San Martín's Failure in Lima," pp. 657–81.

6. "Razón de las fincas del Estado que se han distribuido entre los Jefes del Ejército Libertador," ANP, AHH, OL 7–18; Cabildo to Hipólito Unánue, 22 July 1822, ANP, AHH, OL 45–6; Expediente concerning José Antonio Prada, Madrid, 1824, AGI, Lima 1024; Expediente concerning Juan Bautista Lavalle, Lima, 1821, ANP, AHH, PL 1-34.

7. Order of Supreme Delegate Torre Tagle, Lima, 23 May 1822, ANP, AHH, OL 29-56; *Gaceta del Gobierno*, 26 December 1821.

8. Abascal to Secretary of Ultramar, Lima, 31 July 1814, AGI, Lima 747.

9. Stevenson, "Memorias sobre las campañas," in Núñez, ed., *Re-*

*laciones de Viajeros, CDIP*, tome 27, 3:273; Anonymous report to Spain, 30 April 1821, AGI, Indiferente 1570; Report of Ramón del Valle, Rio de Janeiro, 5 March 1822, AGI, Indiferente 313.

10. *Gaceta del Gobierno*, 28 November 1821.

11. Ibid., 5 and 21 September, 21 November 1821, 17 April and 15 May 1822; *Gaceta Ministerial de Chile*, 24 November 1821, in AGI, Lima 800.

12. Francisco Carrillos, Conde de Vistaflorida, and Francisco de Zea to President of the Department Riva Agüero, Lima, March 1822, ANP, AHH, PL 2-21; John Miller, *Memoirs of General Miller in the Service of the Republic of Peru*, 2:94; Gilbert F. Mathison, "Residencia en Lima entre Abril y Mayo de 1822," in Núñez, ed., *Relaciones de Viajeros, CDIP*, tome 27, 1:284; *Gaceta del Gobierno*, 3 October 1821.

13. Worcester, *Sea Power*, p. 69; Vargas Ugarte, *Historia general del Perú*, 6:194; Stevenson, "Memorias sobre las campañas," in Núñez, ed., *Relaciones de Viajeros, CDIP*, tome 27, 3:306.

14. "Estado general . . . de tropas que defendieron la Plaza del Callao," and the surrender agreement, Callao, 19 September 1821, AGI, Indiferente 1571; Proclamation of La Serna, Huamanga, 28 November 1821, AGI, Indiferente 313; Unsigned report from Rio de Janeiro, 10 January 1822, AGI, Indiferente 1570.

15. *Gaceta de Gobierno*, 7 November, 5 December 1821, 29 May, 2 October 1822; Treasury Administrator to Minister of Finance, Lima, 15 October 1821, ANP, AHH, OL 7-12a.

16. Governing Junta to President of Congress, Lima, 9 October 1822, listing the merchants, ANP, AHH, OL 49-4.

17. *Suplemento a la Gaceta del Gobierno*, 10 October 1821, 9 October 1822.

18. "Estado que manifiesta . . . las entradas actuales ordinarias de la Tesorería General de la Republica," 2 January 1823, ANP, AHH, OL 30-36.

19. *Suplemento a la Gaceta del Gobierno*, 31 October 1821; *Gaceta del Gobierno*, 20 October, 10 November, 14 November, 1 December 1821.

20. Decree of San Martín, 23 October 1821, ANP, AHH, OL 1-9a; *Suplemento a la Gaceta del Gobierno*, 24 November 1821.

21. Cabildo to San Martín, 1 September 1821, ANP, AHH, OL 7-10; *Gaceta del Gobierno*, 20 January 1822.

22. List of contributors to state collection, ANP, Superior Govierno, L. 38, C. 1370; San Martín to Consulado, 28 August 1821, ANP, AHH, OL 3-6; "Expediente sobre un cupo de 150,000 pesos al Comercio de la Capital," ANP, AHH, PL 1-10; Cabildo to Unánue, 11 September 1821, ANP, AHH, OL 7-11; Cabildo to Unánue, 19 September 1821, ANP, AHH, OL 7-12; *Suplemento a la Gaceta del Gobierno*, 22 May 1822. Documents relating to the 150,000 peso collection are published in Alberto Tauro, ed., *Asuntos económicos: Informes y oficios del Tribunal del Consulado, CDIP*, tome 21, 1:373–456.

23. Governing Junta to President of Congress, Lima, 9 October 1822, ANP, AHH, OL 49-4; Secretary of Congress to Minister of Finance, Lima, 19 October 1822, ANP, AHH, OL 30-10, accompanied by letters of Prescott.

24. The treasure consisted of 80,000 pesos in silver and 23,780 ounces of gold. The price of gold was 16 pesos an ounce. Unsigned Diario, Rio de Janeiro, December 1821, AGI, Lima 1023. See also unsigned report from Rio de Janeiro, 10 January 1822, AGI, Indiferente 1570; *Gaceta del Gobierno*, 24 October 1821; and Stevenson, "Memoria sobre las campañas," in Núñez, ed., *Relaciones de Viajeros, CDIP*, tome 27, 3: 307, who says that Cochrane kept only 285,000 pesos that belonged to the government and returned the money on deposit from private individuals.

25. *Gaceta del Gobierno*, 1 December 1821.

26. Stevenson, "Memoria sobre las campañas," in Núñez, ed., *Relaciones de Viajeros, CDIP*, tome 27, 3: 309.

27. Camprubi Alcázar, *El Banco*, p. 25; Report of Antonio Jaranco, Rio de Janeiro, 27 February 1822; Report of Ramón del Valle, Rio de Janeiro, 5 March 1822; Antonio Luis Pereyra to Secretary of State, Rio de Janeiro, 27 February 1822, all in AGI, Indiferente 313; Report of S. A. (true name D. J. Cereño, hacendado de Lima) to Minister of Ultramar, Rio de Janeiro, 9 September 1822; Juan Bazo y Berri to Minister of Ultramar, Rio de Janeiro, 29 May 1822, both in AGI, Lima 798.

28. Order of Torre Tagle, Lima, 28 February 1822, ANP, AHH, OL 29-25.

29. Quoted in Vargas Ugarte, *Historia general del Perú*, 6:240; on the plots see 6:206.

30. Unsigned diario, Rio de Janeiro, December 1821, AGI, Lima 1023.

31. Report of Antonio Jaranco, Rio de Janeiro, 27 February 1822, AGI, Indiferente 313; *El Depositario*, no. 52, Huancayo, 22 October 1821, AGI, Indiferente 313; *Gaceta del Gobierno*, 2 October 1822.

32. Superior order, Lima, 18 February 1822, ANP, AHH, OL 29-22.

33. Report of S. A., Rio de Janeiro, 9 September 1822, AGI, Lima 798; Proctor, "El Perú entre 1823 y 1824," in Núñez, ed., *Relaciones de Viajeros, CDIP*, tome 27, 3: 291.

34. Ruybál to Antonio Luis Pereyra, Rio de Janeiro, 27 July 1822, AGI, Lima 798.

35. *Gaceta del Gobierno*, 10 July 1822, 1 December 1821; Riva Agüero to Minister of Finance, Lima, 20 August 1822, ANP, AHH, OL 53-20; Summary Accounts, September, October, and November 1822, ANP, AHH, OL 52-44a, 52-49, and 52-50.

36. *Gaceta del Gobierno*, 19 September 1821, 2, 12, and 26 January, 2 February, and 30 January 1822.

37. Antonio Luis Pereyra to Secretary of State, Rio de Janeiro, 27 February 1822, AGI, Indiferente 313.

38. *Gaceta del Gobierno*, 24 April 1822; Francisco Xavier de Yzcue to Monteagudo, Lima, 15 April 1822, ANP, AHH, OL 49-1.

39. See Vargas Ugarte, *El episcopado*, pp. 179–84; Vargas Ugarte, *Historia general del Perú*, 6:183–84; Paz Soldán, *Historia del Perú independiente*, part 1, 1:211; Unsigned diario, Rio de Janeiro, December 1821, AGI, Lima 1023; Council of Indies Consulta, Madrid, 26 January 1824, AGI, Lima 604; Order of Monteagudo, Lima, 23 May 1822, ANP, AHH, OL 29-33.

40. Miller, *Memoirs*, 1:352.

41. Mathison, "Residencia en Lima," in Núñez, ed., *Relaciones de Viajeros, CDIP*, tome 27, 1: 290.

42. Martín de Aramburu to Ministry of Ultramar, Rio de Janeiro, 2 September 1822, AGI, Lima 798.

43. Mathison, "Residencia en Lima," in Núñez, ed., *Relaciones de Viajeros, CDIP*, tome 27, 1: 307–15.

44. Stevenson, "Memoria sobre las campañas," in ibid., 3: 331–32.

45. Paz Soldán, *Historia del Perú independiente*, part 1, 1:200.

46. Mathison, "Residencia en Lima," in Núñez, ed., *Relaciones de Viajeros, CDIP*, tome 27, 1: 287–88.

47. BML, Actas de Cabildo, book 45, 25 and 26 July 1822; Vargas Ugarte, *Historia general del Perú*, 6:238; Paz Soldán, *Historia del Perú independiente*, part 1, 1:317; Jorge Basadre, *Historia de la república del Perú, 1822–1933*, 1:101.

48. Vargas Ugarte, *Historia general del Perú*, 6:186; Hall, *Extracts*, 2:88.

49. Hall, *Extracts*, 1:282–83.

50. Report of Ramón del Valle, Rio de Janeiro, 5 March 1822, AGI, Indiferente 313; Unsigned diario from Rio de Janeiro, 10 January 1822, AGI, Indiferente 1570; Cristóval Domingo to Juez de Arribadas, Cádiz, 19 March 1822, AGI, Lima 1619; José María Ruybál to Antonio Luis Pereyra, Rio de Janeiro, 27 July 1822, AGI, Lima 798; Mathison, "Residencia en Lima," in Núñez, ed., *Relaciones de Viajeros, CDIP*, tome 27, 1: 293–95; Miller, *Memoirs*, 1:347.

51. Vargas Ugarte, *Historia general del Perú*, 6:231; *Gaceta del Gobierno*, 24 August 1822.

52. Vargas Ugarte, *Historia general del Perú*, 6:240, "Bolívar y yo no cabemos en el Perú."

53. La Serna to Secretary of Ultramar, Cuzco, 12 March, 26 September 1822, AGI, Lima 1023. A few documents relating to La Serna's administration at Cuzco, particularly his proclamations and propaganda, are published in Horacio Villanueva Urteaga, ed., *Documentación oficial española, CDIP*, tome 22, vol. 3.

54. Proclamation of La Serna, Huancayo, 12 November 1821, AGI, Indiferente 313; Proclamation of San Martín, Lima, 4 December 1821, AGI, Indiferente 313.

55. See *El Depositario* for 22 October, 27 November, and 30 November 1821, in AGI, Indiferente 313.

56. La Serna to Conde de Casa Flores, Andahuaylas, 11 December 1821, AGI, Indiferente 313; La Serna to Minister of Hacienda, Cuzco, 2 April 1824, AGI, Lima 762.

57. La Serna to Conde de Casa Flores, Andahuaylas, 11 December 1821, AGI, Indiferente 313.

58. Francisco Richard to Secretary of State, Burdeos, 14 May 1822, AGI, Indiferente 313; Juan Bazo y Berri to Minister of Ultramar, Rio de Janeiro, 29 May 1822, AGI, Lima 798.

59. Alexander Caldcleugh, "El Perú en Víspera de la jura de la independencia," in Núñez, ed., *Relaciones de Viajeros, CDIP*, tome 27, 1: 196.


CHAPTER 9

1. Quoted in Masur, *Bolívar*, p. 358.

2. Ibid., p. 360; John Lynch, *The Spanish-American Revolutions, 1808–1826*, p. 266; Basadre, *Historia de la república*, 1:75, 84; Paz Soldán, *Historia del Perú independiente*, part 2, 1:44; Vargas Ugarte, *Historia general del Perú*, 6:302.

3. Francisco Valdivieso to Rafael Menendez, Lima, 20 January 1823, ANP, AHH, OL 70-31.

4. James Thomson, "Impresiones de Lima entre 1822 y 1824," in Núñez, ed., *Relaciones de Viajeros, CDIP*, tome 27, 2: 15.

5. Basadre, *Historia de la república*, 1:24–28; Vargas Ugarte, *Historia general del Perú*, 6:241–50.

6. Basadre, *Historia de la república*, 1:31–34; Vargas Ugarte, *Historia general del Perú*, 6:252–54; for a study on the long-term effect of the British loans subsequently taken by Peru see W. M. Mathew, "The Imperialism of Free Trade: Peru, 1820–1870"; and for the history of this first loan see Mathew, "The First Anglo-Peruvian Debt and Its Settlement, 1822–49."

7. Quoted in Basadre, *Historia de la república*, 1:35.

8. BML, Actas de Cabildo, book 45, 5 and 9 September, 1823; Thomson, "Impresiones de Lima entre 1822 y 1824," in Núñez, ed., *Relaciones de Viajeros, CDIP*, tome 27, 2: 36; and Proctor, "El Perú entre 1823 y 1824," in ibid., 3: 206.

9. Thomson, "Impresiones de Lima entre 1822 y 1824," in Núñez, ed., *Relaciones de Viajeros, CDIP*, tome 27, 2: 38–39; Vargas Ugarte, *Historia general del Perú*, 6:277–79.

10. Decrees of Congress (Torre Tagle's supporters), Callao, 21 June 1823; Lima, 16 August 1823; and Lima, 19 August 1823, respectively ANP, AHH, OL 70-80, OL 66-18, and OL 66-19; Order of Congress (Riva Agüero's supporters), Callao, 23 June 1823, ANP, AHH, OL 70-78.

11. Decree of Torre Tagle, Lima, 23 July 1823, ANP, AHH, OL 66-8; BML, Actas de Cabildo, book 45, 2 September 1823.

12. Cabildo of Lima to Torre Tagle, Lima, 30 July 1823, ANP, AHH, OL 85-13; Angel de Alfaro to Minister of Finance, Lima, 20 January 1824, ANP, AHH, OL 4-9.

13. Vergara Arias, *Montoneras y guerrillas*, pp. 49–60; Proctor, "El Perú entre 1823 y 1824," in Núñez, ed., *Relaciones de Viajeros, CDIP*, tome 27, 2: 250.

14. Decree of Torre Tagle, Lima, 18 August 1823, ANP, AHH, OL 66-20.

15. Quoted in Masur, *Bolívar*, p. 360.

16. BML, Actas de Cabildo, book 45, 6 June 1823; Francisco de Echagüe to Berindoaga, Lima, 12 November 1823, ANP, AHH, OL 70-142a; Vargas Ugarte, *Historia general del Perú*, 6:302.

17. Paz Soldán, *Historia del Perú independiente*, part 2, 1:216–17.

18. Reinforcing the sense of absolute anarchy is the absence of documents relating to several key events. A large body of collected reports and correspondence from Viceroy La Serna, being carried to Spain by his commissioners Antonio Seoane and the marqués de Valleumbroso, was thrown overboard when the commissioners were seized by Buenos Aires corsairs off the coast of Brazil; Unsigned note to Secretary of War, Madrid, 5 October 1822, AGI, Ultramar 812. Torre Tagle lost many of his papers in two fires in the palace—one on the night of 13 July 1822, and one set by the Spaniards in July 1823; *Gaceta del Gobierno*, 2 October 1822; Paz Soldán, *Historia del Perú independiente*, part 1, 1:313; Proctor, "El Perú entre 1823 y 1824," in Núñez, ed., *Relaciones de Viajeros, CDIP*, tome 27, 2: 248. The Acts of the Lima cabildo also have significant gaps. There are no records from 10 June to 22 July 1823—during the first royalist occupation, BML, Actas de Cabildo, book 45, 22 July 1823. More seriously, the Acts of the cabildo ceased altogether on 27 January 1824—a few days before the second Spanish occupation. Book 45 is the last Libro de Actas in the Biblioteca Municipal de Lima. Finally, the newly founded National Library, containing San Martín's personal collection of books, was looted by the royalists in 1823 and in 1824.

19. Berindoaga to Minister of Hacienda, Lima, 2 September 1823, ANP, AHH, OL 70-83.

20. Quoted in Masur, *Bolívar*, p. 360.

21. Quoted in ibid., p. 364.

22. Bolívar to Berindoaga, Pativilca, 12 January 1824, ANP, AHH, OL 99-4.

23. Basadre, *Historia de la república*, 1:77–78.

24. Proctor, "El Perú entre 1823 y 1824," in Núñez, ed., *Relaciones de Viajeros, CDIP*, tome 27, 2: 324–28. At the end of March 1824 Proctor and his family fled Lima, without passports, on a British warship.

25. Basadre, *Historia de la república*, 1:82.

26. Quoted in ibid., 1:84.

27. Quoted in Masur, *Bolívar*, pp. 366–67.

28. Cabildo to General Rodil, Lima, 17 March 1824, AGI, Estado 75; *Triunfo del Callao, Extraordinario*, Lima, 20 March 1824.

29. Thomson, "Impresiones de Lima entre 1822 y 1824," in Núñez, ed., *Relaciones de Viajeros, CDIP*, tome 27, 2: 57–58.

30. "El Marqués de Torre Tagle a sus compatriotas," Lima, March 1824, AGI, Estado 75.

31. Vargas Ugarte, *Historia general del Perú*, 6:317.

32. "Estado que manifiesta las cantidades de Plata que ingresado en esta Tesorería," Callao, 31 December 1824, ANP, AHH, OL 112-95; Estados, Lima, 31 December 1824, ANP, AHH, OL 112-96; "Estado . . . de los gastos causados por los Buques de guerra," Callao, 31 December 1824, ANP, AHH, OL 112-97.

33. Vargas Ugarte, *Historia general del Perú*, 6:330.

34. Aliaga to Rodil, Lima, 4 April 1824, AGI, Lima 1270; La Serna to Minister of Finance, Cuzco, 30 June 1824, AGI, Lima 1270; Council of Indies summary, 1824, AGI, Lima 1024; Requests from merchants to Rodil for export licenses, 1824, ANP, AHH, OL 112-14; Decree of Bolívar, Trujillo, 11 March 1824, ANP, AHH, OL 96-4.

35. Quoted in Masur, *Bolívar*, p. 370.

36. La Serna to Minister of Grace and Justice, Cuzco, 15 March 1824, AGI, Lima 762; Gárate to King, Puno, 18 April, 1824, AGI, Indiferente 1325.

37. Masur, *Bolívar*, p. 370; Decree of Bolívar, Trujillo, 11 April 1824, ANP, AHH, OL 96-5.

38. Augusto Tamayo Vargas and César Pacheco Vélez, eds., *José Faustino Sánchez Carrión*, vol. 9 of *Los Ideólogos*, tome 1 of *CDIP*.

39. Masur, *Bolívar*, pp. 369–73.

40. Lynch, *Spanish-American Revolutions*, pp. 279, 281. See the testimony of Valdés in his "Exposición," dated Vitoria, 12 July 1827, in Villanueva Urteaga, ed., *Documentación oficial española, CDIP*, tome 22, 3:315–84.

41. Quoted in Masur, *Bolívar*, pp. 372–73.

42. Domingo Ximenez and others to ministers of government, Madrid, 28 December 1824, AGI, Estado 74; Council of Indies Consulta, Madrid, 6 July 1825, AGI, Lima 604. Olañeta was already dead by this time.

43. Thomson, "Impresiones de Lima entre 1822 y 1824," in Núñez, ed., *Relaciones de Viajeros, CDIP*, tome 27, 2: 80–81.

44. Vargas Ugarte, *Historia general del Perú*, 6:348–49.

45. Ibid., p. 366.

46. Paz Soldán, *Historia del Perú independiente*, part 2, 1:294.

47. Nestor Gambetta, *El "Real Felipe" del Callao* (Lima: Imprenta del Ministerio de Guerra, 1945), p. 59; Mariano Torrente, *Historia de la revolución de la independencia del Perú* (edited version of his *Historia de la revolución Hispano-Americana*, Madrid, 1829–30), in Denegri Luna, ed., *Memorias, Diarios y Crónicas, CDIP*, tome 26, 4: 319–28.

48. Summary of other secondary sources in Vargas Ugarte, *Historia general del Perú*, 6:387; Marqués de Zambrano to Secretary of Hacienda, Madrid, 12 August 1826, AGI, Lima 1480.

49. Zambrano to Secretary of Hacienda, 12 August 1826, AGI, Lima 1480.

50. Quoted in Basadre, *Historia de la república*, 1:261.

# Selected Bibliography

Abascal y Sousa, José Fernando de. *Memoria de Govierno*. Edited by Vicente Rodríguez Casado and José Antonio Calderón Quijano. 2 vols. Seville: Escuela de Estudios Hispano-Americanos, 1944.

Angrand, Leonce, ed. *Imagen del Perú en el Siglo XIX*. Lima: C. Milla Batres, 1972.

Anna, Timothy E. "The Buenos Aires Expedition and Spain's Secret Plan to Conquer Portugal." *The Americas* 34, no. 3 (January 1978): 356–80.

———. "Economic Causes of San Martín's Failure in Lima." *Hispanic American Historical Review* 54, no. 4 (November 1974): 657–81.

———. "The Last Viceroys of New Spain and Peru: An Appraisal." *American Historical Review* 81, no. 1 (February 1976): 38–65.

———. "The Peruvian Declaration of Independence: Freedom by Coercion." *Journal of Latin American Studies* 7, no. 2 (November 1975): 221–48.

Aparicio Vega, Manuel. *El Clero patriota en la revolución de 1814*. Cuzco, 1974.

Arias-Schreiber Pezet, Jorge. *Los médicos en la independencia del Perú*. Lima: Editorial Universitaria, 1971.

Barra, Felipe de la, prol. and comp. *Asuntos Militares, Estado Militar en 1820–22*. 4 vols. to date. Tome 6 of *Colección documental de la independencia del Perú*. Lima: Comisión Nacional del Sesquicentenario de la Independencia del Perú, 1971.

Barreda Laos, Felipe. *Vida intelectual del virreinato del Perú*. Lima: Universidad Nacional Mayor de San Marcos, 1964.

Basadre, Jorge. *Historia de la república del Perú, 1822–1933*. 10 vols. 6th ed., aug. Lima: Editorial Universitaria, 1968–70.

———. *La iniciación de la república: Contribución al estudio de la evolución política y social del Perú*. 2 vols. Lima: F. y E. Rosay, 1929.

———. *Introducción a los bases documentales para la historia de la república del Perú*. 2 vols. Lima: Ediciones P.L.V., 1971.

———. *La multitud, la ciudad y el campo en la historia del Perú*. Lima: Imprenta A. J. Rivas Berrio, 1929.

273

Bonilla, Heraclio. "La coyuntura comercial del siglo XIX en el Perú." *Revista del Museo Nacional* (Peru) 35 (1967–68): 159–87.

Bonilla, Heraclio, and Spalding, Karen. "La independencia en el Perú: Las palabras y los hechos." In *La independencia en el Perú*, ed. Heraclio Bonilla, et al., pp. 15–63. Lima: Instituto de Estudios Peruanos, 1972.

Brading, D. A. and Cross, Harry E. "Colonial Silver Mining: Mexico and Peru." *Hispanic American Historical Review* 52, no. 4 (November 1972): 545–79.

Buechler, Rose Marie. "Technical Aid to Upper Peru: The Nordenflicht Expedition." *Journal of Latin American Studies* 5, no. 1 (May 1973): 37–77.

Burkholder, Mark A. "From Creole to *Peninsular*: The Transformation of the Audiencia of Lima." *Hispanic American Historical Review* 52, no. 3 (August 1972): 395–415.

———. "José Baquíjano and the Audiencia of Lima." Ph.D. diss., Duke University, 1970.

Campbell, Leon G. "The Army of Peru and the Túpac Amaru Revolt, 1780–83." *Hispanic American Historical Review* 56, no. 1 (February 1976): 31–57.

———. "The Changing Racial and Administrative Structure of the Peruvian Military under the Later Bourbons." *The Americas* 32, no. 1 (July 1975): 117–33.

———. "A Colonial Establishment: Creole Domination of the Audiencia of Lima during the Late Eighteenth Century." *Hispanic American Historical Review* 52, no. 1 (February 1972): 1–25.

———. "The Foreigners in Peruvian Society during the Eighteenth Century." *Revista de Historia de América* 73–74 (January-December 1972): 153–63.

———. *The Military and Society in Colonial Peru, 1750–1810*. Philadelphia: American Philosophical Society, 1978.

Camprubi Alcázar, Carlos. *El Banco de la Emancipación*. Lima, 1960.

———. "El Banco de la Emancipación." *Revista Histórica* (Peru) 23 (1957–58): 91–206.

Céspedes del Castillo, Guillermo. *Lima y Buenos Aires: Repercusiones económicas y políticas de la creación del Virreinato del Plata*. Seville: Escuela de Estudios Hispano-Americanos, 1947.

Dale, William Pratt. "The Cultural Revolution in Peru, 1750–1820." Ph.D. diss., Duke University, 1941.

Denegri Luna, Felix, comp. and prol. *Memorias, Diarios y Crónicas*. 4 vols. to date. Tome 26 of *Colección documental de la independencia del Perú*. Lima: Comisión Nacional del Sesquicentenario de la Independencia del Perú, 1971.

Díaz Venteo, Fernando. *Las campañas militares del Virrey Abascal*. Seville: Escuela de Estudios Hispano-Americanos, 1948.

Dunbar Temple, Ella, comp. and prol. *La acción patriótica del Pueblo en la emancipación: Guerrillas y montoneros*. 3 vols. to date. Tome 5 of *Colección documental de la independencia del Perú*. Lima: Comisión documental de la independencia del Perú. Lima: Comisión Nacional del Sesquicentenario de la Independencia del Perú, 1971.

Febres Villaroel, Oscar. "La crisis agricola en el Perú en el ultimo tercio del siglo XVIII." *Revista Histórica* (Peru) 27 (1964): 102–99.

Fisher, J. R. *Government and Society in Colonial Peru: The Intendant System, 1784–1814*. London: Athlone Press, 1970.

―――. "The Intendant System and the Cabildos of Peru, 1784–1810." *Hispanic American Historical Review* 49, no. 3 (August 1969): 430–53.

―――."Royalism, Regionalism, and Rebellion in Colonial Peru, 1808–1815." *Hispanic American Historical Review* 59, no. 2 (May 1979):232–57.

―――. *Silver Mines and Silver Miners in Colonial Peru, 1776–1824*. Centre for Latin American Studies, Monograph Series no. 7. Liverpool: University of Liverpool, 1977.

Friedrich, Carl J. *Tradition and Authority*. New York: Praeger, 1972.

*Gaceta del Gobierno de Lima Independiente* (16 July 1821–December 1822). Facsimile reproduction. 3 vols. La Plata, Argentina: Universidad Nacional de la Plata, 1950.

*Gaceta del Gobierno del Perú: Período de gobierno de Simón Bolívar*. Prologues by Cristóbal L. Mendoza and Felix Denegri Luna. 3 vols. Caracas: Fundación Eugenio Mendoza, 1967.

Galatoire, Adolfo José. *Cuáles fueron las enfermedades de San Martín*. Buenos Aires: Editorial Plus Ultra, 1973.

Gamio Palacio, Fernando, ed. *La municipalidad de Lima y la emancipación de 1821*. Lima: Concejo Provincial de Lima, 1971.

Ganster, Paul. "A Social History of the Secular Clergy of Lima during the Middle Decades of the Eighteenth Century." Ph.D. diss., University of California, Los Angeles, 1974.

Hall, Basil. *Extracts from a Journal Written on the Coasts of Chile, Peru, and Mexico, in the Years 1820, 1821, 1822*. 2 vols. 3d ed., Edinburgh, 1824. Reprinted Upper Saddle River, N.J.: Gregg Press, 1968.

Jos, Mercedes. "Manuel Lorenzo Vidaurre, Reformista Peruano." *Anuario de Estudios Americanos* 18 (1961): 443–545.

Leguía y Martínez, Germán. *Historia de la emancipación del Perú: El Protectorado*. Prologue by Alberto Tauro. 7 vols. Lima: Comisión Nacional del Sesquicentenario de la Independencia del Perú, 1972.

Llontop Sánchez Carrión, Susana. "Las deserciones en el ejército realista (1810–1821)." *Boletín del Instituto Riva-Agüero* 8 (1969–71): 317–62.

Lynch, John. *The Spanish American Revolutions, 1808–1826*. New York: W. W. Norton, 1973.

―――. *Spanish Colonial Administration, 1782–1810: The Intendant System in the Viceroyalty of the Río de la Plata*. London: Athlone Press, 1958.

Markham, Clements R. *A History of Peru*. New York, 1892. Reprinted

New York: Greenwood Press, 1968.

Masur, Gerhard. *Simón Bolívar*. Albuquerque: University of New Mexico Press, 1948.

Mathew, W. M. "The First Anglo-Peruvian Debt and Its Settlement, 1822–49." *Journal of Latin American Studies* 2, no. 1 (May 1970): 81–98.

———. "The Imperialism of Free Trade: Peru, 1820–1870." *Economic History Review* 21 (1968): 562–79.

Mendiburu, Manuel de. *Diccionario histórico-biográfico del Perú*. 2d ed. 11 vols. Lima: Evaristo San Cristóbal, 1934.

Miller, John. *Memoirs of General Miller in the Service of the Republic of Peru*. 2 vols. London: Longman, 1828.

Miró Quesada Laos, Carlos. *Historia del periodismo peruano*. Lima: Librería Internacional del Perú, 1957.

Moore, John Preston. *The Cabildo in Peru under the Bourbons*. Durham: Duke University Press, 1966.

Neiro Samanez, Hugo. *Hipólito Unánue y el nacimiento de la patria: Nueve ensayos sobre Hipólito Unánue y su tiempo*. Lima, 1967.

Nieto Vélez, Armando. "Contribución a la historia del fidelismo en el Perú (1808–1810)." *Boletín del Instituto Riva-Agüero* 4 (1958–60): 9–146.

———. comp., ed., and prol. *La Iglesia*. 1 vol. to date. Tome 20 of *Colección documental de la independencia del Perú*. Lima: Comisión Nacional del Sesquicentenario de la Independencia del Perú, 1971.

———. "Notas sobre la actitud de los obispos frente a la independencia Peruana (1820–1822)." *Boletín del Instituto Riva-Agüero* 8 (1969–71): 363–73.

Núñez, Estuardo, preliminary study and comp. *Relaciones de Viajeros*. 4 vols. to date. Tome 27 of *Colección documental de la independencia del Perú*. Lima: Comisión Nacional del Sesquicentenario de la Independencia del Perú, 1971.

Odom, James Larry. "Viceroy Abascal versus the Cortes of Cádiz." Ph.D. diss., University of Georgia, 1968.

Odriozola, Manuel de. *Documentos históricos del Perú*. 10 vols. Lima: Tip. de A. Alfaro, 1863–77.

Ortiz de Zevallos, Javier, ed. *Correspondencia de San Martín y Torre Tagle*. Lima: J. Mejía Baca, 1963.

Paz Soldán, Mariano Felipe. *Historia del Perú independiente*. 2 parts, 2 vols. each. Lima, 1868–74. Facsimile reproduction, Buenos Aires: Instituto Nacional Sanmartiniano, 1962.

Peña Calderón, Isabel de la. "La mujer Peruana en la emancipación." *Revista del Centro de Estudios Histórico-Militares del Perú* 19 (1971): 112–22.

Pezuela y Sánchez Muñoz de Velasco, Joaquín de la. *Memoria de Gobierno*. Edited by Vicente Rodríguez Casado and Guillermo Lohmann Villena.

Seville: Escuela de Estudios Hispano-Americanos, 1947.

Pike, Fredrick B. *The Modern History of Peru*. New York: Praeger, 1967.

Pons Muzzo, Gustavo, comp. and prol. *La expedición libertadora*. 3 vols. to date. Tome 8 in *Colección documental de la independencia del Perú*. Lima: Comisión Nacional del Sesquicentenario de la Independencia del Perú, 1971.

Porras Barrenechea, Raul. *Los ideólogos de la emancipación*. Lima: Editorial Milla Batres, 1974.

Puente Candamo, José A. de la. "Un esquema de la tematica 'fidelista.' " *Boletín del Instituto Riva-Agüero* 8 (1969–71); 597–622.

Raffeld, Herbert. "The Viceroyalty of Peru: Bulwark of Royalism, 1808–1821." Ph.D. diss., University of California, Berkeley, 1951.

Riva Agüero, José de la. *Emancipación y la república*. Vol. 7 of *Obras Completas*. Lima: Instituto Riva Agüero, 1971.

———. *Memorias y documentos para la historia de la independencia del Perú y causas del mal exito que ha tenido*. 2 vols. Paris: Garnier hermanos, 1858.

Robertson, William Spence. *Rise of the Spanish American Republics as Told in the Lives of Their Liberators*. New York, 1918. Reedition New York: Free Press, 1965.

Rojas, Ricardo. *San Martín: Knight of the Andes*. New York: Cooper Square Publishers, 1967.

Seminario de Historia del Instituto Riva Agüero. *La causa de la emancipación del Perú: Testimonios de la época pre~ursora*. Lima: Instituto Riva Agüero, 1960.

Sparks, María Consuelo. "The Role of the Clergy during the Struggle for Independence in Peru." Ph.D. diss., University of Pittsburgh, 1972.

Tamayo Vargas, Augusto, and Pacheco Vélez, César, ed. and prol. *José Faustino Sánchez Carrión*. Vol. 9 of tome 1, *Los Ideólogos*. In *Colección documental de la independencia del Perú*. Lima: Comisión Nacional del Sesquicentenario de la Independencia del Perú, 1974.

Tauro, Alberto, ed. and prol. *Asuntos económicos: Informes y oficios del Tribunal del Consulado*. 1 vol. to date. Tome 21 in *Colección documental de la independencia del Perú*. Lima: Comisión Nacional del Sesquicentenario de la Independencia del Perú, 1971.

Tibesar, Antonine. "The Lima Pastors, 1750–1820: Their Origins and Studies Taken from Their Autobiographies." *The Americas* 28, no. 1 (July 1971): 39–56.

———. "The Peruvian Church at the Time of Independence in the Light of Vatican II." *The Americas* 25, no. 4 (April 1969): 349–75.

Torata, Fernando Valdés, Conde de, ed. *Documentos para la historia de la guerra separatista del Perú*. 4 vols. Madrid: Imp. de la Viuda de M. Minuesa de los Rios, 1894–98.

Vargas Ugarte, Ruben. "Don Ricardo Palma y la historia." *Journal of*

*Inter-American Studies* 9, no. 2 (1967): 213–24.

———. *El episcopado en los tiempos de la emancipación*. Lima: Librería e Imprenta Gil, 1962.

———. *Historia general del Perú*. 6 vols. Barcelona: I. G. Seix y Barral Hnos., 1966.

Vergara Arias, Gustavo. *Montoneras y guerrillas en la etapa de la emancipación del Perú (1820–1825)*. Lima: Editorial Salesiana, 1973.

Vicuña Mackenna, Benjamin. *La independencia en el Perú*. 5th ed. Prol. by Luis Alberto Sánchez. "Colección Vicuña Mackenna," no. 5. Buenos Aires: Editorial Francisco de Aguirre, 1971.

Villalobos, Sergio. *El comercio y la crisis colonial*. Santiago: Ediciones de la Universidad de Chile, 1968.

Villanueva Urteaga, Horacio, comp. and prol. *Documentación oficial española*. 3 vols. to date. Tome 22 in *Colección documental de la independencia del Perú*. Lima: Comisión Nacional del Sesquicentenario de la Independencia del Perú, 1971.

Wiesse, Carlos. *Historia del Perú colonial*. Lima: Librería Francesa científica E. Rosay, 1918.

Woodham, John E. "The Influence of Hipólito Unánue on Peruvian Medical Science, 1789–1820: A Reappraisal." *Hispanic American Historical Review* 50, no. 4 (November 1970): 693–714.

Worcester, Donald E. *Sea Power and Chilean Independence*. Gainesville: University of Florida Press, 1962.

# Acknowledgments

IT IS A PLEASURE for me to acknowledge several institutions and friends who made this book possible. The research and writing were conducted with the assistance of research grants and a Leave Fellowship from the Canada Council. I received countless favors and advice from the directors and staffs of the chief archives employed: the Archivo General de Indias in Seville, the Archivo Nacional del Perú, and the Biblioteca Municipal de Lima. Various individuals in the Elizabeth Dafoe Library of the University of Manitoba assisted through rapid acquisition and cataloging of research material. John J. TePaske and Mark A. Burkholder read the manuscript and offered valuable comments. My particular thanks go to my wife, Mary, for everything she did to help complete this project.

# Index